Total Quality Management

Total Quality Management

Three Steps to Continuous Improvement

Arthur R. Tenner
Irving J. DeToro

Addison-Wesley Publishing Company
Reading, Massachusetts
Menlo Park, California   New York
Don Mills, Canada
Wokingham, England   Amsterdam
Bonn   Sydney   Singapore   Tokyo
Madrid   San Juan   Paris   Seoul
Milan   Mexico City   Taipei

Many of the designations used by manufacturers and sellers to distinguish their products are claimed as trademarks. Where those designations appear in this book and Addison-Wesley was aware of a trademark claim, the designations have been printed in initial caps (i.e., Symphony).

The publisher offers discounts on this book when ordered in quantity for special sales. For more information please contact:
Corporate & Professional Publishing Group
Addison-Wesley Publishing Company
One Jacob Way
Reading, Massachusetts 01867

Library of Congress Cataloging-in-Publication Data

Tenner, Arthur R.
    Total quality management: three steps to continuous improvement /Arthur R. Tenner, Irving J. DeToro
        p.   cm.
    Includes bibliographical references and index.
    ISBN 0-201-56305-3 (hardback)
    1. Total quality management.   I. DeToro, Irving J.   II. Title.
    HD62.15.T46   1992
    658.5′62—dc20   91-19024
                                                                  CIP

Cover design by James Brisson
Text design by Joyce C. Weston
Set in 10.5 point Palatino by Camden Type 'n Graphics, Camden, Maine

ISBN 0-201-56305-3

Text printed on recycled and acid-free paper.
6 7 8 9 10 11 12 CRW 96959493
Sixth printing, November 1993

Contents

Foreword

Total Quality Management: Three Steps to Continuous Improvement will prove to be a classic for both service companies and the service side of manufacturing alike. True Total Quality Management, which has been the key to success for world class manufacturing companies, is described and detailed simply and effectively for immediate application to the service process. The clear and interesting explanations in *Total Quality Management* should help readers assess their current situation then develop an effective plan for total quality.

In this book, a manager's perspective of the technical aspects of Total Quality Management coupled with excellent examples of strategies used by several leading North American companies provide a blueprint to successfully champion a quality initiative.

We need to understand history in order not to repeat our mistakes. *Total Quality Management* starts with these history lessons and then focuses them to form the quality concepts that create the framework for the rest of the book.

Three major themes emerge: *Customer Focus, Process Improvement,* and *Total Involvement.* Total Quality Management requires that a company be driven by customers' needs. This should be understood and pursued by everyone in the company. Many examples, approaches, and tools are provided in the book to accomplish this in any organization, given the will to continuously seek this information. Understanding customer expectations launches the ongoing pursuit of excellence.

The most successful companies are fanatical about Process Improvement. "If it ain't broke, make it better" must be the battle cry of every employee. Proven tools, methods, and strategies are provided here to support both the technical as well as the behavioral environment needed to create the teamwork that makes revolutionary quality improvement a reality.

Total Involvement from the CEO to the newest employee is essential to ensure Customer Focus and Process Improvement. The authors provide the ways and means to understand the existing infrastructure while creating a new corporate culture. This effective marriage of cultural and organizational awareness makes possible the accomplishment of the difficult goal of total company involvement—the key to success.

The final section—one of the most effective in the book—clearly demonstrates how all the tools, techniques, strategies, approaches, principles, mechanisms, frameworks, and processes have been effectively implemented at several companies: Banc One, Xerox Corporation, and Ford Motor Company.

There will be no doubt in your mind about *what* to do, *how* to do it, and *when* it should be done. You will certainly understand because of the clear, crisp, informative, and interesting style of the writing complete with wonderful examples and exhibits. The company case studies will provide you with the examples you need to create a world class organization through the three steps to continuous improvement—Total Quality Management.

Charles A. Aubrey II, Chief Quality Officer and Vice President,
Banc One Corporation
President Elect, American Society for Quality Control

Preface

Total quality management was first applied to repetitive manufacturing operations, and many have encountered difficulties extending its concepts and tools to other functions. Some question whether quality applies at all to businesses whose outputs are information or professional services rather than tangible products. Building on Dr. W. Edwards Deming's principle that "experience alone teaches nothing," a hypothesis and methodology were developed and tested.

This book introduces a systematic approach for implementing total quality management outside of manufacturing. It relies on the ability to model all work as a process and features a step-by-step plan within which the basic quality tools are used. The book also presents the results of tests through examples of success as well as difficulties encountered when attempting to shortcut the prescribed methodology.

Focusing the organization's attention on understanding and responding to customer needs is the first of three core principles. Interactions with customers to understand their level of satisfaction or to predict their future expectations represent processes designed to tie business efforts to the customer. A framework is offered to help define the criteria against which customers base their expectations for quality service.

Systematically and continuously improving all products, services, and processes is the second core principle. Successful application begins by identifying each process in its totality, measuring its performance, and then building a fundamental understanding of its underlying limitations. Although simplest to apply to repetitive manufacturing operations, the basic quality tools can now be extended to all types of work, including information systems, marketing, finance, transportation, health care, education, administration, engineering, and R&D.

Total involvement of all participants is the third core principle. Readers will understand the role of leadership and how to improve systems used to align, motivate, and empower employees. Examples are provided on how to integrate the involvement of suppliers and measure progress in objective terms.

Finally, total quality management strategies used by recognized leaders in the field are explained. Specific examples reveal how to transform an organization's culture into one that stimulates everyone to contribute toward common goals.

Our objective in writing this book was to offer a single, comprehensive guide for extending the concepts and techniques of total quality management beyond the manufacturing operations for which they were originally developed. This book is designed to enable service leaders to capture the competitive advantage of total quality management. Although the approach is designed primarily for supporting functions within manufacturing companies, it is equally applicable to businesses in the service sector.

In compiling this book, we did not discover new facts about the principles of management, nor did we create new methods for improving the quality of products and services. Instead, this book offers the following features:

- Three simple, yet comprehensive principles for understanding the key concepts of total quality management

- Six core elements available for leading the cultural change required in order to implement the key concepts

- Basic criteria against which customers base their expectations for quality service and approaches that suppliers can use to build a better understanding of their customers at three successive levels

- A six-step process-improvement road map that enables the basic quality tools to be applied to any type of work process

- A model showing how to stimulate total involvement and lead everyone toward the common goals of systematic improvement and total satisfaction of customers, employees, shareholders, and the public at large

Examples and graphics are presented to clarify the key concepts. Work-sheets and checklists are provided to help in their application.

Arthur R. Tenner and Irving J. DeToro
November 1991

Acknowledgments

The authors wish to acknowledge others who helped to make this book possible. Although there are too many to enumerate, the following deserve special recognition for their contributions.

The visionary leadership of Dave Clair, as president of the Exxon Research & Engineering Company, helped the process to begin. Other Exxon leaders who shared the experience of learning about total quality management and helped formulate many of the ideas embedded in this book include Joe Browne, Kathy Herald, Bob Hofstader, Fred Horowitz, Al Lopez, Trent McComas, and Gerry Shea.

Portions of the book took shape through the specific contributions of a number of individuals. The authors are grateful to Chuck Aubrey (Banc One Corporation), Joel Berenter (Ford Motor Company), David Cox (Imperial Oil, Ltd.), and Michael Hepworth (Michael Hepworth Associates).

Background

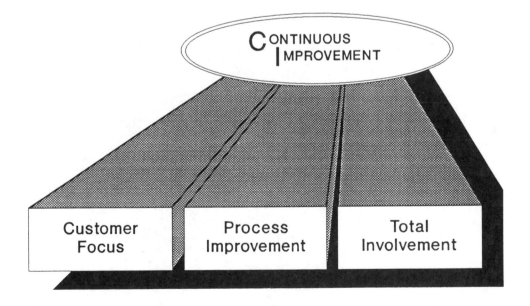

1 *Why Quality?*

The United States economy expanded throughout the decade of the 1980s. Unemployment reached a low of 5.2 percent; total industry utilization approached full capacity at 85 percent; and the total value of goods and services produced grew 2.5 percent annually.[1]

Even the size of the U.S. economy is an indication that we are still the most significant economic force in the world. Our national output (gross national product) is approximately three times the size of the Japanese economy and twice as large as the combined economics of France, the new Germany, and Britain.[2]

Why, then, is there a concern about our ability to compete internationally? Why have the domestic car manufacturers lost market share to the Japanese? Why are "well-managed" U.S. companies laying off workers and managers? And why has the center of the financial world moved from New York City to Tokyo?

We begin our examination of these questions in Chapter 1 by providing background information on our competitive position and its impact on the U.S. economy. In Chapter 2, we discuss the history of the quality movement and the leaders in the field, such as Taylor, Shewhart, Deming, Juran, Crosby, and Feigenbaum. In Chapters 3 and 4, we update the definitions of quality and begin application by exploring a series of basic concepts as a foundation to understanding total quality management (TQM).

Trade Imbalance

When the federal government publishes trade figures, we are again reminded that American consumers continue to prefer foreign goods to

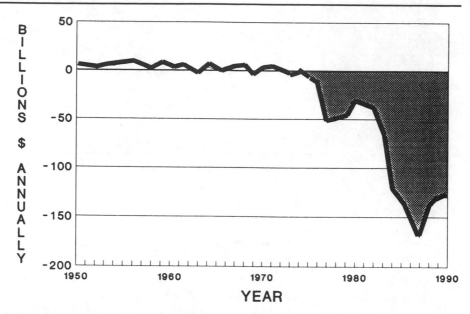

Figure 1.1   United States Trade Balance.   *Source:* Commerce Department.

those made in America. We import these goods because of their quality and value, because they are innovative, and because they incorporate leading technology. However, our taste for foreign products has caused an imbalance in the merchandise portion of our current account, the broadest measure of U.S. foreign trade. This trade imbalance is one indication that our ability to participate in world markets has eroded and that we have lost our competitiveness! (See Figure 1.1.)

What Happened?

At the conclusion of World War II, demand for consumer goods was so strong that U.S. producers of goods and services had difficulty meeting market demands. The lessons learned during the war about how to produce quality materials were ignored, and American manufacturers went about the business of meeting the needs of the largest market in the world with quantity, not quality. The huge production capability we built to produce war material was converted to the mass production of cars, refrigerators, and other consumer products.

Other countries recovering from the devastation of the war had little infrastructure left and a much smaller market to serve. Starting with a "clean slate," they designed new, more efficient, more flexible

4   *Total Quality Management*

manufacturing capabilities, which enabled them to meet the needs of their smaller market and niches in our market. This new flexibility and capability, coupled with a keen understanding of what customers desired, has led to an economic revolution in which much smaller countries—such as Japan, Korea, Taiwan, and Germany—have captured large segments of the U.S. market and have also displaced U.S. manufacturers as suppliers in some segments of world markets.

This postwar reversal in roles has caused U.S. imports to overwhelm our exports, thereby creating a huge trade imbalance and an outflow of U.S. dollars to other countries. Statistics released in December 1989 showed that Germany enjoyed a whopping $71 billion trade surplus, followed by Japan with a $58 billion surplus.[3]

Trade Deficit Impacts

As producers in Europe and Asia continue to gain market share in the United States and displace domestic manufacturers in world markets, the question for Americans is, What can we do about this? What can we do to stem the tide of imports and increase our ability to export our goods and services and to compete internationally?

Made in America, a book written by the MIT Commission on Industrial Productivity, cites four possible options:[4]

1 "One option is to place tariffs, quotas, domestic-content requirements, on all imported goods and services and stem the flow of imports by raising their cost and by restricting volumes that can be introduced into U.S. markets."

2 Another possibility is that a recession in the United States will at some point dampen the demand for more expensive foreign goods and free up domestic manufacturing capacity for the production of goods for export. Thus, the commission states, "a recession in the United States, greater prosperity in Europe, or the resumption of economic growth in the paralyzed countries of Latin America would automatically improve the trade balance."

In both options 1 and 2, the cure may be worse than the disease! Raising tariffs and establishing import quotas would create an environment in which other countries would retaliate, and trade could be restricted to the detriment of everyone. The commission outlines two other, more realistic options:

3 Still another way to reduce our trade deficit is to devalue our currency. It sounds rather odd to consider a devaluation of the dollar, much as a poor third world country does when it mismanages its economy, yet a cheaper currency would allow us to offer goods on the world markets at attractive and competitive costs. The MIT Commission states: "It should be kept in mind that the U.S. balance of trade was in small surplus as recently as 1981. The drastic deterioration in the U.S. trade position coincided with the sharp appreciation of the dollar in the early 1980s, brought on in large part by the high interest rate that attracted foreign capital. Since 1985 the dollar has been depreciating, and the trade balance has already improved considerably; this has contributed to a strong revival of American manufacturing."[5]

4 The most viable option, one that is directly under our control, is that we simply improve the quality of the goods and services we produce. That is, we must better understand the requirements of the American consumer, then find the means to meet those requirements, with every product manufactured, with every service provided, every time!

Depreciation of U.S. Currency

Because we have elected not to impose tariffs, domestic-content requirements, or restrictions on imports, and because we are not providing the goods and services American consumers require, our currency has been impacted. Indeed, our currency has been on a "wild ride" during this past decade. "In September 1985," writes Kenneth Gilpin, "a group of finance ministers from five nations gathered on an Indian summer Sunday at the Plaza Hotel in Manhattan and agreed the value of the dollar had grown too high. They decided to try to push it down, and they succeeded."[6] The dollar peaked against the Japanese yen on February 25, 1985, at 263 yen to the U.S. dollar, and the following day, it peaked against the West German mark at 3.5 deutsche marks to the dollar.

Five years later, the exchange rate for the dollar was approximately 130 yen and 1.7 deutsche marks, or a drop in value of 50 percent, respectively. The effect has been to lower the price of U.S.-produced goods in the export markets, thereby causing a surge in U.S. exports and a resumption of the growth of U.S. business.

But the major side effect of our currency's losing value versus the yen and the deutsche mark is the transfer of wealth to others.

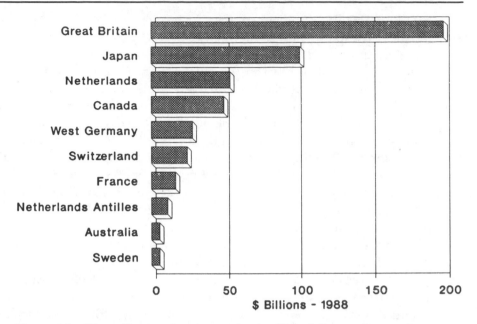

Figure 1.2   Direct Foreign Investment in the United States. *Source:* Commerce Department.

Transfer of Wealth

The U.S. dollars flowing to foreign countries as a result of our purchasing their goods and services have not come back to us in kind. That is, foreign consumers have not purchased American goods in sufficient quantities to offset their trade surplus. Rather, what has happened is that foreign holders of U.S. currency have purchased well-known U.S. firms, landmark commercial real estate, and prime farmland (see Figure 1.2).

The Japanese, for example, hold a smaller fraction of the total U.S. assets owned by foreigners, but they are the most visible because they purchased signature buildings, and they are projected to overtake the British by 1994. The Mitsubishi Estate Company of Tokyo puchased the controlling interest in the Rockefeller Group—owners of Rockefeller Center, Radio City Music Hall, and other midtown Manhattan office buildings—for $846 million.[7] In 1989, Sony Corporation purchased Columbia Pictures for $3.4 billion. The Exxon Building in New York was sold to Mitsui Fudosan of Tokyo in 1985 for $620 million, and the Pebble Beach Company, owner of one of America's best-known golf resorts, was purchased by General Coast Enterprises, a Japanese company, in the latter half of 1990.

Foreigners own 12.5 million acres of U.S. farmland in forty-nine states, 10 percent of the U.S. manufacturing base, 53 percent of the commercial and industrial loans in New York, and 42 percent in Los Angeles. Many other landmarks have been acquired, including, in California, San Francisco's Mark Hopkins and Los Angeles's Century City; Chicago's Hyatt Regency; Washington's Willard Hotel; and in New York, the Tishman Building, Citicorp Center, Manhattan Tower, the ITT Building, the Pershing Square Building, the Sperry Building, and the World Financial Center. Famous names such as Tiffany's, Talbots, Firestone Tires, Smith-Corona Typewriters, and Ball Park Franks are either owned or controlled by Japanese interests.[8]

And so it goes. The Japanese, the British, and the Canadians are purchasing U.S. assets to such an extent that foreign holdings in the United States climbed in 1989 by $280 billion, to $2.1 trillion—a gain of 15.6 percent over the previous year. U.S. holdings of assets in other countries grew only $147 billion, or 12 percent, to a total of $1.4 trillion. The $664 billion imbalance between what Americans own overseas and what foreigners own in the United States is the country's net debtor position. Many private economists believe it will top $1 trillion within a few years.[9]

A study by Paul Krugman and Edwin Graham for the Institute for International Economics indicates that foreign ownership is not harmful and should not be of concern.[10] The study reports that foreign companies accounted for 7 percent of total United States employment in manufacturing in 1986, compared to 21 percent in France, 14 percent in Britain, and 13 percent in West Germany.

But what should be of concern to all of us is that we are transferring our wealth to others, that our assets are falling rapidly in value and are a bargain to those who enjoy a stronger currency, that we are putting our standard of living in jeopardy, and that we are losing our economic position in major world markets!

Loss of Traditional Markets

We have lost our competitiveness! We no longer supply the world with steel, copiers, cameras, cars, or consumer electronics. In the early 1980s, we were a net exporter of semiconductors and sophisticated electronic

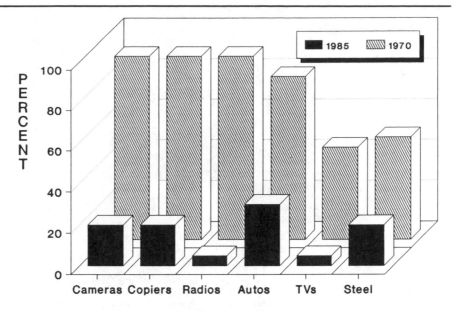

Figure 1.3 U.S. Share of World Production. *Source:* Boston Consulting Group, 1987.

components. By the late 1980s, we became a net exporter of only wheat, soybeans, lumber, and aircraft.[11]

What's happening here?

During the thirty-year period ending in 1980, the United States dominated a number of industries and world markets. We supplied the majority of the world's need for cars, radios, TVs, cameras, and copiers (see Figure 1.3) because we were the most efficient producer. Since the 1980s, we have lost our role as supplier to the world!

More important, we Americans may have lost the one advantage we prized most. We know that the Japanese, for example, have supplanted us not only in our traditional markets, such as consumer electronics, but in what was once a unique American competitive advantage—"know-how." Comparing the Japanese edge in manufacturing to our own capabilities, we find that our friendly Japanese competitor has bested us in a very critical dimension (see Figure 1.4). For every hour of labor the Japanese use to produce a product, we require more labor to produce the same item. For example, to produce a color TV set requires 1.3 hours of U.S. labor for every 1.0 hour of Japanese labor. In the production of auto transmissions, we require

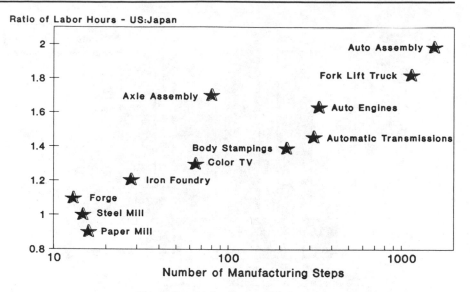

Ratio of Labor Hours - US:Japan

The ratio of labor-hours (US:Japan) increases
with the complexity of the job and indicates a possible
disadvantage of U.S. management practices.

Figure 1.4   Japanese Edge in Manufacturing. *Source:* Boston Consulting Group, 1987.

1.41 hours to 1.0 hour required by the Japanese. Only in the production of sheet steel and paper do we seem to have the same capability as the Japanese.

What Are We Doing About It?

Twenty-six studies were completed in the United States during the last decade on ways to improve our international competitiveness, yet none of the study recommendations has been adopted. We seem unable to dramatically rally our national resolve to address this inability to compete internationally.[12] We continue to be only vaguely aware of the reasons for our inability to compete and resort to "Japan bashing" as if it were a real solution.

Since 1980, the United States has been displaced in these markets by foreign competitors that seem to be more innovative, more cost-effective, and more capable of meeting the consumer's requirements. Figure 1.5 details this change in our world position for products first invented and sold here in the United States.

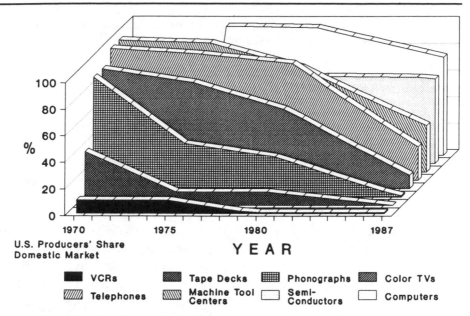

Figure 1.5   Invented Here, Made Elsewhere. *Source:* Council on Competitiveness, Commerce Dept.

The result of this superior performance by foreign firms is that the United States has been pushed out of supplying the world's major markets, some of which we developed and once dominated. The easy answer is that the problem is one of worker productivity, that we're paying too much compared to the cheap wages paid by others, and that we're less effective because our work force is less skilled.

Loss of Economic Leadership

The loss of our position as supplier of goods and services to the world is due less to the cost and skill of our labor than perhaps to the way in which management and labor interact.

First, the issue of wages. In 1985, the United States was at a clear cost disadvantage due to the high wages paid to American workers. The average hourly wage for the U.S. worker then was $12.82, compared to the Japanese worker at $6.45 and the West German worker at $9.60. However, by 1987, the appreciation of the Japanese yen and the West German mark forced the hourly wages of the Japanese worker to

$11.44 and the West German worker to $16.30. Wages have become less of an issue in determining differences in cost.[13]

But productivity is still an issue because we are less efficient than our Asian and European competitors. Peter Drucker puts the case this way: this lack of productivity can be laid at the feet of unions and management for allowing the creation of restrictive work rules and job restrictions.[14] This situation produces inflexibility, in that a foreman cannot do work, more workers are required to complete a task because they are represented by different unions, and time is wasted while waiting for the designated worker to become available. He cites as an example a Nissan plant in the Midlands in England where a Nissan worker produces twenty-four cars per year compared to six for an English Ford plant. After eliminating some of the reasons for Nissan's increased productivity, such as purchasing parts rather than fabricating on site, Drucker attributes the increased productivity at the Nissan plant to Nissan's having 5 job classifications to Ford's 125. Drucker faults Western management for creating this inefficient work climate by accepting work rules to avoid providing job retraining, outplacing, job security, and to have slightly lower wage rates.

American workers working for foreign-managed firms seem to be more productive than American workers working for American-managed firms. Autoworkers at Honda in Ohio or at New United Motor Manufacturing, Inc. (NUMMI) in California produce cars at lower cost, with higher reliability, and with greater perceived quality than domestic car manufacturers. And they do their work with less absenteeism (3 percent versus 20 percent) and with what appears to be a greater commitment to the success of their firm. The issue seems to be less one of individual worker productivity than one of the management system in which people work.

Summary

U.S. business leaders are realizing, to a greater extent than ever before, that they must take decisive action to preserve our position as a world supplier of goods and services. Increasing numbers of firms are revamping their management styles and work processes in favor of those that are more effective in meeting the needs and expectations of customers. The lessons taught by the trade imbalance, the transfer of American wealth, the buying of America by foreign interests, and the loss of economic leadership have not been lost on U.S. business leaders.

There are more and more success stories of U.S. firms, such as Motorola and Xerox, exporting to Japan and Germany products and services that are superior to those produced elsewhere. We need to accelerate that trend!

Notes

1. *Economic Indicators,* prepared for the Joint Economic Committee by the Council of Economic Advisers (June 1990).

2. OECD, CIA, Defense Intelligence Agency (1990).

3. "Economic and Financial Indicators," *Economist* (Dec. 22–Jan. 4, 1991).

4. Michael L. Dertouzos, Richard K. Lester, Robert M. Solow, and the MIT Commission on Industrial Productivity, *Made in America: Regaining the Productivity Edge* (Cambridge, Mass.: MIT Press, 1989), 33–35.

5. Ibid., 34.

6. Kenneth L. Gilpin, "The Dollar's Wild Ride," *New York Times* (June 19, 1988), p. 7.

7. Robert J. Cole, "Control of Rockefeller Center Is Sold to a Japanese Company," *New York Times* (October 31, 1989), p. 1.

8. Congressional Economic Leadership Institute, as reported in *USA Today* (July 28, 1988).

9. "The Size of Our Debt and Where Is It Going?," *Star-Ledger,* Newark, N.J. (July 3, 1990).

10. Paul Krugman and Edwin M. Graham, "Foreign Direct Investments in the U.S.," *Foreign Affairs* (Summer 1990), p. 174.

11. Charles H. Ferguson, "From the People Who Brought You Voodoo Economics," *Harvard Business Review,* no. 3 (May–June 1988).

12. "The Cuomo Commission on Trade & Competitiveness," *Business Week* (June 27, 1988).

13. Lawrence A. Veit, "Competitive Labor Costs," *New York Times* (June 6, 1987).

14. Peter F. Drucker, "Workers' Hands Bound by Tradition," *Wall Street Journal* (Aug. 2, 1988).

2 *History of Quality*

Readers of management books published in the 1980s must have the impression that writers were suggesting Americans adopt the Japanese style of management in order to compete with our Asian and European counterparts. We may even have developed the impression that we should adopt some Japanese customs and social conventions and forego our individualism. Not likely! We're Americans, with our own values, uniqueness, and peculiarities, which not only suit us but are our strengths.

But the question still remains: how can we retain our values and still compete successfully in the international marketplace? This chapter provides an overview of the basic quality concepts and the men who developed them and advocated their adoption.

Our Prewar Experience

Prior to World War II, the notion of quality was based on the physical characteristics of the product. According to this "product-based" approach, quality reflects differences in measurable attributes of the product; the implication is that more of an attribute may be desirable.[1] This definition of quality is balanced somewhat by the "manufacturing-based" view of quality, in which the manufacturer measures the quality of the product by its conformance to a predetermined set of specifications. Deviations from these specified characteristics are a cause for concern since, by definition, they are a reflection of a lower level of quality. Clearly, these definitions of quality reflect a view that is internal to the organization producing the product or providing the service.

Only indirectly do these definitions represent the wishes of the end user, the consumer.

During this era, the quality mandate was to measure the variation in the product or service characteristic from some predetermined standard and then confront the manufacturing or service-delivery process that contributed to this variation. This task fell to a group of inspectors, usually quality control engineers, who were part of a specialized department. This department most often reported to the highest level within an organization and only indirectly worked with the employees or managers who actually produced the output. This is a problem caused by the success of an engineer, Frederick Taylor.

Quality Leaders

The development of total quality as a management system began in the United States at the turn of this century. Several individuals played key roles in the development, implementation, and dissemination of this important new approach to managing an organization. While they may have previously labored with little recognition for their contributions, since 1980 their involvement in Total Quality Management has become appreciated throughout the world.

Taylor

Frederick W. Taylor (1856–1915) is credited with being one of the first to attempt to use new approaches to improve the work of unskilled workers in industrial organizations. Taylor, a chief engineer, developed a series of concepts that laid a foundation for work improvement during this century. The systemic approach of analysis and the application of some basic concepts to manual work earned Taylor the title of "father of scientific management."[2]

In his book *The Principles of Scientific Management*, Taylor reveals a few elements of his management theory:

A Daily Task—each person in every organization should have a clearly defined, large task which should take one day to complete.

Standard Conditions—the worker should have standard tools and conditions to complete the task.

High Pay for Success—significant rewards should be paid for the successful completion of the task.

High Loss for Failure—failure for completing the task should be personally costly.

Tasks in large, sophisticated organizations should be made difficult so as to require skilled, accomplished workers.[3]

Taylor was able to demonstrate for the first time that the economic pie could be increased not only by the application of capital and labor but by the application of knowledge to work. However, Taylor also created a monumental problem that was to become apparent later. He separated planning from work improvement and thereby isolated the worker from responsibility for improving work. In the words of J. Juran, "the result is that Taylor delivered a devastating blow to craftsmanship."[4]

This division of responsibility, reports Juran, resulted in the creation of a separate department of inspectors to monitor the quality of the output and, in effect, diffused the responsibility for quality within the organization.[5] This group of inspectors, reporting to a chief inspector, became known as the quality assurance department.

Shewhart

Walter A. Shewhart (1891–1967) was a statistician employed by Bell Labs during the 1920s and 1930s. His book *The Economic Control of Quality of Manufactured Products* was considered by statisticians as a landmark contribution to the effort to improve the quality of manufactured goods. Shewhart reported that variations exist in every facet of manufacturing but that variations could be understood through the application of simple statistical tools such as sampling and probability analysis.[6]

Shewhart's techniques taught that work processes could be brought under control by defining when a process should be left alone and when intervention was necessary.[7] He was able to define the limits of random variation that occur in completing any task and said that intervention should occur only when these limits have been exceeded. He developed "control charts" to track performance over time, thereby providing workers with the ability to monitor their work and predict when they were about to exceed limits and possibly produce scrap!

Shewhart's work in sampling and control charts attracted the interest of another statistician, W. Edwards Deming.

Deming

Only with the airing of the NBC television program "If Japan Can, Why Can't We?" on June 24, 1980, did Americans become aware of a man, living less than five miles from Washington, who had a major impact on the world. Dr. W. Edwards Deming, a simple statistician by his own account, had trained Japanese engineers in the 1950s and was credited by the Japanese with significantly assisting in their remarkable recovery from the devastation of World War II.

Born in 1900 and educated at the University of Wyoming and Yale (Ph.D., 1927), Deming both taught and used statistics in his work. Deming was impressed with Shewhart's work, visited and studied with him, and employed his techniques. Deming became known as an expert on sampling and was hired away from the Department of Agriculture in the late 1930s to help the Census Bureau institute a new sampling approach for collecting census data. As a student of Shewhart, he learned that the statistical tools used at the plant were equally applicable at the office. Deming, for example, improved the accuracy of keypunch operators by training the operators and then inspecting only a third of their work.[8]

When World War II broke out, Deming was asked to assist the war effort, and assist he did. He and others working with him taught Shewhart's statistical techniques to thirty-one thousand engineers who were involved in the production of war material. But to consider Deming a simple statistician would be to seriously undervalue his contribution.

Deming learned that after the war, the lessons of quality that he had taught so well were being ignored. "Quality in those postwar years took a back seat to production . . . getting those numbers out."[9] Deming realized he had been teaching engineers, not the managers responsible for the enterprise. He learned then that quality is not determined on the shop floor but in the executive suite.

When invited to Japan in 1947 to assist in the 1951 census, Deming became personally aware of the complete devastation of the country, and the Japanese became aware of his knowledge of Shewhart's techniques. In 1950, the Union of Japanese Scientists and Engineers (known by its telex code, JUSE) invited Deming to come to Japan and deliver a series of lectures on quality. The rest is history.

Deming has summarized his concepts and principles in a series of fourteen points and seven deadly diseases[10] (see Table 2.1). However, his approach can be described as follows:

Quality is primarily the result of senior management actions and decisions and not the result of actions taken by workers. Deming stresses that it is the "system" of work that determines how work is performed and only managers can create the system. Only managers can allocate resources, provide training to workers, select the equipment and tools that workers use, and provide the plant and the environment

Table 2.1: Deming's Management Principles

7 Deadly Diseases

1. Lack of constancy of purpose

2. Emphasis on short-term profits

3. Evaluation of performance, merit rating, or annual review

4. Mobility of management

5. Management by use of visible figures

6. Excessive medical costs

7. Excessive costs of liability

14 Points

1. Create and publish to all employees a statement of the aims and purposes of the company or other organization. The management must demonstrate constantly their commitment to this statement.

2. Learn the new philosophy, top management and everybody.

3. Understand the purpose of inspection, for improvement of processes and reduction of cost.

4. End the practice of awarding business on the basis of price tag alone.

5. Improve constantly and forever the system of production and service.

6. Institute training (for skills).

7. Teach and institute leadership.

8. Drive out fear. Create trust. Create a climate for innovation.

9. Optimize toward the aims and purposes of the company the efforts of teams, groups, staff areas, too.

10. Eliminate exhortations for the workforce.

11. (a) Eliminate numerical quotas for production. Instead, learn and institute methods for improvement.
    (b) Eliminate M.B.O. (management by objectives). Instead, learn capabilities of processes, and how to improve them.

12. Remove barriers that rob people of pride of workmanship.

13. Encourage education and self-improvement for everyone.

14. Take action to accomplish the transformation.

Source: Mary Walton, *The Deming Management Method* (New York: Dodd, Mead & Company, 1986), 34–36.

necessary to achieve quality. Only senior managers determine the markets in which the firm will participate and what products or services will be sold.

The worker, in turn, is responsible for the resolution of those *special* problems caused by actions or events directly under his or her control. In a production environment, for example, if a lathe operator measuring the diameter of a finished part sees that the tolerances are beginning to vary widely, the operator can change the cutting tool and correct the problem. If, however, the worker has attained process stability (removed all the special variations that could occur within the work process) and the output is still unacceptable, then Deming would advise that management redesign the system and eliminate the *common* problems.

Deming attempts to separate the *common* from the *special* causes that contribute to the variation in product or service quality and thereby allocate correctly the task of improving quality between the manager and the worker. He advocates the use of statistical quality control, since he believes it is "the statistical understanding of systems that allows accurate diagnosis and solution of problems."[11]

Juran

Dr. Joseph M. Juran, born in 1900 in an area that is now part of Romania, came to the United States in 1912 and settled in Minnesota. He attended college at the University of Minnesota and, after graduating in 1924, joined the inspection department at Bell Telephone's Hawthorne Works. Working within the Bell System until the start of World War II, Juran was also familiar with Shewhart's work and was personally involved in applying these and other statistical approaches in the production of telephone equipment.

Juran visited Japan in 1954 and, like Deming, assisted Japanese leaders in taking charge of restructuring their industries so they could export products to world markets. He was able to help the Japanese to adapt the quality concepts and tools designed primarily for the factory into a series of concepts that would become the basis for an overall "management process."[12]

Juran has documented three fundamental managerial processes that were originally used to manage the finances of an organization—financial planning, financial control, and financial improvement—and has applied this approach to the task of managing quality. The three elements of the Juran Trilogy[13] are as follows:

1 *Quality planning:* A process that identifies the customers, their requirements, the product and service features the customers expect, and the processes that will deliver those products and services with the correct attributes and then facilitates the transfer of this knowledge to the producing arm of the organization.

2 *Quality control:* A process in which the product is actually examined and evaluated against the original requirements expressed by the customer. Problems detected are then corrected.

3 *Quality improvement:* A process in which the sustaining mechanisms are put in place so that quality can be achieved on a continuous basis. This includes allocating resources, assigning people to pursue quality projects, training those involved in pursuing projects, and in general establishing a permanent structure to pursue quality and maintain the gains secured.

The approach Juran then advocates to implement quality is to identify team "projects" that can be targeted and scheduled for improvement. He believes this focus is required to concentrate attention on quality improvement. Juran, who has done a great deal of original work to quantify the benefits of pursuing quality improvement, indicates that project teams, on average, return about $100,000 in savings. If an

Table 2.2: Quality Costs: The Good, the Bad, and the Ugly

Good	Prevention	Costs associated with prevention activities, such as planning, training, design, and analysis	
Bad	Detection	Costs associated with appraisal and inspection, such as inspection of incoming work, auditing, verifying, checking, and final inspection	
Ugly	Quality not provided	Internal Failure	Rework and repair prior to delivery to customers
		External Failure	Repair, replace, refund after delivery to customers
		Exceeding Requirements	Costs incurred by providing product/service characteristics not valued by customers
		Lost Opportunity	Lost revenue resulting from customers' purchasing from your competitors

Source: Adapted from Xerox Corporation, *Leadership through Quality,* 1983.

organization agrees with the notion of the "cost of quality" (see Table 2.2) and accepts that the costs of imperfection can equal 30 percent of a firm's revenues, then dividing that value by $100,000 gives one an idea of the number of projects that must be underway in order to effectively reduce the cost of poor quality.[14]

Crosby

Philip B. Crosby, a quality advocate made famous in 1979 by his best-selling book *Quality Is Free,* started his career in manufacturing in 1952 at Crosley Corp. in Indiana. After he worked at a series of related manufacturing jobs, Crosby became director of quality for the Pershing missile project at Martin Marietta Corp. He was eminently successful in reducing the manufacturing defects in the production of the missile by embarking on a "zero-defects" program, which later became a government policy.[15] Crosby became famous in government circles because of his success with zero defects, but others who attempted to install the program were less successful, in part says Crosby, because of the lack of management commitment.[16]

Crosby moved to ITT, where he became the corporate vice president of quality and where he started the Quality College to impart the concepts of quality to ITT employees. In 1979, he retired to Winter Park, Florida, where he established the "Quality College" under his new firm, Philip Crosby Associates.

Crosby's approach to quality is also summarized in fourteen steps (see Table 2.3) but is built around the following four fundamental beliefs, which he calls "absolutes":[17]

1 Crosby defines quality as "conformance to requirements, not elegance." This differs from the conventional definition of quality in that it does not reference the manner in which the item is constructed or the method by which a service is provided. Rather, this definition is strategic, in that it focuses on trying to understand the full array of expectations that a customer has and drives organizations to meet these expectations. Clearly, this external view of quality is energizing, because it establishes targets that may be far more demanding and realistic than those established internally.

2 The quality system for suppliers attempting to meet customers' requirements is to do it right the first time—prevention, not inspection. This notion attempts to correct the problem created by Taylor by

ensuring that the worker manufacturing the product or providing the service does not pass defective work. There will be few, if any, inspectors in a quality organization, since everyone has the responsibility for his or her own work. There is no one else to catch errors.

3 The performance standard is zero defects. Crosby has advocated the notion that zero errors can and should be a target. Certainly, he would cite the fact that we would probably always choose an airline that strives for zero accidents or a surgeon who strives for zero fatalities as examples where no tolerance for failure is acceptable. Crosby advocates not expecting any less in the performance of our own work!

Table 2.3: Crosby's Quality Management

	Quality Absolutes		*Quality Improvement Process*
	Conventional Wisdom	*Reality*	
1. Definition	Goodness	Conformance to Requirements	1. Management Commitment
2. System	Appraisal	Prevention	2. Quality Improvement Team
3. Standard	That's Close Enough	Zero Defects	3. Measurement
4. Measure	Indices	Price of Nonconformance	4. Cost of Quality
			5. Quality Awareness
			6. Corrective Action
			7. Zero Defects Planning
			8. Employee Education
			9. Zero Defects Day
			10. Goal Setting
			11. Error Cause Removal
			12. Recognition
			13. Quality Councils
			14. Do It All Over Again

Source: Creative Factory, Inc. All rights reserved. Reprinted with permission.

4 The measurement of quality is the cost of quality. Costs of imperfection, if corrected, have an immediate beneficial effect on bottom-line performance as well as on customer relations. To that extent, investments should be made in training and other supporting activities to eliminate errors and recover the costs of waste. Crosby and others cite the costs of quality as equal to 20 percent to 40 percent of a firm's revenues.

Two of Crosby's absolutes, zero defects and cost of quality, have been particularly difficult to implement. These two concepts have not been universally accepted, and many organizations have failed to successfully apply them. But in deference to Crosby, these failures may not necessarily reflect the validity of the concepts; instead, they may reflect failures on the part of senior management to implement these approaches correctly.

Feigenbaum

Dr. Armand V. Feigenbaum, a former manager of manufacturing operations and quality control for General Electric, has contributed significantly to the worldwide quality movement by developing the approach that the responsibility for quality extends well beyond the manufacturing department. Feigenbaum, currently a quality consultant, developed the concept that quality in manufacturing could not be achieved if the products were poorly designed, inefficiently distributed, incorrectly marketed, and improperly supported in the customer's site. Thus, Feigenbaum's idea that every function within the organization is responsible for quality was developed and became known as total quality control (TQC).

Feigenbaum also originated the concept known as the "cost of quality" as a means of quantifying the benefits of adopting a total quality management approach. He developed this approach as a result of working with a number of departments in which he encouraged managers to track the costs of failure and the rework necessary to correct the problems. "The sum of these costs represents 10 to 40 percent of companies' annual sales," says Feigenbaum.[18]

The Gurus' Common Teachings

The common thrust behind the teachings of each of these quality gurus is the concept of continuous improvement. Although their approaches differ in technique, emphasis, and application, the objective is the same—continuous improvement of every output, whether it be a product or a service, by removing unwanted variation and by improving the underlying work processes.

Emergence of the Japanese Economy

Deming, Juran, and others visited with business leaders around the world in the cause of improving quality. Why is it, then, that their messages were heard, adopted, and embraced by leaders in Japan and not by leaders in other countries?

The answer lies, in part, with the fact that the Japanese economy was completely devastated after World War II. Their factories were demolished, and those that remained intact were designed solely for the production of war material, not very useful in a conquered country. Another problem facing the Japanese was their prewar reputation for shoddy goods, an unacceptable problem for a country that must rely on exports to survive.

Japanese managers studied foreign manufacturing practices, scoured the literature for the best practices employed by others, and invited guest lecturers like Deming and Juran to address their national leaders.[19] Since this was such a critical issue for the country, senior managers became involved and personally drove the effort to improve the quality of their exports. They reinforced all these efforts by establishing mechanisms to ensure that quality was pursued on a continuous basis; they supported their drive with extensive training; and they involved their employees through such techniques as quality circles.

The effect has been that by the end of the 1980s, Japan, a country with no natural resources and insufficient land to grow enough crops to feed its people, has become the second largest industrial power in the world, with a trade surplus of U.S. dollars exceeding $50 billion and the third highest per capita GNP in the world.[20]

The Customer Is King—Again!

American consumers have elected in the 1990s to purchase the goods and services that best meet their needs, regardless of their country of origin. The relative absence of trade barriers, tariffs, and restrictions on the entry of goods has turned the United States into the largest open market in the world. This has subjected American producers to intense competitive pressure from the best-managed firms in the world and has shifted the consumer to a position where the availability of superior products and services is no longer an issue. The consumer now selects from a full array of offerings from suppliers from around the world. The consumer is king—again!

Philip Kotler, a well-known professor of marketing at Northwestern University's Kellogg School, contrasts organizations that secure their profits through the pursuit of sales volume versus those that secure their profits through customer satisfaction. He states that most firms "don't embrace the [customer satisfaction] marketing concept and are driven to it by circumstances."[21] He describes these circumstances as "sales declines, slow growth, changing buying patterns, increasing competition, and increasing market expenditures."[22]

As General Motors has discovered, ignoring customers' needs, expectations, and requirements can be dangerous to the well-being of an organization. Roger Smith, CEO of GM, stated in *USA Today* in August 1989 that GM lost market share in the 1980s "because our quality wasn't where it should be."[23] Smith, preoccupied with the restructuring of GM to achieve low operating costs during his eight and a half years with the company, lost sight of satisfying the auto customer. During this period in the eighties, GM's share of the U.S. car and truck market declined from 44 percent to 35 percent.[24]

In mid-1990, GM began aggressively embracing the concept of quality and the need to meet its customers' requirements. Whether it will succeed in regaining its customer focus is open to some debate.

Summary

The post–World War II economy has given way to a new era in which consumers can choose from a full array of goods and services. The relative openness of U.S. markets to all foreign firms means that U.S.-managed firms are subjected to increasingly intense competition from emerging economies with lower wage rates, from economies that enjoy a lower cost of capital, and from economies whose employees have a different work ethic. These conditions, coupled with the fact that American consumers will always choose those goods and services that best meet their full range of requirements, mean that American managers must change the way they manage if they are to survive and if we as a nation are to maintain our standard of living.

The MIT Commission reported in *Made in America* that the problems plaguing American industries are not just random events that, given

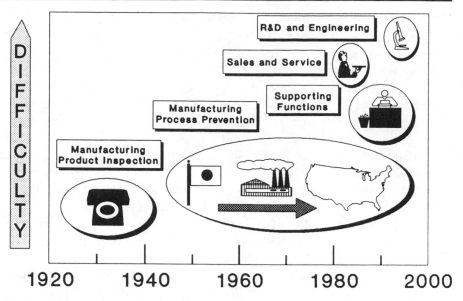

Figure 2.1   History of Quality Improvement

time, will correct themselves but rather are signs of "systematic and pervasive ills" that cannot be corrected by working "harder to do the same things that failed in the past." We have to adapt ourselves to the new economic environment in which we find ourselves.[25]

Yet a brief review of history would reveal that efforts to improve quality were initiated here in the United States in the early part of this century by men like Shewhart, Deming, Juran, Feigenbaum, Crosby, and others. Their approach was to move from the *inspection* of manufactured products to uncover defects to the *prevention* of defects. This approach recognizes the expense and waste associated with reworking defective products and emphasizes the need to *improve* the fundamental *processes* employed by an organization (see Figure 2.1).

Although perfected by the Japanese in the 1960s and 1970s, quality management returned to North America in the 1980s, and our challenge is to extend these successful manufacturing-improvement concepts to the service sector. The application of process improvement to the creation and delivery of services—health services, transportation services, information services, research and development services, engineering services, and marketing services, to name a few—is the subject of this book.

Total Quality Management

Notes

1. David A. Garvin, *Managing Quality: The Strategic and Competitive Edge* (New York: Free Press, 1988).

2. Wayne K. Hoy and Cecil G. Miskel, *Educational Administration: Theory, Research and Practice*, 2d ed. (New York: Random House, 1978).

3. Frederick W. Taylor, *Scientific Management* (New York: Harper, 1947), 63–64.

4. J. M. Juran, *Juran on Leadership for Quality: An Executive Handbook* (New York: Free Press, 1989), 4.

5. Ibid.

6. Garvin, *Managing Quality*.

7. Ibid.

8. Mary Walton, *The Deming Management Method* (New York: Dodd, Mead, 1986).

9. Ibid., 9.

10. W. E. Deming, *Management of Statistical Techniques for Quality and Productivity* (New York: New York University, Graduate School of Business, 1981).

11. Chapman Wood, "The Prophets of Quality," *Quarterly Review*, American Society for Quality Control (Fall 1988).

12. Ibid., 21.

13. Juran, *Juran on Leadership for Quality*, 20. ("Trilogy" is a registered trademark of the Juran Institute.)

14. J. M. Juran, "Prescription for the West: Four Years Later" (presented as the closing address at the 29th Conference of the European Organization for Quality Control, Estoril, Portugal, June 1985).

15. Wood, "Prophets of Quality," 25.

16. Ibid.

17. Philip B. Crosby, *Quality Is Free: The Art of Making Quality Certain* (New York: Mentor Books, New American Library, 1979).

18. Ibid., 24.

19. Ibid., 7.

20. "Economic and Financial Indicators," *The Economist*, July 7–13, 1990, 99–100.

21. Philip Kotler, *Marketing Management: Analysis, Planning, and Control* (Englewood Cliffs, N.J.: Prentice-Hall, 1984), 23.

22. Ibid., 24.

23. James R. Healy, "Quality in the '80s Wasn't Where It Should Be," *USA Today*, sec. B, Money (Aug. 1, 1989).

24. Ibid., 1B.

25. Michael L. Dertouzos, Richard K. Lester, Robert M. Solow, and the MIT Commission on Industrial Productivity, *Made in America: Regaining the Productivity Edge* (Cambridge, Mass.: MIT Press, 1989), 8.

3 *Quality Redefined*

The word *quality* has many different definitions, ranging from the conventional to those that are more strategic. Conventional definitions of quality usually describe a quality item as one that wears well, is well constructed, and will last a long time. Still another definition conveys the image of excellence, first-rate, the best. However, managers competing in the fierce international marketplace are increasingly concerned with the strategic definition of quality: *meeting the needs of customers.*

Well-respected senior executives like J. Houghton from the Corning Corporation declare that "quality is the critical business issue. This means quality in the broadest sense from Manufacturing to Administration."[1] What is Houghton talking about? How does he define quality, and how does that definition account for meeting the needs of the customer?

This chapter explores the seemingly divergent definitions of quality and develops a definition for those of us who are charged with the responsibility of improving service performance.

Evolution of Marketing Concepts

In his text *Marketing Management*, Professor Philip Kotler discusses several different philosophies under which organizations manage their businesses:

- *The production concept:* This approach assumes that the customer is primarily interested in low cost and widely available products and services. This concept implies that producers concentrate their efforts on increasing volumes by standardizing goods and services and by applying mass-production technology. This approach requires high volumes over which all costs can be allocated and, presumably, provides low-unit-cost goods and services that then become widely available.

- *The product concept:* This approach holds that consumers prefer products that are well made and contain a full array of features and benefits, and services that are performed properly, and that these consumers will be loyal to these products and services even if a trend toward newer products and services develops. These consumers are willing to pay more for these attributes, and producers of the goods or services that operate under this concept will be focused internally, constantly improving their product or service. The risk, of course, is that producers may become so internally focused that they fail to recognize the emergence of new trends, new fashions, new demands from their customers.

- *The selling concept:* This concept is based on the assumption that the customer will not buy a product or service solely on the merits of the offering by the provider and must therefore be moved to action—a buying decision—by an aggressive selling strategy. Kotler describes this approach as one that is often used with "unsought goods"—items we normally do not consider unless brought to our attention: "insurance, encyclopaedias, and funeral plots."

- *The marketing approach:* This approach is totally different from the others in that it is based on the belief that the business objectives of the organization can best be achieved through the complete satisfaction of the end user—the customer.[2]

Kotler, having described the various concepts that organizations have used to attain their profit objectives, is quick to point out, *"most companies don't really grasp or embrace the marketing concept until driven to it by circumstances."*[3] These circumstances, described earlier, have been the very pressures to which U.S. businesses have been subjected from international competitors that have entered our markets with an unprecedented intensity.

Evolution of Quality Concepts

David Garvin, in his book *Managing Quality,* describes five major approaches to quality, several of which parallel the development of the marketing approaches described by Kotler:

1 *Transcendent:* Quality is understood only after exposure to a series of objects that develop its characteristics. The example that is often used to explain this definition is that the quality of a particular artist only becomes apparent when a number of his or her works have been viewed. The idea here is that quality can't be defined, and you recognize it only when you see it.

2 *Product-based:* Quality is based on the presence or absence of a particular attribute. If an attribute is desirable, greater amounts of that attribute, under this definition, would label that product or service as one of higher quality.

3 *Manufacturing-based:* Quality in manufacturing is defined as the conformance of a product or service to a set of predetermined requirements or specifications. Failure to meet these requirements is, by definition, a deviation and, as such, represents a lack of quality. This approach assumes that the specification is a valid surrogate for a customer requirement and that, if met, it would satisfy the customer.

4 *User-based:* Quality "lies in the eye of the beholder." The ability to satisfy the customers' requirements, expectations, or wants is the sole criterion by which quality will be determined. This definition supports Kotler's "marketing concept," in which the ultimate aim of the organization is the complete satisfaction of the customer.

5 *Value-based:* Quality under this definition consists of offering a product or service to a customer with certain characteristics at an acceptable cost or price. This definition combines the idea of worth or value with the offering.[4]

These definitions are essentially ones that have been developed within manufacturing organizations, but even with that constraint, it is evident that the evolution in the firm's response to the marketplace as described by Kotler and the definition offered by Garvin are converging.

Evolution of the Total Quality Management Concept

The concept of quality, as described by the foregoing definitions provided by Kotler and Garvin, first began in manufacturing organizations producing physical, tangible products. Indeed, it's clear that one worker might receive immediate feedback if the subassembly being passed on were faulty. As a result, much progress has been made in the pursuit of product- and user-based quality as firms pursued either the production or product philosophy in their organizations. But we need to recognize that we moved in the 1980s to a new consumer-oriented economy that brings the concept of quality closer to the user-based/value-based approach described by Garvin and the marketing approach used by Kotler.

The quality gurus introduced in Chapter 2 offer a variety of definitions of quality, but they, too, are all structured around satisfying the customer. Juran describes quality as "fitness for use,"[5] and Deming cites in his first point for top management that they "must satisfy customer needs."[6] Crosby, in his absolutes of quality, defines quality as "conformance to [customer] requirements."[7]

What is needed, then, is a new operational definition of quality that organizations can employ to describe the management approach that they intend to use in order to achieve their organizational objectives. Clearly, such a definition must account for the customer, but we have come to realize that an organization must satisfy many different types of customers. To accommodate the need to meet these varying requirements, we offer the following definition:

Quality: A basic business strategy that provides goods and services that completely satisfy both internal and external customers by meeting their explicit and implicit expectations.

Furthermore, this strategy utilizes the talents of all employees, to the benefit of the organization in particular and society in general, and provides a positive financial return to the shareholders.

What Is a Total Quality Management System?

It has become clear in the last forty-five years—thanks to Crosby, Deming, Feigenbaum, Juran, and others—that quality is not determined by the worker on the shop floor, nor is it determined by the service technician working at the customer's site. Quality is determined by the senior managers of an organization, who by virtue of the positions they hold, are responsible to customers, employees, suppliers, and shareholders for the success of the business. These senior managers allocate resources, decide which markets the firm will enter, and select and implement the management processes that will enable the firm to fulfill their mission and, eventually, their vision.

Combining the various teachings of the quality gurus with practical experience has led to the development of a simple but effective model

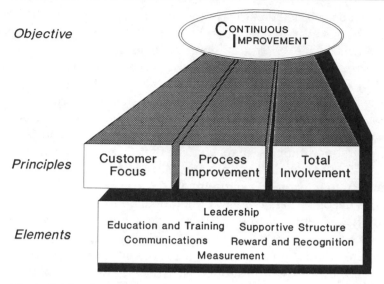

Figure 3.1 Implementation Concepts

for implementing total quality management (TQM; see Figure 3.1). This model builds on three fundamental principles of total quality—focus on the customers, internal and external; focus on improving work processes to produce consistent, acceptable outputs; and focus on utilizing the talents of those with whom we work—and six supporting elements. This model is expanded throughout the remainder of this book.

Quality Principles

- *Customer focus:* Quality is based on the concept that everyone has a customer and that the requirements, needs, and expectations of that customer must be met every time if the organization as a whole is going to meet the needs of the external customer. This concept requires a thorough collection and analysis of customer requirements, and when these requirements are understood and accepted, they must be met.

- *Process improvement:* The concept of continuous improvement is built on the premise that work is the result of a series of interrelated steps and activities that result in an output. Continuous attention to each of these steps in the work process is necessary to reduce the variability of the output and improve the reliability of the process. The first goal of continuous improvement is processes that are reliable—reliable in the sense that they produce the desired output each time with no variation. If variability has been minimized and the results are still unacceptable, the second goal of process improvement is to redesign the process to produce an output that is better able to meet the customer's requirement.

- *Total involvement:* This approach begins with the active leadership of senior management and includes efforts that utilize the talents of all employees in the organization to gain a competitive advantage in the marketplace. Employees at all levels are empowered to improve their outputs by coming together in new and flexible work structures to solve problems, improve processes, and satisfy customers. Suppliers are also included and, over time, become partners by working with empowered employees to the benefit of the organization.

Supporting Elements

- *Leadership:* Senior management must lead this effort by example, by applying the tools and language, by requiring the use of data, and by recognizing those who successfully apply the concepts of TQM. When installing TQM as the key management process, the importance of the role of senior managers as advocates, teachers, and leaders cannot be overstated.

    The senior officer of any organization should fully appreciate the implications of managing in an international economy in which the world's best-educated, most competent, and most successful managers may be employed by the competition. This hard reality will awaken senior managers to the fact that they must develop, in a participative manner, their mission and their vision as well as a management process that they can use to attain both. Business leaders must understand that total quality management is such a process and is composed of principles and supporting elements that they must manage in order to achieve continuous quality improvement.

- *Education and training:* Quality is based on the skills of every employee and his or her understanding of what is required. Educating and training all employees provides the *information* they need on the mission, vision, direction, and strategy of the organization as well as the *skills* they need to secure quality improvement and resolve problems. This core training ensures that a common language and a common set of tools will be used throughout the firm. Additional training on benchmarking, statistics, and other techniques is also required to pursue and achieve complete customer satisfaction.

- *Supportive structure:* Senior managers may require support to bring about the change necessary to implement a quality strategy. Such support may be provided by outside consultants, but it is clearly far superior for an organization to be self-sufficient. To gain this self-sufficiency, a small support staff can help the senior management team understand the concepts of quality, assist by networking with other quality managers in other parts of the organization, and serve as a resource on the topic of quality for the senior management team.

- *Communications:* Communications in a quality environment may need to be addressed differently in order to communicate to all employees a sincere commitment to change. For example, most newsletters have low credibility because they are viewed as a means of conveying just management's point of view, or propaganda. If readership surveys and other data collected support this view, then different means of communication have to be developed to overcome this problem. Ideally, managers should meet personally with employees to disseminate information, provide direction, and respond to questions from everyone.

    Success stories recognizing individuals, examples of the application of quality tools, and cases of improved customer satisfaction are all material for quality communications.

- *Reward and recognition:* Teams and individuals who successfully apply the quality process must be recognized and possibly rewarded, so that the rest of the organization will know what is expected. Failure to recognize someone who achieves success using the touted quality management process will convey the message that this is not the true path to job success, possible promotion, and overall personal success. In the early stages of any new fundamental change, especially a new management process, employees are looking for subtle signals as to management's true intention, its true motives. Recognizing successful quality practitioners provides role models for the rest of the organization.

- *Measurement:* The use of data becomes paramount in installing a quality management process. Clearly, opinions must give way to data and everyone must understand that it's not what you think that's important, it's what you know! To set the stage for the use of data, external customer satisfaction must be measured to determine the extent to which customers perceive that their needs are being met. The collection of customer data provides an objective, realistic assessment of performance and is useful in motivating everyone to address real problems.

Summary

Since the end of World War II, organizations attempting to achieve their business objectives of improved market share, increased return on assets, and improved margins have come to appreciate that those objectives can only be achieved by moving from internally to externally focused management systems.

Clearly, any of the internally focused approaches to marketing described by Kotler or the internally focused definitions reported on by Garvin cause an organization to be unaware of changes in marketplace requirements and thereby render its products or service, over time, ineffective. Conversely, paying close attention to the needs of the external customers and meeting those needs is a route to achieving increasing success in the marketplace.

Extending the concept of satisfying all external customers to include the notion that everyone has an internal customer who must be satisfied is a powerful, driving, realistic force in directing the activities of everyone in an organization. This view of satisfying customers, both internal and external to the organization, and using assessments of how well customers perceive that their requirements are being met is the only valid strategy to ensure the survival of any organization.

Notes

1. James R. Houghton, "The Age of the Hierarchy Is Over," *New York Times,* September 24, 1989, D2.

2. Philip Kotler, *Marketing Management* (Englewood Cliffs, N.J.: Prentice-Hall, 1984), 17–29.

3. Ibid., 23.

4. David A. Garvin, *Managing Quality: The Strategic and Competitive Edge* (New York: Free Press, 1988), 41–46.

5. Joseph M. Juran, *Juran's Quality Control Handbook,* 4th ed. (New York: McGraw-Hill, 1988), 2.8.

6. Mary Walton, *Deming Management at Work* (New York: G. P. Putnam and Sons, 1991), 21.

7. Philip B. Crosby, *Quality Is Free* (New York: New American Library, 1979), 111.

4

Applying Quality Concepts

This chapter helps readers begin the application of the total quality management (TQM) concepts that were introduced in Chapter 3. The approach relies on understanding all work as a process. The continuous improvement of work processes represents one of the key principles of TQM, but many quality practitioners have struggled when applying this basic principle beyond the manufacturing operations for which it was developed. To enable this principle to be extended to other functions, this chapter clarifies three key differences that have been obstacles and introduces a method to overcome them.

When comparing various types of work processes, manufacturing stands out as unique in that (1) its customers are isolated from production, (2) its outputs are tangible, and (3) its operations are highly repetitive. By contrast, nonmanufacturing processes differ in one or more of these key features. Customers are usually involved directly in the delivery of services, and the value added by nonmanufacturing processes is often characterized as intangible. Further, some nonmanufacturing processes are repeated infrequently, and their outputs can be unique every time.

Application of the quality improvement concepts and tools beyond the manufacturing processes for which they were designed requires overcoming the obstacles imposed by these three key differences. In some cases, this requires clarifying the underlying work processes. In other cases, it requires identifying objective measures. And in still other cases, it requires taking both of these steps.

Although it sounds simple, overcoming these key differences can be very difficult. How do we establish measurable objectives for professional services that completely capture the full set of customer expecta-

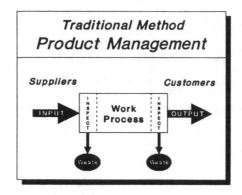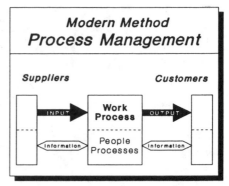

Figure 4.1   Quality Process Management

tions? How do we measure and analyze administrative processes that are repeated quarterly, annually, or perhaps only once every few years? How do we predict the behavior of customers who are involved in service transactions? This chapter helps readers to begin probing for answers to these questions.

Product versus Process

The migration of quality improvement from product management to process management paved the way for extending improvement techniques beyond manufacturing. As shown in Figure 4.1, the traditional method focused on the product or output. Quality improvement required tighter inspection of both incoming raw materials and outgoing finished products. With this approach, better quality was achieved at the expense of increased waste and higher costs. This is contrasted with modern, process-centered quality improvement, in which better quality can be achieved without necessarily increasing costs.

Improving quality through the process relies on an integrated approach along the entire customer-supplier chain. Process improvement is broader than just quality assurance or inspection. It is broader than just operations and production alone. Furthermore, process

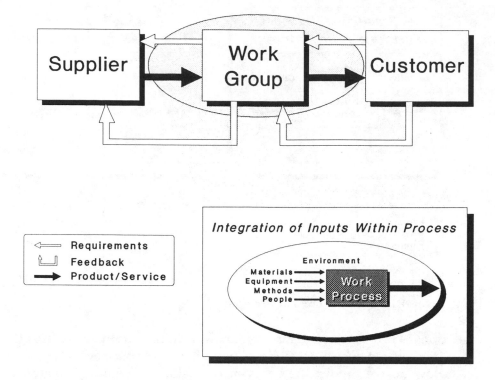

Figure 4.2   Work Process Model. *Source:* Adapted from W.W. Scherkenbach, *The Deming Route to Quality and Productivity* (Rockville, Md.: Continuing Engineering Education Press, 1987), 36.

improvement can be applied to nonmanufacturing as well as manufacturing functions. The extension beyond manufacturing is explained in this chapter.

Figure 4.1 shows the integrations of process management along the customer-supplier chain. At its core are the work processes themselves, the processes on which product quality improvement efforts had traditionally focused. Process management recognizes the value of the line workers who produce and deliver products/services and integrates them into the improvement processes. Process management also recognizes the role of customers and suppliers and integrates the systems that exchange information with them.

Figure 4.2 shows the basic elements of the work process model. The process begins with the flow of information in the form of requirements from the customer to define the characteristics of the desired output. The work group then integrates materials, equipment, methods, and people within an environment to produce these outputs. Customer satisfaction forms the feedback loop that drives corrective action to improve performance. This same model is mirrored upstream to suppliers. This basic model serves as the foundation for understanding and improving processes, regardless of the output—e.g., products, services, or information.

To extend the work process model beyond manufacturing, it might be helpful to clarify one element at this point—materials. The materials delivered by suppliers to manufacturers include such items as raw materials, subassemblies, and component parts. By contrast, the basic materials supplied to work groups in information services are information and data. Engineers add value to technical and business data, and dental hygienists perform their craft on their customers' teeth. Although these materials may look and feel very different than such classics as iron and coal, they do not preclude use of the process model.

Quality process management offers an inherent competitive advantage over alternative practices because it permits the improvement of quality while simultaneously reducing waste and costs. This advantage is available to all organizations, regardless of whether their outputs are manufactured products, marketing data, financial services, information services, health care, technical consulting, engineering designs, or administrative services. Since quality improvement techniques were developed for manufacturing, successfully applying them to other functions requires identifying the inherent differences between these work processes and adapting the techniques to the desired function.

Manufacturing versus Nonmanufacturing Processes

Manufacturing can be defined as the making of goods and products, especially by machines or on a large scale. But what about all of the other types of work performed—the delivery of services instead of products, one-of-a-kind production instead of large-scale? These other types of operations can be referred to as nonmanufacturing.

Nonmanufacturing processes differ from their manufacturing counterparts in a number of ways, and Table 4.1 compares several attributes. This table should not be read to imply universal differences between manufacturing and nonmanufacturing, merely general

Table 4.1: Comparing Typical Process Attributes

	Manufacturing	*Nonmanufacturing*
Output properties	Tangible	Intangible or tangible
Production and delivery	Separate	Integrated
Customer interface	Focused: sales and marketing	Spread across line employees
Feedback	Through process	Through customer
Organizational focus	Process efficiency	Customer relations
Process ownership	Clearly defined	Multiple
Process boundaries	Defined	Unclear
Process definition	Documented	Unclear
Control points	Defined	None
Quality measures	Established and objective	Subjective
Corrective action	Preventive	Reactive

tendencies. Furthermore, the differences displayed represent "historical" perspective, not "ideal" performance. Our intention is to show that some businesses tend to be characterized better by the attributes in the right column (nonmanufacturing) and others by those in the center column (manufacturing).

Consider the following differences: output properties that are tangible versus intangible; processes that are well documented versus unclear; quality measures that are objective and formally established versus subjective; and work processes that are separated from customers versus subject to customer intervention. Quality improvement techniques were designed for applications typified by the first rather than the second characteristic in each pair. Thus, the following can be concluded about the attributes of applications that are best suited to classic quality improvement techniques:

1 Tangible outputs that permit direct physical measurement, determination of objective customer requirements, and translation into definitive engineering specifications.
2 Processes that are clearly documented, including raw material and equipment specifications, product movement, operating procedures, and performance standards.

3 Functional delineation of production, sale, and delivery that clarifies organizational boundaries, process ownership, and logical control points. In combination with items 1 and 2, quality measures can be established and controlled within each step of the process.

As business characteristics diverge from those of the ideal applications, successful use of classic quality improvement techniques can be expected to require adaptation. Furthermore, the importance of adaptation increases in relation to the number of attributes deviating from those defined in the center column of Table 4.1.

Improving Nonmanufacturing Processes

The preceding array of differences in the attributes of manufacturing and nonmanufacturing processes can be simplified to three key characteristics: coproduction, tangibility, and repetition. This simplification enables the extension of classic quality improvement techniques.

Coproduction: Customer Participation in Your Work

Customer participation in the production of the output is the first key characteristic that distinguishes manufacturing from nonmanufacturing processes. Referred to as coproduction, this characteristic is found in most nonmanufacturing functions.

As coproducers, customers frequently provide the material input into the service process. Customers supply the automobiles, appliances, and buildings on which maintenance and repair services are performed. Customers supply their own bodies to the work processes in the health care, travel, and entertainment fields. Customers supply the money managed and the data processed in financial and information services. Customers supply the conceptual designs and real estate used in construction.

The feature of coproduction brings the customer directly into the service process. As a result, the process itself represents an experience of vital interest, importance, and value to the customer. Coproduction also exposes a broad array of employees in face-to-face contact with customers. In fact, coproduction influences the basic design of service processes.

Tangibility and Repetition

Tangibility and repetition are the other two key characteristics that distinguish manufacturing from nonmanufacturing functions. Defining

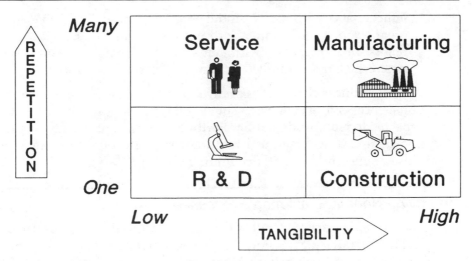

Figure 4.3 Output Characteristics. *Source:* G. J. Kidd, "A Scientific Approach to Quality in R&D," *ASQC Quality Congress Transactions* (Toronto: American Society for Quality Control, May 1989), 848. ℗The American Society for Quality Control. Reprinted by permission.

specifications and measuring conformance of tangible outputs are relatively straightforward procedures that can rely on physical characteristics such as size, weight, shape, volume, thickness, and material composition. Repetitive processes generate large quantities of data over relatively short periods of time. The combination of tangible outputs with repetitive processes facilitates the measurement, comparison, analysis, and systematic improvement of operations, as well as the inspection, grading, and sorting of outputs.

As shown in Figure 4.3, outputs that are both tangible and repetitive are a combination unique to manufacturing. By contrast, construction has tangible outputs, but they are often nonrepetitive and can be unique. Although often repetitive, outputs from the service sector are characterized as intangible. Professional services—such as research, engineering, or technical consulting—show the greatest difference relative to manufacturing, since the principal attributes of their outputs are intangible, and each output is unique.[1]

Overcoming Obstacles

There is nothing mystical about nonmanufacturing processes that precludes use of the work process model developed for manufacturing.

Table 4.2: Simplifying Ten Service Characteristics to Three Key Differences

Ten Characteristics of Service Identified by Albrecht and Zemke in Service America	Key Differences
1. Service is produced at the instant of delivery and cannot be created in advance and stored in inventory.	C T R
2. Service cannot be centrally produced, inspected, or stockpiled.	C T R
3. Service cannot be demonstrated, nor can a sample be sent in advance for approval.	C T
4. In the absence of tangible product, customers value service on the basis of their own personal experience.	T
5. The service experience cannot be resold or passed on to a third party.	C T
6. Faulty service cannot be recalled.	C T
7. Quality assurance is required before production. [Authors' note: Differentiation on when quality assurance is performed represents the difference between product management and process management presented earlier in this chapter. Albrecht and Zemke's point 7 is always valid for services in which customers participate in the delivery process (coproduction). Quality assurance is also required before production in manufacturing under the concept of quality improvement through prevention instead of detection.]	C
8. Delivery of service usually requires human interactions.	C
9. Customers' assessments of service quality are subjective and strongly influenced by expectations.	T R
10. Customers' assessments of service quality tend to decrease in proportion to the number of employees they encounter during the delivery of services.	C

Source: K. Albrecht and R. Zemke, *Service America* (Homewood, Ill.: Dow Jones–Irwin, 1985), 36–37.

Note: C = coproduction by customer; T = tangibility (lack of); R = repetition (lack of).

Nonmanufacturing processes merely represent various combinations of differences in the three key characteristics: coproduction, tangibility, and repetition.

Accommodations for these three differences pervade the design and operation of work processes outside of manufacturing. In their book *Service America*, Karl Albrecht and Ron Zemke offer ten characteristics to differentiate physical products from services.[2] Table 4.2 shows the relationship between their ten features and the three key characteristics introduced in this chapter.

In order to apply quality tools beyond the manufacturing processes for which they were designed, it is necessary to overcome the obstacles imposed by the three key differences. In cases where the outputs are intangible, successful application requires the identification of appropriate measures, either subjective or objective. In cases where the outputs are unique or in which customers are coproducers, successful application requires the clarification of the underlying work processes that are repeated. And in other cases, application requires taking both of these steps.

Measurement at Three Levels

The measurement of performance also becomes more difficult as business characteristics diverge from those of the ideal applications. This obstacle to quality improvement can be overcome by taking advantage of measurement at three levels: process, output, and outcome. Unfortunately, when performance parameters are difficult to define or measure, the tendency has been to substitute other measures without recognizing that they represent different levels. The following is an explanation of the three measurement levels:

1 *Process measures* define activities, variables, and operations of the work process itself. Measures at the process level also include measuring the products and services that suppliers input to the work process. These measures represent parameters that directly control the integration of people, materials, methods, machines, and the environment within the work process. Although frequently understood and used in manufacturing operations, measures at the process level are often absent from other functions. Understanding and applying measures at the process level help to predict the characteristics of the outputs *before* they are delivered to customers.

2 *Output measures* define specific features, values, characteristics, and attributes of each product or service. Furthermore, output measures can be examined from two sides. One side represents the output characteristics desired by the customer, and the other side represents the output characteristics actually delivered by the process. The former is referred to as requirements, expectations, or the voice of the customer. The latter is referred to as capability or the voice of the process. Measures at the output level reveal what *is* delivered to customers.

3 *Outcome measures* define the ultimate impact of the process on the customer and are dependent on what the customer does with the

product or service. Although this is the most important level, outcome measures are the most difficult to define and analyze because they are confounded by the customer's work process. To simplify the array of performance measures, customer satisfaction can be used as the key measurement of outcome. Measures at the outcome level reflect the impact of outputs on the customer's processes and can only be determined *after* the product has been delivered or the service provided.

Training-Division Example of Measurement Levels

An example of training for the customer service representatives of an appliance manufacturer will help clarify the three measurement levels. This example deals with a work process that differs from manufacturing in all three characteristics: (1) customers are coproducers; (2) outputs are mostly intangible; and (3) the output is repeated only a few times. With the aid of Figure 4.4, this example also shows how the level of measure is dependent on the frame of reference as service transactions pass along the customer-supplier chain.

Participants in the example process include Carl Thoren, Michael Roberts, and the company's 240 service representatives who attend the training program and apply its teachings. Thoren and Roberts are both assigned to the training division. Thoren was responsible for developing and designing the training program, and Roberts then delivered the course to the service representatives.

Carl Thoren is an instructional designer in the training division of the customer service department. He developed a four-hour training session to improve service representatives' ability to answer maintenance questions on a new household appliance. Although Michael Roberts, the classroom instructor, is the direct customer of Thoren, attention must be paid to the needs of customers all along the chain, and especially to the ultimate end users. Activities in Thoren's work included identifying the training needs of the service representatives, developing the required training program, preparing an instructor's guide, and producing classroom materials.

Measures at the process level of Thoren's work are somewhat vague and only partly defined. One obvious measure is the length of time required for each activity, but the training division has not clarified any others. Instead, it focuses on output measures and develops internal process measures as needed to understand and improve performance.

Outputs from Thoren's work include the design of the four-hour

The Customer-Supplier Chain

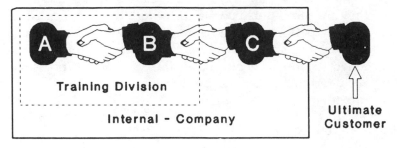

Key	Role		Example Measures
A	Instructional designer	**PROCESS**	Time to develop new course
		OUTPUT	72-page guide; 26-page manual; 34 visual aids; 4-hour design;
		OUTCOME	10 classes delivered
B	Classroom instructor	**PROCESS**	Time to plan lessons
		OUTPUT	10 classes delivered
		OUTCOME	5 skills gained by 240 reps
C	Service representative	**PROCESS**	5 skills gained
		OUTPUT	24 contacts added weekly
		OUTCOME	$60,000/month higher sales; happier customers

Figure 4.4   Relating Measurement Levels.

course, a seventy-two-page instructor's guide, a twenty-six-page participant's manual, and thirty-four visual aids for use in the classroom. These items are the tangible outputs from Thoren, but their measurement does not represent all of the most critically important parameters. Other output measures relate to the intangible characteristics required of these outputs, such as accuracy, completeness, clarity, and ease of use.

Michael Roberts, a classroom trainer, delivered ten sessions of the course that Thoren designed to 240 customer service representatives.

The inputs into Roberts' work process include outputs from Thoren. Furthermore, outputs from Roberts' work are outcomes of Thoren's process. Activities within Roberts' work included lesson planning, classroom preparation, and presentation of the actual course. As with Thoren, a complete set of process and output measures has not been defined for Roberts.

As an outcome of the training process, service representatives are now able to answer twenty-four additional customer inquiries each week. These additional calls are outputs of the customer service department. One outcome of these calls is an increase in sales of the new product by $60,000 per month. Another outcome is the improvement of customer satisfaction attributable to the new skills of the service reps.

Figure 4.4 shows how the level represented by any particular measurement is defined by its frame of reference. To see how this works, examine one measurement from three reference points. Training 240 service reps is an *outcome* of Thoren's work as the course designer. This same measure is a direct *output* from Roberts' work as the classroom instructor. This same measure is an activity in the daily *process* of the service representatives. This moving frame of reference shows how the measurement level is translated as products/services flow along the customer-supplier chain.

Even though its set of measurements is incomplete, the training division is able to improve its performance in the development and delivery of training programs through use of data from all three levels. By measuring appropriate parameters and results, experiments can be designed to test performance improvement hypotheses.

Summary

In order to apply the quality improvement concepts and tools beyond the manufacturing processes for which they were designed, the obstacles imposed by three key differences—coproduction, tangibility, and repetition—must be overcome. This can require clarifying the underlying work processes and/or identifying appropriate measurements.

Capturing the full set of performance measures is often an idealized dream. Complete measurement is not always practical, particularly when working outside of manufacturing and with intangible, subjective performance characteristics or unique outputs or processes in which customers are coproducers.

Use of measures at the process, output, and outcome levels provides a framework for understanding performance in dimensions beyond those that are objectively measurable. This approach can be thought of as an extension of high-school algebra with "three equations and three unknowns." The unknown values can be postulated and tested, derived through a systematic application of formulas, or guessed through trial and error.

By recognizing the key differences among various types of work processes, and by overcoming the obstacles imposed, the competitive advantage of TQM can be captured by all organizations.

Notes

1. G. J. Kidd, "A Scientific Approach to Quality in R&D," *ASQC Quality Congress Transactions* (Toronto: ASQC, May 1989), 848–853.
2. K. Albrecht and R. Zemke, *Service America* (Homewood, Ill.: Dow Jones–Irwin, 1985), 36–37.

References

Davidow, W. H., and Uttal, B. *Total Customer Service.* New York: Harper & Row, 1989.

Kane, E. J. "IBM's Quality Focus on the Business Process." *Quality Progress* 19, no. 3 (1986): 24–33.

Scherkenbach, W. W. *The Deming Route to Quality and Productivity.* (Rockville, Md.: Continuing Engineering Education Press, 1987).

Customer Focus

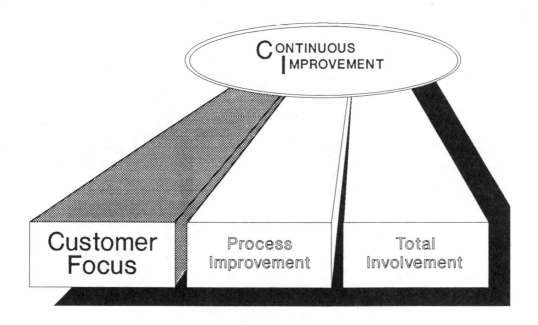

Customer Focus

Process Improvement

Total Involvement

CONTINUOUS IMPROVEMENT

5 *Identifying the Customer*

What is a customer?
A customer is the most important person ever in this office
. . . in person or by mail.
A customer is not dependent on us . . . , we are dependent on him.
A customer is not an interruption of our work.
. . . he is the purpose of it. We are not doing a favor by serving him.
. . . he is doing us a favor by giving us the opportunity to do so.
A customer is not someone to argue or match wits with.
Nobody ever won an argument with a customer.
A customer is a person who brings us his wants.
It is our job to handle them profitably to him and to ourselves.
—L. L. Bean, Freeport, Maine

The key to gaining a long-term competitive advantage is to continually meet customers' expectations in ways that they recognize as adding value. To achieve this advantage, it is necessary to know who your customers are, what they expect, and how well you (and your competitors) are performing from your customers' point of view. Focusing on the customer, then, is the first of three basic quality management principles.

Chapter 5 is the first of three chapters aimed at focusing on the customer and helps to identify *who* the customer is. Chapter 6 helps to identify *what* the customer expects. Understanding the customer's expectations is often referred to as listening to the voice of the customer and requires identifying the full set of product/service characteristics that the customer needs, his or her level of expectations, relative importance, and satisfaction. Chapter 7 explains *how* to listen to the voice of the customer through an array of readily available mechanisms.

Who Is the Customer?

We all assume that we can easily identify our customers. "We sell and service the Blue Chip Corporation," or we boast that "Lack Luster, Inc., is one of our biggest and best customers." But that simple identification of the customer is not useful, since Blue Chip Corp. may have a hundred thousand employees, and Lack Luster may be an international organization with locations throughout the world. We need to know specifically who within Blue Chip Corp. and who within Lack Luster, Inc., is our customer and for what!

We need to know to whom we must talk to assess the level of customer service that we are providing, and we need to identify what we must do in the future to improve. Obviously, to do these things, we need to identify specific people with whom we work within each client organization so that we can become more precise about what we must do to better meet their needs.

This chapter provides a series of guidelines and a framework that can be applied to identify our specific customers, what they expect from us, and the process by which we know how well we are providing the services they have requested. This chapter also expands our approach for identifying customers to include working with internal as well as external customers.

If the task of identifying external customers is difficult, the task of identifying fellow employees as potential customers may be even more complex, especially when dealing with professional or senior-level employees. For example, the worker on the assembly line knows full well that if he or she passes a defective product or performs a service inadequately for a fellow worker, the feedback is immediate and direct. But what happens when a patent attorney, located at headquarters, is not responsive to a field research scientist filing a patent application? Does the attorney realize that, like the assembly-line worker, the research scientist is a customer with needs and requirements that must be met?

The concept of internal customers is significant because it dramatically makes the case that an organization cannot successfully meet the needs of its external customers if each output passed between employees within the company is deficient. Mathematically, it is easy to see that the external customers' requirements cannot be achieved 100 percent of the time if each handoff within is less than 100 percent. For example, a chain of only three internal suppliers who each meet 90 percent of their internal customers' requirements may result in a 73 percent effective delivery from the organization to an external customer ($90\% \times 90\% \times 90\% = 73\%$).

In working with major clients, we have observed that interactions among external and internal customers are so complex that a framework was needed to facilitate the identification of such customers. The first step in developing such a framework is to identify the output—a product or service that an individual produces. Next, we pose the question, "Who is the person to whom I will pass this output?" If no individual can be identified, then, obviously, scrap is being produced and an immediate decision can be made to stop! A framework, such as the one described in Chapter 9, is a useful guide to improving outputs.

If however, we can identify the person to whom we pass the output of our work, then we can secure from that person a list of needs, expectations, and requirements that we as the supplier must meet. Several guidelines on correctly identifying outputs are listed here:

What Outputs Are Not

- *Things that you supervise or approve but that are actually produced by others.* Examples are budgets that are developed by a staff but approved by a senior manager. The budget is the output of the financial staff; the senior manager is a cosupplier.

- *Goals or outcomes for the organization.* Examples are profits, customer satisfaction, revenues, and market share increases. Like morale, these outcomes are the result of a number of outputs produced by a number of people and are usually beyond the capability of a single individual to impact or influence.

- *Steps in the work process.* Generating a work plan or schedule is a step that an individual takes as part of the effort to complete a project but is not an "output" that is passed along to others.

- *The overall function described by an individual's job title or responsibility.* The manager of the computer service department, in all likelihood, does not actually repair computers, even though he or she is certainly responsible for the timely, accurate repair of malfunctioning computers. Rather, the manager generates staffing plans, forecasts, training plans, budgets, and a number of other outputs that are passed to others. The employees in the department actually perform the repair service because they visit the customer's site, diagnose the problems, and effect the repairs.

What Outputs Are

- *The specific products or services that you produce, as part of your work process, and that you pass to others, who, in turn, use them in their work process.*

But Really, Who Is the Customer?

We have tried to describe the customer as the person to whom you pass your output, but there are customers and there are customers. Two examples help to clarify this apparent paradox.

The general services division (GSD) of Blue Chip Corp. provides computer services for internal users. That is, GSD develops software and systems and provides data-processing services for departments within Blue Chip Corp. on a contract basis. In one case, the vice president of administration of Blue Chip requests that GSD develop a new order-entry system for Blue Chip products. GSD develops the system requirements from the headquarters administrative staff, analyzes the work, and submits a project proposal. The vice president of administration and the vice president of GSD agree on the costs, schedule, and systems requirements.

The system is built accordingly and twelve months later delivered to the Blue Chip field administrative offices, which promptly declare that it won't work and they can't use it. The new system does not contain the screens (CRT formats) the field administrators like to use, and work station response times are too slow. What happened?

There are in Blue Chip *buyers* of systems and *users* of systems, and they are different customers with different requirements (see Figure 5.1). Both the administrative and GSD senior managers failed to consider the needs of the end user, the field administrators, who, in fact, are the prime customers for the new system. GSD and the headquarters administration staff should have realized that the field end users would have specific requirements, and to the extent that those requirements differ from the headquarters requirements, they should have been reconciled before work began on building the system. Now GSD must perform "maintenance" on the order-entry system to adapt it to the field administrators' needs—at considerable expense to Blue Chip Corp.

What Do Customers Want?

Once we have identified the customers for the output we produce, we must determine from the customer what he or she expects, requires,

Add value as an internal supplier by breaking down barriers between buyers and users

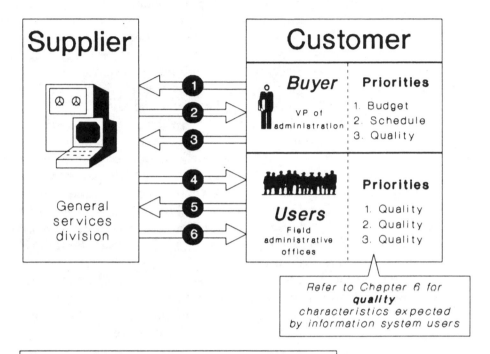

Figure 5.1   Identifying the Customer: Adding Value as an Internal Supplier

and needs from us, the supplier. We must accept the concept that quality is defined by the customer and meeting the customer's needs and expectations is the strategic goal of total quality management (TQM). As stated by Donald E. Petersen, former CEO of Ford Motor Company, "What we adopted is a definition of quality driven by the customer and focused on the customer's wants and needs. This change put us back on track to make substantial improvements in the quality of our products and services."[1]

Sometimes, the customers are unsure of their precise needs and expect the supplier to assist in the clarification of their requirements (see Chapter 6). This situation can be turned into an advantage, since it creates an opportunity to develop a "partnership" between customer and supplier that is beneficial to both. In many TQM systems, the customer brings the supplier in early in the new-product development cycle to take advantage of the supplier's specialized skill.

A second example shows the advantage that can be created through the clarification of requirements between users and buyers of an external customer (see Figure 5.2). A transportation company in North America formed a team with its customer, an auto company, to visit the auto company's dealers to determine what dealers required of the parent company in the delivery of new-model cars. Armed with this information, the transportation company and the auto company developed a set of requirements that, when met, completely satisfied both the dealers and the auto manufacturer.

The transportation company secured a unique position of "partner" with the auto company that provided it a small degree of protection from price competition. The transportation company earned this enhanced status by providing added value to its customer's organization.

Customer Satisfaction

The objective of implementing this disciplined approach of determining outputs, identifying customers, and identifying requirements is to enhance the supplier's ability to meet the customers' needs and expectations and thereby increase customer satisfaction. Clearly, as discussed in Chapter 3, the only viable means for organizations to achieve their objectives is to meet the requirements of their customers by continually improving work processes. Customer needs and expectations are constantly escalating as customers have their requirements met and learn of new possibilities from competitors. Any company that is too internally focused and not mindful of the dynamics of the marketplace will eventually lose market share.

The task, then, is to pursue customer satisfaction in an organized, disciplined manner. Xerox Corporation uses a framework similar to the one shown in Figure 5.3 to guide its efforts to improve customer satisfac-

Add value as an external supplier by clarifying Requirements of both buyers and users

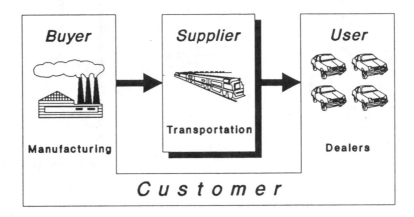

*Role of transportation supplier
in delivering new cars to dealers*

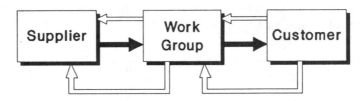

Classic Model of Customer-Supplier Chain

Figure 5.2   Identifying the Customer: Adding Value as an External Supplier

tion. Beginning with an external assessment of the customers' perceptions of the products and service provided by Xerox, internal work processes impacting customer satisfaction are identified and improved to remove unwanted variation in performance. Xerox then eliminates unnecessary work steps, and variation is minimized so that consistent, reliable delivery of service can be achieved. Improvements are captured and made a permanent part of the new process, and the exercise is repeated. Once process stability is achieved, Xerox tries to improve the overall process by moving performance to a new level that better matches what its customers are demanding. This approach enables

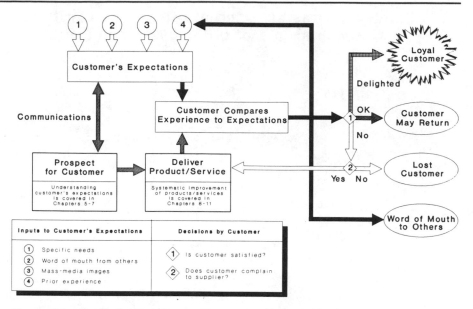

Figure 5.3   Customer Satisfaction Framework

Xerox to continuously improve its output and meet its customers'
needs. (Readers may wish to refer to Chapter 9, which offers a road map
for following this type of approach.)

A Word of Caution!

While internal suppliers are focusing on meeting the needs of their
immediate customer (the next person to whom they are providing a
product or service), they should also be mindful of the final end user,
the external customer who will eventually consume the product or service and pay the bills. This awareness provides a reality check on an
organization, in that all individuals in the organization must understand
how their products and services are being accepted in the marketplace.
Later, when customer satisfaction data are reported, everyone sees his
or her value in contributing to the success of the organization.

Summary

Identifying our customer is best started by determining the output we
are producing and then identifying the individual to whom we will pass

our output. If we cannot identify an individual who receives and uses our output in his or her work process, *stop!* We are producing scrap!

Once we have identified our customers, and they agree that they are our customers, then we must gather and clarify their requirements and build a complete understanding of what they want, need, and expect of us. If we go further as suppliers, and identify latent requirements (features that our customers may not have been aware of but really want), then we begin to become a more valued supplier—and possibly, in the eyes of the customer, a partner.

Having identified the customers' requirements, meeting those requirements every time—100 percent of the time—is the essence of achieving *quality*.

Note

1. D. E. Petersen, "Beyond Satisfaction," *Creating Customer Satisfaction*, research report no. 944 (New York: Conference Board, 1990), 33.

Understanding Customer Expectations

What do customers want? In essence, they want their expectations to be met completely and consistently. Consumers tend to perceive the quality of a service by comparing the actual service experienced to what their expectations were before purchasing it. Service is judged to be unsatisfactory when expectations are not met, satisfactory when they are met, and more than satisfactory when they are exceeded.

Successful organizations are able to diagnose the full set of customers' expectations and satisfy them completely, every time. World-class organizations have the uncanny ability of understanding implicit and even latent requirements. These latent requirements are features that customers want but do not know are available and hence are unable to articulate in discussions with their suppliers.

Once the customers are identified in the targeted market niche for a particular product or service, their expectations can be determined by answering four key questions:

1 What product/service characteristics do customers want?
2 What performance level is needed to satisfy their expectations?
3 What is the relative importance of each characteristic?
4 How satisfied are customers with performance at the current level?

Finding answers to these questions begins by postulating a set of features and characteristics that customers might want. This list of hypothetical criteria should next be tested by directly *asking* customers. The process of learning customers' needs, requirements, expectations, and level of satisfaction is commonly called listening to the voice of the customer.

This chapter helps service leaders begin the process of listening to the voice of the customer. It offers a comprehensive set of criteria as a foundation on which initial lists of customers' expectations can be built. This chapter next helps in understanding the performance levels that might be expected by customers as well as the relative importance they attach to each characteristic and their relative level of satisfaction with that characteristic. Research by the Quality Assurance Institute on corporate information systems is presented as an example application. The chapter concludes by briefly introducing quality function deployment, a technique for translating customer expectations into design specifications.

An overview of various mechanisms available for communicating with customers to learn their expectations is provided in Chapter 7.

What Are the Characteristics of Quality Service?

Customers expect to receive *value* in the products and services they purchase or use. In this context, value can be defined as the relationship between what customers get in exchange for what they give. Although this has often been considered as the trade-off between price and quality, a detailed analysis shows that far more is involved. For example, what about convenience? A customer may sacrifice convenience in search of lower price or higher quality. Therefore, in a global sense, the characteristics of quality service are those that enable customers to feel they have made a fair exchange and received value.

Scores of models and frameworks have been developed to help clarify how customers define quality or value. This chapter describes the five models listed below, which offer the best balance between simplicity, completeness, and applicability to services. Readers can use these models to define the product and service characteristics that their own customers want.

- Faster, better, cheaper
- Eight dimensions of quality
- Ten determinants of service quality
- Five "rater" criteria
- Compendium of quality characteristics

Faster, Better, Cheaper

Value can be viewed most simply as getting things that are faster, better, and cheaper than available elsewhere. Figure 6.1 shows these basic

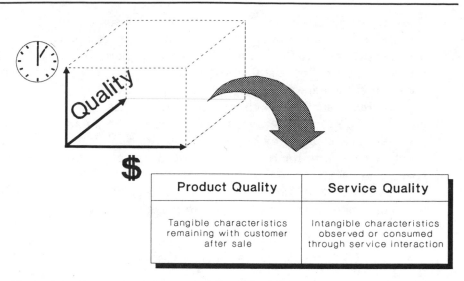

Product Quality	Service Quality
Tangible characteristics remaining with customer after sale	Intangible characteristics observed or consumed through service interaction

Figure 6.1   Customer Wants: Faster, Better, Cheaper

expectations as three dimensions against which trade-offs can be made. The first dimension, time, represents how quickly, easily, or conveniently a product or service can be obtained. The second dimension, cost, equates to how expensive the item is. The third dimension, quality, is the most difficult one to characterize.

To begin clarifying this complex dimension of quality, it is useful to subdivide it into two major sets. The first is *product* quality and includes the tangible attributes that are retained by the customer. The second is *service* quality and includes the characteristics observed or experienced by the customer during the transaction.

As explained previously (Chapter 4), customers are often involved directly in the service process. Therefore, some portion of the value in service consists of *how* it is delivered. Service quality is judged by the customer *during* the service. In air travel, for example, service quality involves the behavior of the cabin attendants and the comfort of the flight.

The product represents *what* is delivered and can be measured *after* the service has been performed. Continuing with the air travel example, product quality includes safe delivery of passengers and their luggage to the expected destination at the scheduled time.

Four additional frameworks are introduced in this chapter to expand on the elements of product and service quality. The first offers eight dimensions that are especially useful for understanding customers' expectations of product quality and apply equally well to service quality. The next two frameworks complement this set by further clarifying the elements of service quality. The fourth serves as a compendium of all of the sets that were introduced.

Eight Dimensions of Quality

David Garvin has defined eight dimensions that can be used at a strategic level to analyze quality characteristics. Some of the dimensions are mutually reinforcing, whereas others are not—improvement in one may be at the expense of others. Understanding the trade-offs desired by customers among these dimensions can help build a competitive advantage. Garvin's eight dimensions can be summarized as follows:

1 *Performance:* The product's primary operating characteristic. For example, performance of an automobile includes traits such as acceleration, handling, cruising speed, and comfort; performance of an airline includes on-time arrival.

2 *Features:* Secondary aspects of performance. These are the "bells and whistles" that supplement the basic functions. Examples include free drinks on planes and sunroofs on cars. The line separating primary performance characteristics from secondary features is often difficult to draw. Further, customers define value in terms of flexibility and their ability to select among available features, as well as the quality of those features.

3 *Reliability:* Probability of successfully performing a specified function for a specified period of time under specified conditions. Reliability of durable goods is often measured as the mean time to first failure or mean time between failures. These measures, however, require a product to be in use for a specified period of time and are not relevant in the case of products and services that are consumed instantly.

4 *Conformance:* Degree to which a product's design and operating characteristics meet established standards. Although this is sometimes defined as "conformance to requirements," a sounder analysis will be obtained by examining each characteristic's divergence from its target value. This more robust measure of conformance is built on the teachings of a prizewinning Japanese statistician, Genichi Taguchi.

5 *Durability:* A measure of product life. Durability can be defined as the amount of use obtained from a product before it deteriorates to the point that replacement is preferred over repair. Durability is closely linked to both reliability and serviceability. Consumers weigh the expected costs of future repairs against the investment in and operating expenses of a newer, more reliable model.

6 *Serviceability:* The speed, courtesy, competence, and ease of repair. The cost of repairs includes more than the simple out-of-pocket costs. Serviceability covers this full dimension by recognizing the loss and inconvenience due to downtime of equipment, the nature of dealings with service personnel, and the frequency with which repairs fail to correct the outstanding problems.

7 *Aesthetics:* How a product looks, feels, sounds, tastes, or smells. Aesthetics is largely a matter of personal judgment and a reflection of individual preference; it is a highly subjective dimension.

8 *Perceived quality:* Reputation. Consumers do not always have complete information about a product's or service's attributes; indirect measures or perceived quality may be their only basis for comparing brands.[1]

Ten Determinants of Service Quality

Research by Len Berry, Parsu Parasuraman, and Valerie Zeithaml in the early 1980s provides a strong foundation for understanding the attributes of service quality. Through interviews with business executives and customer focus groups, Berry and his colleagues identified ten determinants of service quality. Their categories, which provide a useful complement to the eight dimensions offered by Garvin, are as follows:

1 *Reliability:* Consistency of performance and dependability; performing the right service right the first time; honoring promises; accuracy.
2 *Responsiveness:* Willingness or readiness of employees to provide service; timeliness.
3 *Competence:* Possession of the skills and knowledge required to perform the service.
4 *Access:* Approachability and ease of access; waiting time; hours of operation.
5 *Courtesy:* Politeness, respect, consideration, and friendliness of contact personnel.

6 *Communication:* Keeping customers informed in language they can understand; listening to customers; adjusting language to different needs of different customers; explaining the service itself, how much it will cost, and how problems will be handled.

7 *Credibility:* Trustworthiness, believability, honesty; company reputation; personal characteristics of personnel.

8 *Security:* Freedom from danger, risk, or doubt; physical safety; financial security; confidentiality.

9 *Understanding the customer:* Making the effort to understand the customer's needs; learning the customer's specific requirements; providing individualized attention; recognizing the regular customer.

10 *Tangibles:* Physical evidence of the service; physical facilities; appearance of personnel; tools or equipment used to provide service; physical representation of the service, such as a plastic credit card or a bank statement; other customers in the service facility.[2]

Five "Rater" Criteria

As an outgrowth of their work in developing the ten determinants of service quality, Berry, Parasuraman, and Zeithaml distilled their list to five broader categories. Although they called this set "servqual," the five elements can easily be remembered through the acronym "rater." Some organizations find the list of ten characteristics to be confusing and overlapping, but others contend that essential details are lost by reducing it to only five elements. The five dimensions are listed below, and readers can choose for themselves which set they prefer.

1 *Reliability:* Ability to perform the promised service dependably and accurately.

2 *Assurance:* Knowledge and courtesy of employees and their ability to inspire trust and confidence.

3 *Tangibles:* Physical facilities, equipment, and appearance of personnel.

4 *Empathy:* Caring, individualized attention the firm provides its customers.

5 *Responsiveness:* Willingness to help customers and provide prompt service.[3]

Compendium of Quality Characteristics

By synthesizing the four previously described models, we are able to build a single comprehensive set of quality characteristics. Shown in

Table 6.1: Compendium of Quality Characteristics

	Deliverables	Interactions
Faster	Availability	Responsiveness
	Convenience	Accessibility
Better	Performance	Reliability
	Features	Security
	Reliability	Competence
	Conformance	Credibility
	Serviceability	Empathy
	Aesthetics	Communications
	Perceived quality	Style
Cheaper	Price	

Application of this Compendium

Quality is characterized through two sets of elements:

Deliverables: Describe *what* attributes are provided.

Interactions: Describe characteristics of staff and equipment that impact on *how* customers experience the service process while it is performed.

Both elements apply to all products and services, and this description can be used to confirm that all major characteristics have been considered.

Table 6.1, this compendium integrates Garvin's eight dimensions and Berry et al.'s ten determinants into the macroset of faster, better, cheaper.

However, rather than distinguishing between elements of product and service quality, this set reclassifies quality into two components: deliverables and interactions. The deliverables define *what* attributes are provided to customers. The interactions characterize *how* behaviors and styles impact on customers while they are experiencing the service process.

The delineation between deliverables and interactions offers an explicit framework within which to identify improvement opportunities. Furthermore, interactions are not limited to face-to-face contact. As

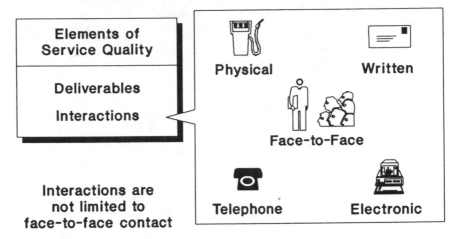

Elements of Service Quality	
Deliverables	
Interactions	

Physical   Written

Face-to-Face

Telephone   Electronic

**Interactions are
not limited to
face-to-face contact**

Assure quality in all modes

Figure 6.2   Modes of Service Interactions

shown in Figure 6.2, your staff also interacts through the telephone as well as through electronic and print media. The service experience is further impacted by physical facilities, and customers can interact with many services without any human interface. The quality characteristics expected by customers must be assured in all modes.

Use Table 6.1 as a worksheet in your dialogue with customers to test the attributes of your own business. Which characteristics differentiate you from your competitors? Which ones represent your strengths? Your weaknesses? Which ones are most important to the customers in your targeted market niche?

What Performance Level Is Needed to Satisfy Expectations?

Some people have argued that product quality can be measured but service quality cannot. Although the two sets of characteristics might be different, and one might be more difficult to measure, data can be obtained and analyzed for both sets. Service quality features are often measured in subjective, qualitative terms based on observations and comparisons. Product quality is usually measured in absolute, quantitative terms based on physical or chemical properties. Exceptions to these generalizations are numerous, but an overall comparison of these differences is presented in Table 6.2.

Table 6.2: Comparing Typical Quality Measurements

	Product Quality	Service Quality
Attributes	Objective	Subjective
	Tangible	Intangible
	Measured in absolute terms such as physical or chemical properties	Observed in comparative terms relative to expectations or prior experience
Examples	Size	Attitude
	Weight	Courtesy
	Volume	Cooperation
	Delivery time	Attentiveness
	Material	Reputation
	Count	Dependability
	Color	Friendliness

Two examples of exceptions to these general tendencies might be instructive. The physical design of a car is certainly a product quality attribute, but how can "style" be measured? It is measured in the same way described for service quality, by subjective judgment in comparison to other cars. What about customer comfort while eating in a restaurant? This is certainly a service quality characteristic, yet the features of chairs are measured the same way as product quality.

In essence, in order to measure quality, you begin by defining the characteristics that are important to customers. The next step is to determine how to obtain meaningful data. This approach is the same whether the feature is an element of product quality or service quality.

Implicit, Explicit, and Latent Requirements

The characteristics of products and services expected by customers can be viewed as a progressive hierarchy of three levels: base expectations, specifications/requirements, and delight (see Figure 6.3). These three levels are often referred to as implicit, explicit, and latent. Delineation in this fashion provides a model for understanding the level of performance needed to satisfy customers' expectations.

The customers' base expectations form the lowest level. These are the characteristics (or levels of performance) that are always assumed to

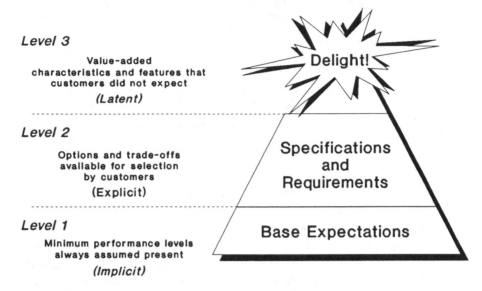

Level 3

Value-added
characteristics and features that
customers did not expect
(Latent)

Level 2

Options and trade-offs
available for selection
by customers
(Explicit)

Level 1

Minimum performance levels
always assumed present
(Implicit)

Delight!

Specifications
and
Requirements

Base Expectations

Figure 6.3   Levels of Customers' Expectations

be present, and if they are missing, customers will always be dissatisfied. When buying a car, customers assume certain basic attributes will be included without any discussion with the dealer. Examples of base expectations include the following implicit requirements:

- *Cornering stability:* The vehicle will not be prone to roll over when subjected to sudden evasive maneuvers.
- *Collision protection:* The vehicle is not likely to burst into flames as the result of a rear-end collision.
- *Motor vehicle inspection:* The vehicle is built in compliance with applicable state regulations and will pass any mandated inspections.
- *Rustproofing:* The vehicle will not rust prematurely.

The next level is represented by the specifications and requirements that are visible to customers and are actively involved in their selection process. This is the level at which explicit trade-offs are made and terms negotiated. Staying with cars as the example, this level of performance covers the features that are advertised and those that are discussed with dealers. They include such characteristics as fuel economy, horsepower, acceleration, color, number of seats, body style, interior decor, price, delivery, and warranty protection.

Table 6.3: Example Performance Characteristics at Three Levels

Level	Cornering	Acceleration
Violates base expectation	Vehicle rolls over on evasive maneuver	Vehicle cannot be driven at 60 mph
Meets specification	Lateral acceleration in range 0.65–0.85	0 to 60 mph in 7.0–10.0 seconds
Provides delight	Lateral acceleration exceeds 1.0	0 to 60 mph in less than 4 seconds

The highest level of performance is represented by the value-added features that the customer did not even know about but is delighted to receive. Performance at this level can be described as delivering all of the explicit requirements as well as latent ones. Latent requirements are real but are not visible or obvious to the customer. From your own experience, think about a product or service that absolutely thrilled you. What were the features or characteristics that caused you to feel this way? Were they attributes that you did not even know enough to ask for?

Some people define quality as simply "conformance to requirements," whereas others argue that this is an incomplete definition. The latter view is particularly evident when your competition is able to ascertain and provide features that exceed expectations and delight customers. As an example, consider Thomas Edison's invention of the light bulb at a time when customers did not even have electricity. How could he be bound by the "requirements" of a population that did not even know what questions to ask: direct current or alternating; incandescent or fluorescent; high or low voltage; sixty or one hundred watts; long-life or standard; soft white or clear? In comparison to the specifications of gas lamps, the electric light satisfied latent requirements for bright, safe, reliable, and inexpensive lighting. It represented a level of delight.

Note, however, that performing at the level of delight is not simply a matter of delivering more than specified. For example, a company that blends lubricants in a batch process orders twenty thousand gallons of a particular component. The supplier, thinking that more is better, delivers a full railcar containing twenty-two thousand gallons. But this does not delight the customer, since the batch must then be reformulated for the greater-than-expected amount of this component. As

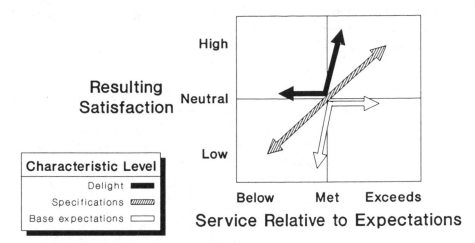

Figure 6.4 Satisfaction versus Expectations. *Source*: Adapted from conversations with B. Zions, The Quality Network, 1990.

another example, this same lubricant blender orders feedstock for delivery in four weeks. Faster delivery—in, say, one week—might not delight the customer, if the customer is then billed for three weeks of demurrage on the railcar.

Table 6.3 offers another example to help clarify the three-level performance model. This table compares two characteristics of automotive performance through the three-level hierarchy.

Customer satisfaction ratings respond differently to changes in performance at each of these three levels. As explained by Bernard Zions (Figure 6.4), meeting base expectations can be thought of as a defensive strategy. The implicit characteristics at this lowest level must always be present to earn merely a neutral rating from customers; their absence leads to disaster. By comparison, delivery against agreed-upon explicit specifications yields a proportionate gain in customer satisfaction. Assuming both the lower levels have been achieved, providing the unanticipated value-added features at the highest level yields delighted customers.

Application of the Three Expectation Levels

Recognizing the performance level of any particular product/service characteristic offers three advantages. First, it clarifies which characteristics should be discussed in detail with current or prospective customers. Second, it helps to predict how the level of customer satisfaction might respond to a change in characteristics. Third, it indicates possible future trends in expectations. This knowledge can be applied as follows:

- Focus discussions with customers around the characteristics that represent the conspicuous specifications and requirements (level 2). Customers take the base expectations (level 1) for granted and assume that knowledgeable suppliers know this. Similarly, customers cannot be expected to appreciate level 3 features until they are experienced.

- Meeting level 1 expectations is a defensive requirement that at best will help avoid creating dissatisfied customers. The information systems division (ISD) within one large company conducted an extensive survey of its customers to learn how important ISD service features were and how satisfied customers were with each. ISD had thought it was doing an excellent job in offering security and data protection and could not understand why customers regarded this service as unimportant and only average in satisfaction level. Had ISD recognized that security is a base expectation, it would have known that "average" was the best that could be expected.

- High levels of customer satisfaction can be expected by consistently delivering the implicit base expectations (level 1) and every explicit specification (level 2), as well as including the value-added features (level 3) that delight customers.

- Customers' expectations will escalate, and performance levels will migrate down through the hierarchy over time. For example, at one time, U.S. motorists did not understand or appreciate the benefits of radial tires. Those who found them on their foreign cars were delighted with how long radial-ply tires lasted in comparison to the bias-ply tires they had always known (level 3 characteristic). Later, radials became a desirable option (level 2), and by the 1980s, radial tires became embedded in consumers' base expectations (level 1). The escalation of motorists' expectations moved radial tires from a latent requirement to an explicit specification to an implicit expectation.

Responding to Complaints: The Hidden Level

There is one more level of performance—a hidden one that is only discovered after unhappy customers bring problems back to their sup-

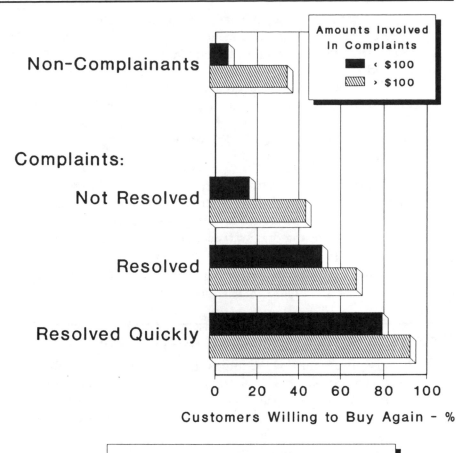

Figure 6.5 Converting Complaints to Loyalty. *Source*: Adapted from John A. Goodman, "The Nature of Customer Satisfaction" (Paper delivered at the ASQC National Quality Forum, New York,October 1988).

pliers. A study by the Technical Assistance Research Program shows that a positive response to complaints can create advantage out of adversity (Figure 6.5). Rather than seeing disappointed customers defecting to your competitors, your ability to "recover" by handling complaints effectively can actually build customer loyalty.[4]

One course of action available to a dissatisfied customer is to accept the problem begrudgingly and not complain to the supplier. Unfortunately, this customer is likely to complain to friends and influence them to avoid buying from this supplier.

The other course of action for a dissatisfied customer is to seek compensation from the supplier (replacement, refund, repair, etc.). By providing convenient avenues for complaining, dissatisfaction will be reduced. Depending on how the problem is handled, three outcomes are possible:

1 If the supplier's corrective action does not meet the customer's expectations, the original feeling of dissatisfaction will be exacerbated.
2 If the supplier's corrective action meets the customer's expectations, the original feeling of dissatisfaction will likely be neutralized.
3 If the supplier's prompt, effective, complete, and courteous action exceeds the customer's expectations, the original feeling of dissatisfaction can potentially be converted into delight.

What Is the Relative Importance of Each Characteristic?

The literature is filled with studies and advice trying to define which are the most important quality characteristics. In our experience, no universal prescription has been developed. The relative importance of each quality characteristic varies in relation to the specific expectations of the customer at any particular time.

As evidence of variability in the relative importance of characteristics, consider something as simple as your own purchase of groceries. Under one set of circumstances, the quality of the food might be paramount to you, and at another time, the ambiance of the supermarket could be of major importance. At another time, convenience might be the critical factor, as in the case of running out of soda for a party you are giving late at night on a holiday weekend. Finally, there may be situations when price alone dictates your shopping decisions.

Rather than attempting to prioritize customers' needs on a global basis, we suggest that the relative importance of performance characteristics should be determined with customers for each product and service, and then updated frequently. The relative rating of importance can be used to guide the allocation of resources for quality improvement efforts.

Unfortunately, building an understanding of how customers rank the relative importance of quality characteristics is not a simple task and can be confounded by customers' lack of perspective. For example, how important is safety in selecting a flight on a commercial airline? Although safety might be the single most important characteristic, the majority of passengers take safety for granted. Many feel that "accidents always happen to the other guy."

Suppliers who understand the three levels of quality explained earlier in this chapter can avoid contaminating their findings by recognizing that characteristics like flight safety are among customers' base expectations. As long as base expectations are satisfied, they will not command the attention or interest of customers. An airline with a pattern of safety incidents will be shunned by passengers, since it has violated their implicit expectations.

Another degree of complexity occurs because customers will seemingly change their priorities overnight. Whereas the types of features and characteristics expected by customers might remain stable for long periods of time, their relative importance and level of expectation will *appear* to change with headline news, weather, competitors' advertising, and technology advances. The word *appear* is emphasized to draw attention to the need to differentiate between fads and fundamental beliefs, or between topical headlines and underlying values.

When asking customers about the importance of a characteristic, their reply might be confused with their level of satisfaction. For example, many customers will underrate the importance of telephone system reliability because of complacency resulting from their satisfaction with current performance. On the other hand, if this same characteristic were tested with customers who are experiencing telephone service interruptions, a significantly higher level of importance will be attached to reliability.

Example of the Determination of Customer Expectations: Quality Characteristics of Information Systems

The Quality Assurance Institute (QAI) issued a research report in 1989 entitled *Measurement of the Customer's View of Information Systems Quality Characteristics.*[5] The findings in this report serve as a specific example showing how to implement the concepts presented in this chapter for understanding customers' expectations. The QAI report identified

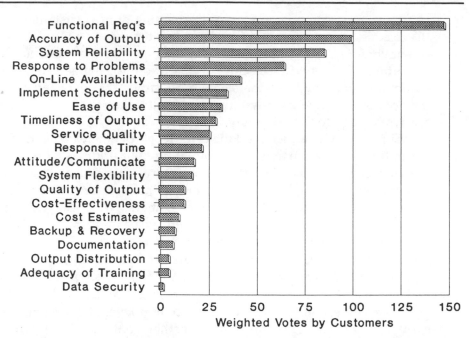

Figure 6.6   Ranking Quality Characteristics for Information Systems. *Source*: W. J. Boll et al. *Measurement of the Customer's View of Information Systems Quality Characteristics* (Quality Assurance Institute, Suite 750, 7575 Dr. Phillips Blvd., Orlando, FL 32819, (407) 363-1111, 1989), 12.

twenty characteristics of information systems that customers expect, and it determined the relative importance among these characteristics.

QAI surveyed users of information systems in 124 of its member companies. The survey was conducted through the information systems department of the volunteering companies. Each organization was free to use whatever terms it chose to characterize quality service, with three provisions: define their terms; indicate how each term would be measured; and determine nonconformance of each quality characteristic.

Approximately eighty characteristics were identified through the survey. The research team consolidated these characteristics into twenty generic categories. The generic quality characteristics were documented and sent back to the participants for them to perform three tasks:

1 Confirm the twenty generic characteristics to be representative.
2 Select the five believed to be the most important.
3 Recommend measures to evaluate each characteristic.

The results from these three tasks were then consolidated by the research team and returned to the participants as a preliminary report. Ninety-three percent of the respondents agreed with the ranking.

Based on this process, the QAI project identified twenty quality characteristics for information systems. These are listed below, along with their corresponding measures. The relative ranking of their importance according to system users is shown in Figure 6.6.

1 *Functional requirements:* Number of change requests submitted from start of customer acceptance testing through first ninety days of production.

2 *Accuracy of output:* Number of errors in output per month as a percentage of the customer's total output received.

3 *System reliability:* Number of times per month, by type of problem, when the customer's system fails to function properly.

4 *Response to problems:* Average elapsed time between the customer's reporting a problem and receiving a response, by severity of problem.

5 *On-line availability:* Percentage of time during the month when a single customer can access the computer to process agreed-upon work during scheduled hours.

6 *Implementation schedules:* Number of actual calendar days required to implement a project, based on the customer's acceptance, as a percentage of scheduled calendar days.

7 *Ease of use:* A subjective measurement of the customer's degree of difficulty in learning the system and utilizing it efficiently.

8 *Timeliness of output:* Number of outputs not received on time as a percentage of the customer's total scheduled monthly output.

9 *Overall service quality:* A subjective measurement of overall service quality received during the month from computer operations, systems, and information center.

10 *Response time:* Average elapsed time between the customer's pressing a function key and receiving first presentation of computer response, by type of transaction processed during the month.

11 *Attitude and communications:* A subjective measurement of data processing's (staff) willingness to be of assistance and to provide useful information on system changes, opportunities, and problems.

12 *System flexibility:* A subjective measurement of the degree of difficulty and timeliness in making modifications to an operational system.

13 *Quality of output:* Number of outputs that the customer is unable to use for its intended purpose, by type of problem, as a percentage of the customer's total monthly outputs. Types of problems include blurred or improperly aligned reports and fiche.

14 *Cost-effectiveness:* Postimplementation audit, including return-on-investment analysis of the implemented system.

15 *Cost estimates:* Total actual implementation costs as a percentage of approved estimated costs.

16 *Backup and recovery procedures:* A quantitative subjective measurement of the adequacy of existing backup and recovery procedures and the potential impact of an extended system outage on the customer's operation.

17 *Adequacy of documentation:* A subjective measurement of the accuracy, clarity, comprehensiveness, and overall usefulness of the documentation.

18 *Distribution of output:* Number of times per month that the customer receives output intended for someone else as a percentage of the customer's total number of output deliveries.

19 *Adequacy of training:* A subjective measurement of the comprehensiveness, timeliness, skill level, and overall effectiveness of training received.

20 *Data security:* A subjective measurement of the customer's confidence that data are secure and unauthorized access is prevented.[6]

QAI Analysis of Findings

The results of the ranking caused concern among the researchers as well as with several of the participants. For example, security, which has been a high priority for information systems departments, ranked last among the twenty characteristics. A follow-up review yielded a better understanding, and the following selected learning points from QAI's report are worth noting:

- Cumulative rankings cannot be assumed to represent expectations of specific customers. Although the twenty quality characteristics have strong commonality among the participating companies, the ranking of each characteristic varied significantly.

- Ranking represents current concerns. Items that ranked high represent characteristics with which customers are not satisfied. Low-ranked quality criteria generally represent problems that have been solved. Highly ranked quality characteristics will drop in perceived importance when they are no longer problems to customers, and low-ranked ones will rise on the list if they become problem areas.

■ Performance characteristics expected by customers involve both product and service quality. In some instances, characteristics involve both a product and a service.

■ Measures are both objective and subjective.[7]

Quality Function Deployment

This chapter has offered a process for listening to the voice of the customer in order to learn expectations. Once those expectations are understood, the next step is to translate them into product and service specifications. The concept of this translation was introduced in Chapter 4 through the establishment of two sets of measures at the output level: customer requirements and process capability. However, the translation between this pair of measures is sometimes complicated. Help is available through a technique known as quality function deployment (QFD).

The quality characteristics required by customers, the level of their expectations, and the relative importance attached to each criterion will often be inconsistent and seemingly impossible to achieve. Consider how the voice of the customer contradicts itself in the following examples:

■ Automobiles with fast acceleration and excellent fuel economy
■ Restaurants with courteous service, delicious food, and low prices
■ Computer systems with high security and easy access
■ Research results with instantaneous application of major break-throughs
■ Engineering designs that are safe, reliable, efficient, and inexpensive

QFD can be used to translate customer requirements into appropriate technical specifications. The technique helps in defining units of measurement, and it provides a framework for evaluating trade-offs among various combinations of design features.

QFD was formalized in 1972 at Mitsubishi's shipyard in Kobe, Japan. It has been used to reduce development time for introducing new products and to reduce disruptive and expensive engineering changes. The heart of QFD is a large matrix that relates *what* customers require with *how* products and services will be designed and produced in order to satisfy those requirements.

A full description of QFD is beyond the scope of this book. The intention here is merely to show how this technique fits into the scheme of total quality management. One excellent first source of information is a 1986 article by L. P. Sullivan entitled "Quality Function Deployment."[8] Additional literature has been published on the subject, and a number of organizations offer QFD training courses.

Summary

Customers tend to perceive the quality of services by comparing the actual level experienced to their expectations. The process of satisfying customers therefore begins by fully understanding their expectations. This process can be referred to as listening to the voice of the customer and requires learning what features and characteristics customers want, the performance level they expect, the importance they attach to each characteristic, and how satisfied they are with performance at the current level.

Faster, better, cheaper is the most fundamental set of characteristics to describe how customers define value and provides a springboard for understanding other, more complex models. The array of quality features can be subdivided into the categories of product and service or of deliverables and interactions.

All products and services contain some elements of service quality. For example, an automobile includes elements of service quality in both the purchasing process and the inevitable maintenance and repair. The value added by the dealer in the purchasing process includes attributes as simple as availability of the desired vehicle in inventory and convenience of the location. The overall quality perceived by the customer is also impacted by interactions with the sales staff.

The level of performance expected by customers can be measured, although some data will be obtained through subjective comparisons instead of objective measures against absolute standards. The three-level hierarchy helps in the analysis of performance measures. At the base level are the implicit expectations, which must never be violated. The intermediate level contains the explicit specifications, which can be discussed and negotiated. The highest level addresses latent requirements, which might not be evident to customers but which, when provided, will lead to their delight. Furthermore, customers' expectations escalate: features that currently delight customers may eventually become embedded in their base expectations.

Building an understanding of customer satisfaction and the relative importance customers attach to each quality characteristic is a complex and difficult task. For example, a customer survey might tend to underrate the importance of a vital performance characteristic because customers are satisfied with its current delivery and distracted by other irritants. Knowledgeable suppliers are able to discern customers' true underlying values.

Once understood, customers' expectations must then be translated into product and service specifications. Quality function deployment is a technique for accomplishing this translation.

Notes

1. D. A. Garvin, "Competing on the Eight Dimensions of Quality," *Harvard Business Review* (Nov.–Dec. 1987): 101–109.

2. L. L. Berry, V. A. Zeithaml, and P. Parasuraman, "Quality Counts in Service, Too," *Business Horizons* 28, no. 3 (1985): 44–52.

3. V. A. Zeithaml, L. L. Berry, and P. Parasuraman, *Delivering Quality Service: Balancing Customer Perceptions and Expectations* (New York: Free Press, 1990).

4. J. Goodman, "The Nature of Customer Satisfaction," *Quality Progress* 22, no. 2 (1989): 37–40.

5. W. J. Boll et al., *Measurement of the Customer's View of Information Systems Quality Characteristics* (Orlando, Fla.: Quality Assurance Institute, 1989).

6. Ibid., 9–11.

7. Ibid., 13–16.

8. L. P. Sullivan, "Quality Function Deployment," *Quality Progress* 19, no. 6 (1986): 39–50.

References

Farley, J. M., Carson, D. F., and Pearl, D. H. "Service Quality in a Multinational Environment." *ASQC Quality Congress Transactions*, 96–101. San Francisco: 1990.

Garvin, D. A. *Managing Quality*. New York: Free Press, 1988.

King, C. A. "A Framework for a Service Quality Assurance System." *Quality Progress* 20, no. 9 (1987): 27–32.

Peters, T. *Thriving on Chaos*. New York: Knopf, 1987.

Peters, T., and Waterman, R. H. *In Search of Excellence*. New York: Harper & Row, 1982.

Rosander, A. C. *The Quest for Quality in Services*. Milwaukee: Quality Press, 1989.

Mechanisms for Understanding Customers

Giving customers what they want
isn't nearly as hard as finding out what they want.
　　　　　—Amanda Bennett[1]

Understanding customers' expectations is a prerequisite for improving quality and achieving full customer satisfaction. Significant research has been conducted in understanding customers' expectations of products, but what has been done for service? Further, what has been done for service groups within large manufacturers? What techniques can be applied to understand the expectations for seemingly unique, somewhat monopolistic, and often intangible services?

This chapter provides a two-dimensional framework for defining the mechanisms available for understanding customers' expectations. The first dimension classifies the approach initiated by the supplier, moving from reactive to proactive. The second dimension indicates the level of understanding likely to be achieved by each mechanism. Although this approach was developed for service groups within large organizations, it can be used to understand the requirements of any type of customer.

The reactive mode of waiting to hear complaints reveals only a minimal understanding of the customers' expectations. A better understanding will be gained by initiating more active approaches to listening to customers. Examples include help desks, hot lines, analysis of sales data, obtaining feedback from customer representatives, and conducting informal surveys.

Full understanding, however, can best be achieved through mechanisms specifically initiated to listen to customers. These approaches include personal interviews, focus groups, structured surveys, and benchmarking. The key is to build a profound understanding of your customers' needs and expectations. What are the distinguishing characteristics of the products or services that are important to your customers? How satisfied are your customers with the product and service characteristics delivered by you? By your competitors? By the best available technology?

The chapter concludes by showing how one organization progressed through the framework to build its level of understanding of its customers' needs. The example uses the computer acquisition group of Imperial Oil, Ltd., a major Canadian oil company. The group is responsible for planning, scheduling, ordering, and delivering computer hardware and software to fifteen thousand employees in three operating companies and a number of head-office departments.

Internal Services—The Least Understood Market

Tools and techniques for understanding customers' needs and expectations of consumer products have been honed carefully over decades. Market research, combined with engineering analysis and testing, help define the physical and chemical specifications of products and subcomponents to maximize their value in the marketplace. Quality function deployment, which was introduced in Chapter 6, helps translate customers' requirements into product designs and specifications.

But what about the other end of the spectrum? How can customers' requirements be defined and measured for services instead of for products; or when expectations are subjective rather than objective; or when the customers and suppliers are captive within the same organization; or without the support of professional market researchers? Amanda Bennett reports:

> Pinning customers down, though, isn't easy. When asked to describe the perfect service provider, customers often answer in vague terms. They say, "I'd like them to be nice, helpful, courteous."
>
> But even as companies are relying more on customer feedback, they are finding consumers more reluctant to be queried. American Airlines says that cooperation on the company's surveys has dropped from about 40% in the early 1980s to about 33% today. [In 1990] as an incentive, American Airlines provided a $25 travel certificate to those who responded to one survey, and it tries to keep telephone surveys down to 10 minutes.[2]

Probably the least understood sets of requirements are those for internal services, such as financial and information services, administrative

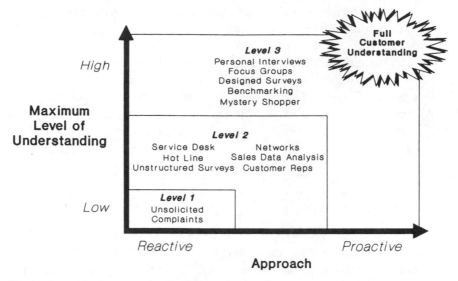

Figure 7.1 Mechanisms for Understanding Customers. *Source:* Adapted from conversations with D. A. Cox, Imperial Oil, Ltd., 1990.

support, and human resources development. When appointed as continuous improvement adviser for the information systems and technology department of Imperial Oil, Ltd., in 1988, David Cox found himself a pioneer in the search for ways to understand the expectations of his organization's internal customers. This chapter is built around his insight and experience, and his work is gratefully acknowledged.

Development of the Framework

As shown by the work process model introduced in Chapter 4, two sets of information flow from customers to suppliers: (1) requirements—a description of the product or service expected by customers before it is produced or delivered; (2) satisfaction—feedback on what the customers liked or did not like about the work that was performed for them. Numerous approaches are used to define requirements and measure satisfaction of external customers for use in new-product development and advertising. However, such systematic processes are rarely used for understanding internal customers.

Figure 7.1 shows the two-dimensional framework that has been developed for categorizing mechanisms commonly used to gather information from customers. The first dimension displays the degree of activity initiated by the supplier. The second dimension maps the level of understanding that might be attained. Although actually following a continuum, the framework is shown with three discrete levels to simplify its explanation.

Level 1

The reactive mode, categorized as level 1, is likely to reveal only a minimal understanding of the customers' expectations. Approaches here are primarily ones of gathering complaints. Examples include logging irate phone calls from dissatisfied customers and responding to letters to employees' bosses.

The effectiveness of learning customers' expectations and satisfaction through these reactive approaches is impeded by four factors. First, the data are obtained from a biased, nonrepresentative set of customers who are sufficiently unhappy to initiate complaints, frequently in the form of a solution: "We need more CPU capacity." Second, only a limited sampling of these unhappy customers actually volunteer information to suppliers through these mechanisms. Third, systems to synthesize and analyze these data are often lacking. Fourth, employees receiving information through these channels are often distracted by the need to fix their customers' problems or defend themselves against the accusations. However, actions can be taken to minimize these four shortcomings and maximize the value of level 1 mechanisms.

The Technical Assistance Research Program (TARP) found that only ten out of twenty customers who are dissatisfied with products or services bother complaining to the supplier. Of these, nine will be directed to the front-line personnel, and one will go to management. Thus, a system designed to analyze and understand complaints received by the front-line employees reveals less than half the picture. Even worse, decisions based exclusively on complaints received by management may focus on only 5 percent of the problems.[3]

Customers' failure to complain is often the result of their not knowing how to complain or where to direct a complaint, or feeling that complaining just is not worth their effort. Organizations can reduce these barriers through several approaches. They can display clearly the avenues available to customers, including toll-free phone numbers. They can make complaining worthwhile to their customers by responding to their problems and trying to create advantage out of adversity.

In addition, employees receiving complaints can be supported and rewarded for their role to offset the distaste usually inherent in this task. Training programs and user-friendly systems are examples of supporting systems.

Level 2

A higher level of understanding will be gained by initiating active approaches to listen to customers. Mechanisms at level 2 are defined as those approaches that communicate with customers but have listening to customer expectations as their secondary objective. Their primary objective often includes answering customers' questions or selling more/new products. Although they are more effective than the previously discussed reactive approaches, the ability of level 2 mechanisms to capture customers' views is compromised because these mechanisms are designed mainly to satisfy their primary objectives. Level 2 examples include help desks or hot lines, analysis of sales data, feedback from customer representatives, and unstructured surveys.

As with level 1, actions can be taken to maximize the effectiveness of level 2 mechanisms. Additional resources can be allocated to gather and analyze information obtained, and systems can be installed to minimize the effort required to satisfy the secondary objective. Employees involved in these types of functions can be coached and trained to gather customer data in addition to fulfilling their primary objectives, and they can be rewarded for doing so.

Level 3

Full understanding of customers' expectations can only be attained through the use of mechanisms specifically designed to extract this information. Approaches at this third level include personal interviews, focus groups, and designed surveys. Another mechanism at this highest level is the "mystery shopper," which enables suppliers to take the viewpoint of their customers by planting employees in positions to use their own services.

Focus groups can offer insights that are impossible to capture through surveys or even through interviews with individual customers. Forum Corporation, a Boston based service-quality consulting firm, cites a bank whose customers said they simply wanted "friendly service." Through focus groups, bank officials determined that it was most important to customers that in especially busy periods, every bank official be seen helping at service windows. Anyone not working at serving customers directly needed to be doing his or her work out of sight of the public.[4]

Interviewing and surveying *former* customers is a frequently neglected level 3 mechanism. Unlike communications with prospective or current customers, communications with former customers can provide specific, objective data on the shortcomings of your products and services.

F. F. Reichheld and W. E. Sasser, Jr., offer a relevant analogy.[5] They equate "zero defections" of customers from service providers to "zero defects" of manufacturers. Their analogy includes the concept of cost of quality: the cost of scrap and rework of manufactured products equates to the loss in revenues over the lifetime of defecting service customers. The analogy continues to root-cause analysis. Manufacturers seek to understand and eliminate the underlying causes of defective products. Similarly, service providers can seek to understand and eliminate the underlying cause of defecting customers. This process begins by communicating with these former customers.

Benchmarking to Understand Expectations

Benchmarking can be categorized as another level 3 approach. As explained by Bob Camp, author of *Benchmarking*,[6] this is the process of continually researching for new ideas and methods, practices and processes, and either adopting the practices or adapting the good features, and implementing them to obtain the "best of the best." Customers' expectations are influenced by what they learn through comparison shopping. Although they might settle for your particular product or service now, what is to stop them from finding something better next time? Benchmarking enables suppliers to establish performance targets based on best possible practices and continuously improve toward those targets.

Benchmarking is the search for best practices. It is the search for what is best and for an understanding of how the best is achieved. Camp has defined four distinct types of benchmarking:

1 *Internal:* One of the easiest benchmarking investigations is to compare operations among functions within your own organization. This type of investigation is applicable to multidivisional or international firms. Data should be readily available and reportable on a consistent basis.

2 *Competitive:* Direct product or service competitors are the most obvious to benchmark against. Although this information may be difficult to obtain, its value is high.

3 *Functional:* It is not necessary to limit comparisons to direct competitors. In fact, a narrow focus may risk missing potential breakthroughs. Functional benchmarking investigates leaders in dissimilar industries. The relevance of comparison is maintained by defining the performance characteristics that must be similar to your own functions. As an example of functional benchmarking, Xerox Corporation's interest in improving the delivery of small parts to service technicians led it to identify L. L. Bean as the leader in order fulfillment and warehousing operations.

4 *Generic:* Some business functions and processes are the same regardless of dissimilarities across industries. Generic benchmarking is the purest form of benchmarking, in that it may uncover methods that are not implemented in the investigator's own industry. Generic benchmarking extends functional benchmarking by removing the constraints imposed by limiting the investigation to practices with similar characteristics. Generic benchmarking holds the potential for revealing the "best of the best." It requires broad conceptualization. Although it is the most difficult type of benchmarking to use, it probably provides the highest potential payoff.[7]

Example Application: Information Systems Group

Intentionally or unintentionally, information systems groups have traditionally had a reputation for a fortress mentality—for building enough walls and moats around themselves to assure that communications between the "systems experts" and the rest of the organization are kept to a minimum.

As a service group within the information systems and technology department of Imperial Oil, Ltd., the computer acquisition group (CAG) is responsible for the acquisition of all computer hardware and software on behalf of the corporation. The following account describes how the group sought to break down the walls between itself and its customers and employed a level 3 mechanism to learn its customers' expectations.

Like most internal service groups, CAG thought it was doing a pretty good job. After all, expenditures for computer hardware and software, both mainframe and PC, had been rising at a healthy rate, and

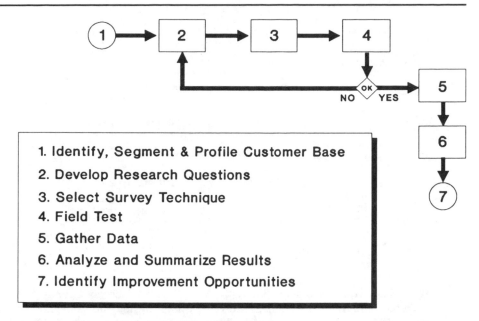

Figure 7.2   The Customer Window^SM Process

the group had been able to respond to this increased workload reasonably well—at least as far as they knew, since the absence of complaints from the group's major customers was interpreted as an indication of overall customer satisfaction.

In the past, CAG had unilaterally determined which services were important to its customers and what performance levels were needed to keep them happy. CAG did not have a formal process for determining its customers' needs and rarely consulted with its customers to validate its assumptions.

This approach ended in 1989 with the introduction of total quality management, or continuous improvement, as it is called in Imperial Oil. Among other initiatives, the group began to employ more active approaches for learning its customers' expectations.

Preparation

ARBOR, Inc., a Philadelphia-based market research and total quality training firm, was contracted to support these efforts and introduced its Customer Window^SM as a structured method to survey customers and interpret the results (see Figure 7.2). The approach begins by clarifying and segmenting the customer base and designing research questions to

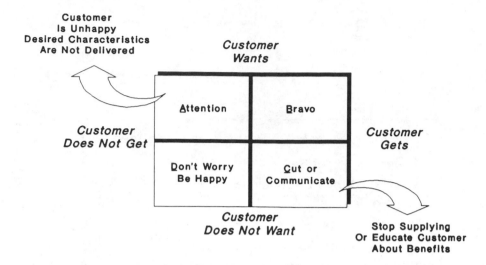

Figure 7.3 The Customer Window[sm] Model. *Source*: David Saunders et al., "Becoming the Internal Vendor of Choice Through Systematic Segmentation and Reasearch," *ASQC Quality Congress Transactions* (San Fransisco, May 1990): 702.

learn the relative satisfaction and importance that customers attribute to each specific product, service, or performance characteristic.[8]

The results are then plotted to prioritize improvement opportunities on a simple grid that represents the heart of the Customer Window[SM] (see Figure 7.3). The grid divides product and service characteristics into four quadrants:

A The customer wants it but does not get it.
B The customer wants it and gets it.
C The customer doesn't want it but gets it.
D The customer doesn't want it and does not get it.

With the help of ARBOR consultants, CAG created a model of its customers and defined three distinct segments (see Figure 7.4). One set of customers comprised the other groups within CAG's own department. The second set consisted of the systems specialists outside of the department, and the third set was represented by the end users in the operating companies and head-office departments. The size of these market segments was examined from the perspectives of CAG's workload, cost of equipment acquired, and number of customers in each segment (see Figure 7.5).

After attending training in the Customer Window[SM] survey techniques, the CAG team developed a questionnaire for use in face-to-face interviews with randomly selected representatives from each customer segment.

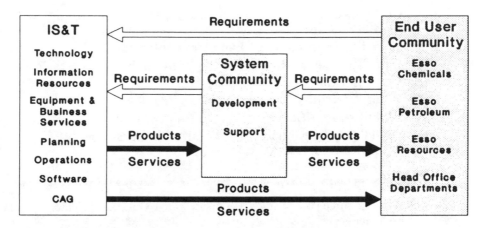

Figure 7.4 Information Systems and Technology Customer Model. *Source*: Adapted from discussions with D. A. Cox, Imperial Oil, Ltd., 1990.

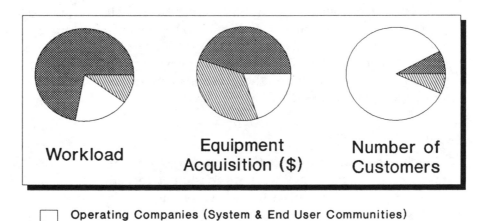

Figure 7.5 Computer Acquisition Group (CAG) Customer Segmentation. *Source*: Adapted from discussions with D.A. Cox, Imperial Oil, Ltd., 1990.

1. Customer Information Profile
2. Do You Know What CAG Does?
3. What Services Does CAG Provide to You?
4. What Do You Like About CAG?
5. Do You Acquire Hardware, Software, Maintenance, or Supplies Not Using CAG?
6. Rate the *Importance* of Each Listed Service
7. Rate Your Level of *Satisfaction* With Each Listed Service
8. How Can Our Services Be Better?
9. What Attributes Should CAG Team Members Have?
10. What Level of Services Should Be Provided?
11. Could Any Services Be Reduced Without Seriously Affecting Your Work?

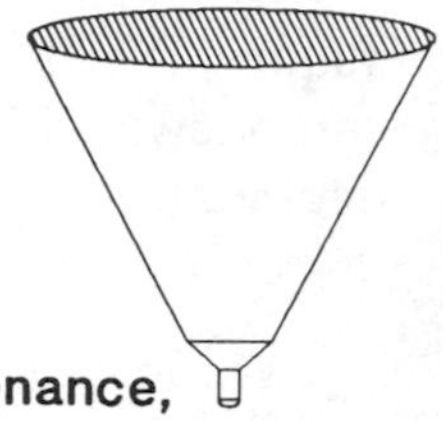

Figure 7.6   Computer Acquisition Group Research Questions. *Source*: Adapted from discussions with D. A. Cox, Imperial Oil, Ltd., 1990.

Field tests helped build skills and experience. The tests also identified shortcomings in the approach and questions. For example, the original set of twenty-one questions was overwhelming, and several questions were essentially duplicates. The eleven questions selected (shown in Figure 7.6) began with broad, nonthreatening subjects and were designed to establish rapport between the customer and the CAG interviewer. Like a funnel, the questions became more focused as the interview progressed.

Results

Much to the surprise of the CAG team, which had no prior experience with formal customer interviews, customer reactions were positive, supportive, and enthusiastic. Many of the services available from CAG were not understood prior to the interviews. One frequently reported comment was, "If we had known you could provide this service, we would have gotten you involved." Customers for the most part were more than willing to spend time with the interviewer

Figure 7.7   Computer Acquisition Group Customer Window[sm]. *Source:* Adapted from discussions with D. A. Cox, Imperial Oil, Ltd., 1990.

and often devoted more time than had originally been planned. Many commented favorably on the process and expected to benefit from it.

Data from the thirty interviews conducted revealed the relative importance and level of satisfaction of the services offered by CAG (see Figure 7.7). Over a hundred improvement opportunities were identified, and several customers even committed themselves to working with CAG on implementation. As a result, employees in CAG can now focus on the service areas that are most important to their customers. CAG has a clear understanding of which service characteristics it needs to improve to achieve greater customer satisfaction.

Summary

In summary, an array of techniques is available to communicate with customers for learning their expectations and level of satisfaction with existing products and services. Use a multiplicity of approaches. Supplement avenues for hearing complaints with mechanisms designed specifically for learning customers' needs.

Notes

1. Amanda Bennett, "Making the Grade with the Customer," *Wall Street Journal* (Nov. 12, 1990), B1. Reprinted by permission of the *Wall Street Journal©*, 1990 Dow Jones & Company, Inc. All Rights Reserved Worldwide.

2. Ibid.

3. J. Goodman, "The Nature of Customer Satisfaction," *Quality Progress* 22, no. 2 (1989): 37–40.

4. Bennett, "Making the Grade."

5. F. E. Reichheld and W. E. Sasser, Jr., "Zero Defections: Quality Comes to Services," *Harvard Business Review* (Sept.–Oct. 1990): 105–111.

6. Robert C. Camp, *Benchmarking* (Milwaukee: Quality Press, 1989).

7. Ibid., 61–65.

8. M. Caplette and D. Saunders, "Becoming the Internal Vendor of Choice through Systematic Segmentation and Research," *ASQC Quality Congress Transactions* (San Francisco: 1990), 700–705. D. Saunders et al., "The Customer Window^SM," *Quality Progress* 20, no. 2 (1987): 37–42.

Process Improvement

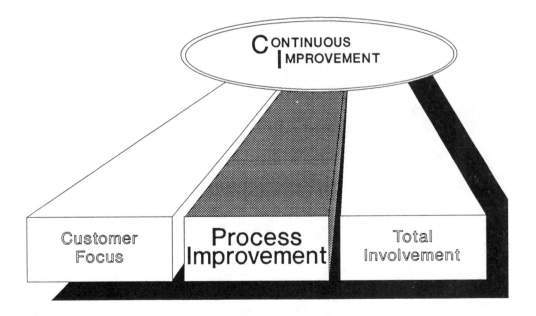

8 Managing Key Processes

Fixing the Product Is Too Late,
Instead, Improve the Process
— *Gerald Shea, Ph.D.,*
Exxon Research and
Engineering Company,
September 1984

Western business leaders have often been criticized for being short-sighted and tending to focus on the near term. One manifestation of this syndrome is the excessive attention to "fire fighting" and the achievement of immediate results. One key to breaking this pattern and building a longer-term perspective is to strengthen the underlying business processes instead of addressing each specific output and deviation. Therefore, process improvement represents the second key principle of total quality management (TQM).

Chapter 8 is the first of four chapters aimed at the systematic and continuous improvement of processes. This first chapter provides a framework for identifying and managing key processes. Chapter 9 outlines a six-step methodology that can be applied to improve the performance of any type of process. Chapter 10 clarifies performance measurement, and Chapter 11 provides examples of improvements to nonmanufacturing processes. Figure 8.1 previews the concepts of process management and lists the chapters in this book that cover each one.

Chapter 8 begins by defining the work process and the six ingredients that are essential for managing any type of business process: ownership, planning, control, measurement, improvement, and optimization. The chapter next helps readers to define their organization's key processes in order to initiate improvement efforts in areas with the greatest impact. Finally, examples of process management are presented.

		Information Sources
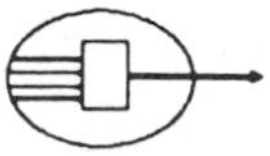	**Identify key processes impacting on success**	Chapter 8
	**Assign ownership**	Chapter 8
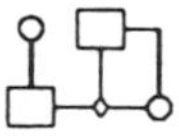	**Plan approach to define and document process**	Chapter 8 + Chapter 9
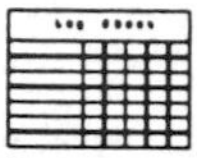	**Measure performance against customers' expectations**	Chapter 9 + Chapter 10
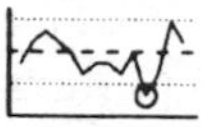	**Control process to assure predictable performance**	Chapter 9
	**Improve capability to meet customers' expectations**	Chapter 9 + Chapter 11
 **$**	**Optimize efficiency and productivity**	Chapter 9

Figure 8.1   Process Management

What Is a Work Process?

As first indicated in Chapter 4, all products and services are produced and delivered through work or business processes. Before explaining how to manage and improve processes, however, it might be useful to review the basic terms and concepts that define work processes.

A process can be defined as the sequential integration of people, materials, methods, and machines in an environment to produce value-added outputs for customers (refer back to Figure 4.2). A process converts measurable inputs into measurable outputs through an organized sequence of steps. Four groups of people are involved in the operation and improvement of processes:

1 *Customers:* the people (or person) for whom the output (product or service) is being produced. Customers are the people who will use the output directly or who will take it as input into their work process.
2 *Work group:* the people (or person) who work in the process to produce and deliver the desired output.
3 *Supplier:* the people (or person) who provide input to the work process. The people in the process are in fact the customers of the supplier.
4 *Owner:* the person who is responsible for the operation of the process *and* for its improvement.

As explained in Chapter 6, customers are the ones who define the output desired from the process. This is accomplished through two broad categories of information that flow from customers to the work group. The first category consists of the requirements: a description of what the customers need, want, and expect. Requirements dictate what the process is supposed to deliver. The second category of communications is feedback: an explanation of how well (or poorly) the output was delivered in comparison to the customers' expectations. This feedback signal is vital for the improvement of the process for future operations.

The flow of information and products with suppliers appears as a mirror image of the processes used to connect the work group to its customers.

Six Ingredients of Process Management

In his book *Quality Process Management*, Gabriel Pall explains the concepts of process management as they relate to quality improvement, and he presents an application plan with specific examples. Pall identifies six ingredients that are essential for process management:

1 *Ownership:* Assign responsibility for the design, operation, and improvement of the process.
2 *Planning:* Establish a structured and disciplined approach to understand, define, and document all major components in the process and their interrelationships.

3 *Control:* Assure effectiveness: all outputs are predictable and consistent with the customers' expectations.

4 *Measurement:* Map performance attributes to customers' requirements and establish criteria for the accuracy, precision, and frequency of data acquisition.

5 *Improvement:* Increase effectiveness of the process by permanently embedding identified improvements.

6 *Optimization:* Increase efficiency and productivity by permanently embedding identified improvements.[1]

These six ingredients are fundamental to the successful management of any type of process. These ingredients are needed for the work processes that produce and deliver products and services to customers, for the processes that clarify requirements and satisfaction along the customer-supplier chain, and for the processes that support employees in their jobs.

Ownership and planning are briefly reviewed in the remainder of this chapter, and the other four ingredients are covered in subsequent chapters. A systematic method for control, improvement, and optimization is featured in Chapter 9, and example applications are offered in Chapter 11. Measurement is the subject of Chapter 10.

Defining Key Processes

Every organization can identify the key processes on which its success depends. How many times have you been frustrated by inefficient service organizations? Some of the difficulties you experienced might have been caused by the failure of those businesses to recognize and manage their key processes. Well-meaning employees are performing their jobs to achieve the objectives of their individual division or department. They may achieve their goals, however, to the detriment of the customer and, hence, the total organization.

The way in which businesses define their organizational structure provides an inherent advantage for the ownership and planning of processes that exactly align within formal organizational boundaries. This generalization contains both good news and bad news. The good news is that the processes that are complemented by the organizational structure tend to have a history of successful control, measurement, improvement, and optimization. The bad news is that the processes that cross organizational boundaries are likely to be in poor condition.

For those interested in more bad news, the performance of the processes that cross organizational boundaries and are in poor condition may be more important to customers than the performance of some processes that fit neatly within administrative boundaries. Furthermore, this importance to the customer may not just involve the outputs from these processes, particularly in service functions, where the customers are active participants in the delivery process (see Chapter 4). The good news behind all this is that the greatest short-term improvement opportunities are likely to be found among these cross-functional processes.

Immunization against unhealthy cross-functional processes can be gained by systematically searching for key business processes, regardless of organizational boundaries. Through their consulting and research, Geary Rummler and Alan Brache ask six questions to help in the identification of key processes that have the greatest impact on customers:

1 Which products and services are most important to the customers?
2 What are the processes that produce these products and services?
3 What are the key ingredients that stimulate action in the organization, and what are the processes that convert these stimuli to outputs?
4 Which processes have the highest visibility with customers?
5 Which processes have the greatest impact on customer-driven performance standards?
6 Which processes do performance data or common sense suggest have the greatest potential for improvement?[2]

Answers to these questions will differ for different types of organizations. No universal formula or prescription has been found. Key processes at a hospital will be different from those at a nationwide fast-food franchise or at an aircraft manufacturer. Nonetheless, all will share some elements of commonality.

One overall, first-pass approximation of key processes can be gained from an examination of what Xerox Corporation has done. Xerox defined sixty-six key processes in ten major areas (refer to Table 8.1). This approach has been generalized and shown as eleven key processes in Figure 8.2. These include four core processes and seven supporting processes.

Once the key processes have been identified, their systematic and continuous improvement can begin. First, assign ownership—responsibility

Table 8.1: Xerox Corporation—Ten Key Business Process Areas

Direct Line Functions	Supporting Functions
Customer marketing	Financial management
Customer engagement	Physical asset management
Order fulfillment	Business management
Product maintenance	Information technology application
Billing collection	Human resource management

Source: Xerox Corporation, internal communications.

for the design, operation, and improvement of the overall system. Next, plan a structured and disciplined approach to understand, define, and document all major components and their interrelationships. Then, follow the process-improvement road map presented in Chapter 9.

Managing Key Processes at Reimer Express

A second example of process management is offered by Reimer Express Lines, Ltd. In our experience, it represents the epitome of simplified process management. Reimer defines its business as being dependent on two key processes: one that delivers freight for customers and the other that collects money from customers. John Perry, vice president for quality, helped shape Reimer's approach, and we gratefully acknowledge his contributions.

Based in Winnipeg, Canada, Reimer Express was the first transportation company and the first service company in North America to win a national quality award. It earned this recognition from the federal government of Canada in 1989 for achieving excellence in transportation services through a commitment to continuous improvement.

Reimer calls its process for handling shipments "Freightflow." As shown in Figure 8.3, eight specific elements combine to form the Freightflow process. Reimer believes it is critical that employees working in one element of the Freightflow service chain understand the impact of their activities on the other elements. This understanding is achieved by training employees in all eight elements. Employees identify "roadblocks to quality" and thereby assist the company in managing the total process for reducing nonconformance.

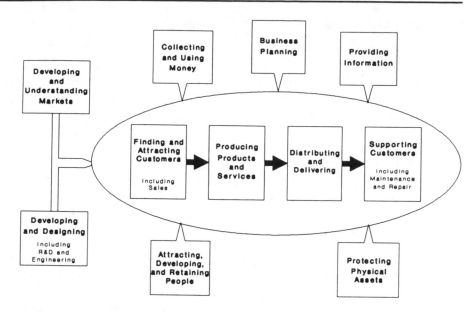

Figure 8.2 Identifying Key Processes

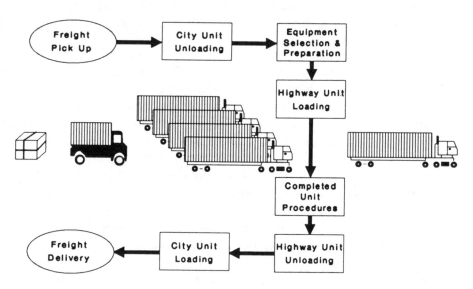

Figure 8.3 "Freightflow" at Reimer Express. *Source*: Adapted from discussions with John Perry, vice president for quality, Reimer Express, Winnipeg, Canada, 1990.

Managing Customer Information Processes

Exchanging information with customers serves as a third example of process management. Whether accomplished through sophisticated systems, word of mouth, or haphazard activities, organizations interchange three types of information with customers. These three types of information represent the outputs from the customer information processes:

1 *Requirements:* Suppliers learn the needs and expectations of former, current, and prospective customers in order to develop, design, and deliver products and services that are valued and desired by customers. This type of information sometimes takes the form of market surveys and analysis.

2 *Advertising:* Suppliers inform former, current, and prospective customers about the features, advantages, and benefits of the products and services they offer.

3 *Satisfaction:* Suppliers learn how customers perceive the value, advantages, and disadvantages of products and services they use. This aspect of the information system forms the feedback loop of the work process model and is a source of data for corrective action and improvement initiatives.

The effective and efficient accumulation and analysis of this information can be regarded as the desired outputs of the customer information processes. The relationship of customer requirements and satisfaction to the work process was explained in Chapter 6. Advertising is a subject in itself and beyond the scope of this book. It is mentioned here merely for the sake of completeness.

It is interesting to note that the outputs from the customer information processes are of critical importance to two of the six process-management ingredients. First, customer requirements dictate the attributes of the products and services that need to be *measured*. Second, quality *improvement* focuses on increasing the effectiveness of work processes for satisfying customers' requirements. On the other hand, the remaining four ingredients—*ownership, planning, control,* and *optimization*—are internal to the supplier's organization and are independent of the customer information processes. Finally, customer satisfaction is the controlling signal through the feedback loop to assure the effectiveness of all efforts.

The preceding discussion about ingredients may raise questions as to the difference between improvement and optimization. Therefore, the meaning of these terms is repeated for clarification. *Improvement* increases the effectiveness of the process for meeting the customer's requirements. *Optimization* increases the efficiency and productivity of the process and may be invisible to the customer. However, since the methods for process improvement and optimization are identical, no further differentiation will be made in this book. The term *improvement* will be used for both ingredients.

Communicating information along the customer-supplier chain is an activity that is both interactive and imprecise. This type of work is certainly very different from jobs in manufacturing operations. For example, the output from the customer information processes cannot be characterized effectively in tangible terms. Furthermore, the customer is an active participant in the information processes, and finally, these processes may be repeated infrequently. These differences, however, do not preclude continuously improving the customer information processes.

Example of Functions Satisfying Multiple Information Objectives

Some activities in the customer information process yield multiple types of data. The role of sales representatives in a large international engineering company provides an example of how all three objectives of the customer information processes can be accomplished simultaneously. The reps' principal objective is to communicate information to customers on the features, advantages, and benefits of the company's engineering services (advertising). In meeting with customers, however, reps also discover information that clarifies customers' requirements and satisfaction. Monthly meetings of the reps at the home office are used to integrate and analyze their findings and to identify service improvement opportunities.

The help desk of the computer systems division of a Houston-based oil company offers another example of achieving multiple information objectives through a single system. The principal objective of the help desk is to serve the company's computer users by answering questions and resolving problems they encounter.

The computer systems division discovered that help desk operators could also contribute to satisfying all three information objectives. This work was facilitated by codifying, categorizing, accumulating, and

Table 8.2: Sampling of Functions to Understand Customer Requirements and Satisfaction

• Formal communications – Proposals – Contracts – Invoices	• Hot lines and help desks
	• Customer complaints – Face-to-face – Written – Telephone – Electronic
• Customer surveys – Formal – Focus groups – Site visits – Industry groups	
	• Informal – Face-to-face – Networks
• Sales data	

analyzing data and information from every call. The help desk satisfied information objectives in the following ways: (1) The help desk served as a sounding board and offered a repeatable, nonthreatening method for learning about user (customer) satisfaction. (2) By analyzing patterns of calls on users' problems, requirements were clarified for electronic mail, and system improvements were identified and implemented. (3) Through listening to users' problems, help was provided to one group by explaining the features of an updated version of their software that would be more effective than the one currently in use.

How do you begin to improve your customer information process? Start by reviewing Chapters 5 and 6, which can help you clarify who your customers are, what they require, and how to measure their satisfaction. Next, assign responsibility for the design, operation, and improvement of the overall system. Identify the processes already in place to accomplish the three objectives. Chapter 7 described various mechanisms available to understand customers, and Table 8.2 lists a sampling of activities typically used. Plan a structured and disciplined approach to understand, define, and document all major components and their interrelationships. Then, follow the systematic process improvement road map presented in Chapter 9.

A Final Word on Process Ownership

Before leaving the subject of process management, it might be appropriate to reemphasize the importance of ownership, particularly the ownership of processes that cross functional boundaries. Process ownership can be identified through two characteristics—authority and responsibility. The owner of any process is the person at the lowest level who has the authority to implement changes and who is responsible for the consequences of these changes.

Many organizations have traditionally focused managers' attention on functional goals and on fixing, maintaining, and running their respective operations. Instead, process owners should focus on the overall system that delivers products and services to customers and on improving the performance of that system. Ideally, compensation and promotion of process owners will include consideration of their ability to continuously improve the performance of their processes.

Summary

TQM achieves quality improvement through prevention and the systematic improvement of key processes rather than through "fire fighting" and focusing on near-term results. Key processes can be defined as the ones that have a material effect on the success of the organization. Since organizations are often structured around their areas of specialization, key processes sometimes cut across functional boundaries and receive less attention than they deserve.

Our experience has revealed three failings that most frequently prevent organizations from systematically improving business processes: (1) the failure to identify key processes and assign *ownership*, (2) the failure to apply a robust improvement *approach* that builds an understanding of fundamental root causes of problems, and (3) the failure to *measure* the right things. The following challenges are offered to help avoid these failings:

Ownership (Chapter 8)

- Have you identified your key processes?
- Have you assigned one individual as the owner of each key process?
- Do the owners recognize their responsibility for maintaining, operating, *and* improving their process?

Approach (Chapter 9)

- Do you look at individual outputs or deviations, or at the whole process?
- Do improvement plans include the development of hypotheses regarding the potential causes of problems?

- Are these hypotheses tested and the results verified?
- Do solutions address root causes?

Measurement (Chapter 10)

- Do you have a comprehensive set of measurements to define the performance of your process and its impact on all stakeholders?
- Do you understand the variation inherent in your measurements?

Notes

1. G. A. Pall, *Quality Process Management* (Englewood Cliffs, N.J.: Prentice-Hall 1987), 31–32.

2. A. P. Brache and G. A. Rummler, "The Three Levels of Quality," *Quality Progress* 21, no. 10 (1988): 46–51.

Six Steps
to Process
Improvement

The six-step process improvement model was prepared specifically to bridge the gap between manufacturing and nonmanufacturing applications of quality methods. It is represented pictorially in Figure 9.1 and can serve as a universal road map for all applications.

It begins by identifying outputs, customers, and the work processes that produce these outputs. The methodology continues by closely examining customer requirements and defining gaps between them and the capabilities of the work processes involved. It next stimulates exploring and analyzing these processes to understand the root causes underlying the gaps. It sparks development of new outputs and processes and requires that these new ideas be tested with data. Appropriate changes are implemented, their effects are evaluated, and the cycle is repeated to secure continuous improvement.

Why Does This Sound So Complicated?

W. Edwards Deming has stated repeatedly, "There is no such thing as instant pudding."[1] Continuous improvement of key business processes cannot be expected to be an exception. The six-step process offered in this chapter was developed through years of frustration and failure, and its application requires discipline. Simpler approaches have been tried and have been successful in some applications, but they have invariably encountered difficulties when generalized to different types of problems. The six-step process has been designed as a universal approach.

Numerous causes can be cited as to why managers outside of manufacturing operations encountered difficulties in their attempts at process improvement. Some may have been seeking short-term

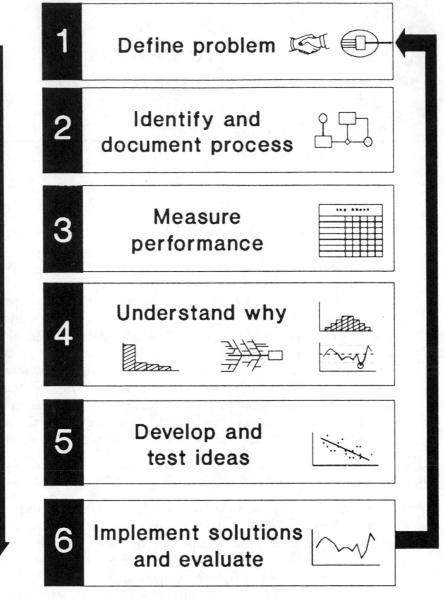

Figure 9.1   Process Improvement Model

breakthroughs. Some failed to recognize the system within which the outputs were produced. Some did not understand what the customers really wanted. Others were unable to establish appropriate measures of the system's performance. Others tried to plug in tools and techniques developed for manufacturing processes. And still others were looking for instant pudding.

The six-step process improvement model introduces a systematic approach for applying quality management to any type of process. It can be applied to any operation: information systems, marketing, finance, administration, R&D, engineering, service, or manufacturing. It can be applied to any system: those that exchange information with the customer, those used to produce and deliver products and services, and those that create the work environment.

Universal application is possible because the approach helps build a fundamental understanding of the business processes before attempting to improve them. Continuous improvement requires knowing *what* these processes are, measuring *how well* they are performing, and understanding *why* they are performing the way they are. This profound knowledge is built through application of the first four steps.

In some applications, one or more of these first four steps can be shortcut because they have already been accomplished through the normal course of business. This does not mean that these steps can be skipped, merely that their requirements are satisfied through existing systems.

Each of the six steps is explained in this chapter. They are described in a straightforward, linear fashion for clarity. Actual application, however, will often be complicated by the need to recycle back to earlier steps as new information is gained and earlier hypotheses are found to be incomplete or incorrect.

Step 1: Define the Problem in the Context of the Process

Unlike manufacturing, service providers or knowledge workers sometimes do not recognize that they are performing within a business system. The process improvement model begins by clarifying which systems are involved, so that efforts can focus on processes, not outputs. Specific activities prescribed within this first step are:

1.1 Identify the output.
1.2 Identify the customers.
1.3 Define the customers' requirements.
1.4 Identify the processes producing these outputs.
1.5 Identify the owner(s) of the processes.

Table 9.1: Defining the Problem in the Context of the Process—Examples

Objective Defined in Terms of a Specific Result	Restated in the Context of the Process	Incremental Process Improvement Realized
1. Expedite production of technical report XYZ	Improve the process for reproducing and distributing technical reports	Average time to produce *all* technical reports reduced by 30% *and* costs reduced by 20%
2. Expedite installation of equipment to test new product ABC	Improve process for setting up tests for new products	Average time to set up performance tests for new products reduced by 30% *and* setup costs reduced by 20%
3. Define appropriate rewards for employees who responded to storm cleanup IJK	Improve system to reward and recognize employee efforts and contributions	Annual opinion survey showed 22% improvement in employees' views of performance management system, *and* compensation levels remained unchanged
4. Select and train 4 additional operators to support increased calls to computer users' help line	Improve systems to support computer users	Annual opinion survey showed 15% improvement in employees' views of computer support, *and* no operators were added
5. Investigate and eliminate cause of computer outage on July 20	Improve reliability of computer system	Downtime reduced by 25% *without* additional equipment or staff

When customers' needs and expectations are not well understood, special efforts must be made to define them clearly and objectively. (Readers can refer to Chapters 5 and 6 for guidance in these activities.) This lack of understanding is often encountered when output properties are difficult to measure, as is commonly the case when the outputs are intangible.

Table 9.1 provides examples of how problems can be defined in the context of the process for continuous improvement. It compares how an objective might be stated in terms of a specific result and how it might be restated in the context of the underlying process. It also shows corresponding examples of the next increment of process improvement that was achieved. Notice that these results are stated in objective, measurable terms.

The owners of the processes involved should also be identified in this first step. Again, this task is often taken for granted because of how clear ownership is in most manufacturing operations. For example, in manufacturing, responsibility is usually defined clearly and documented

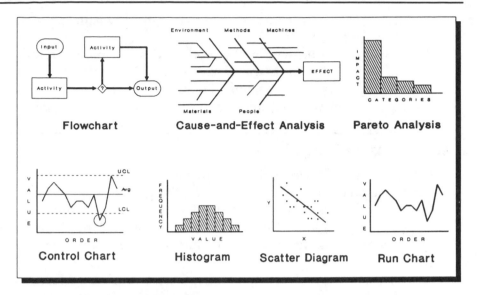

Figure 9.2   Process Improvement Tools

for daily operations, preventive maintenance, and individual manufacturing blocks of process units. On the other hand, this clarity is often lacking in service processes. Understanding who the owners are is an essential step in assuring that appropriate resources are applied and that identified improvements can be authorized. Additional information on process ownership is provided in Chapter 8.

Step 2: Identify and Document the Process

In the absence of clearly defined work processes, work is needed to establish this basis. Since manufacturing processes are usually well documented, this step has historically been taken for granted. This second step in process improvement demands that the process be described in understandable terms, which is usually accomplished with a picture or model, not merely through a written or verbal description.

The flowchart is a commonly used tool for describing processes, and a simplified version is shown in Figure 9.2. The technical literature is filled with methods for flowcharting, and several sources are listed as references at the end of this chapter. Creating a flowchart enables you to perform the following four improvement activities:

2.1 Identify the participants in the process, either by name, by position, or by organization.

2.2 Provide all participants in the process with a common understanding both of all steps in the process and of their individual roles.

2.3 Identify inefficient, wasteful, and redundant steps.

2.4 Offer a framework for defining process measurements.

Step 3: Measure Performance

In the absence of documented performance standards, remedial work is needed to quantify how well (or poorly) the system is performing. Further, these measures must be defined and evaluated in the context of customer expectations. This step is of double importance in situations where neither output requirements nor processes have been defined previously.

Chapter 4 introduced the concept of measuring performance at three levels: process, outputs, and outcomes. Process measures define activities, variables, and operations of the work process itself. Output measures define specific features, values, and attributes of each product or service and can be examined from two sides. One side represents the output characteristics desired by the customer (requirements), and the other side represents the output characteristics actually delivered by the process (capability). The former is referred to as the voice of the customer and the latter as the voice of the process. Outcome measures define the ultimate impact of the process and are dependent on what the customer does with the product or service. Customer satisfaction represents the key measure of outcome.

The cost of quality is one measure of process performance (see Chapter 2), and there are many more. A set of measures is outlined in Table 9.2 and clarified through the following simplified example of purchasing gasoline for passenger cars.

In making decisions as to which brand or grade of gasoline to buy, customers are concerned with how the product itself will perform in their car, the purchase price, and the attributes of service at the point of purchase, such as convenience with regard to time and location, appearance of the facilities, and behavior of the attendants.

To focus on just one characteristic for the purpose of this example, consider the performance of the product itself. The customer's need for smooth, quiet, trouble-free operation of his or her car's engine has been translated into a set of technical specifications for gasoline. One of these

Table 9.2: Relating Customer and Process Measures—Generic

Outcome	Customer satisfaction	
Output	Characteristics desired by customer	Characteristics delivered by process
Process	Performance parameters	

is octane, and one measure of the voice of the process is the actual octane of the gasoline in a specific tank at a specific service station at a given time. Other related measures include the variation of octane within this tank over time, the variation of octane among the tanks of various service stations, and the variation of the octane for this grade of gasoline in the blending tanks of the refinery.

Moving into the processes at the refinery, product specifications such as octane are translated into other performance characteristics for the various feedstreams. One example might be the temperature, pressure, and flow rate of one stream into a reactor.

So what has this example shown? It began by defining the desired outcome as smooth, quiet, trouble-free operation of the customer's car engine. Yet it somehow twisted around to define one aspect of process measures as temperature, pressure, and flow rate into a reactor at a particular refinery. This translation is of fundamental importance because the process is actually controlled by measuring temperatures, pressures, and flow rates in the refinery, not by measuring octane in the service station tanks.

This translation was possible because all of the processes involved were described, modeled, and understood. One model related the customer's satisfaction to the performance of his or her car's engine. A second model related the engine's performance to product specifications of gasoline. A third model related product specifications to refinery operating conditions. These translations, shown in Figure 9.3, follow every link in the customer-supplier chain. (Refer to Chapter 6 for information on measuring customer requirements.)

One snapshot of example measures is shown in Table 9.3. This snapshot offers one specific set of values for each level of measurement. In reality, however, the picture is complicated because the variability of the data must also be understood. Even for a single driver with one car, the required octane will vary with weather, altitude, and condition of the engine (e.g., wear, deposits, and intake and cooling system performance). Likewise, the process characteristics and performance will vary simultaneously.

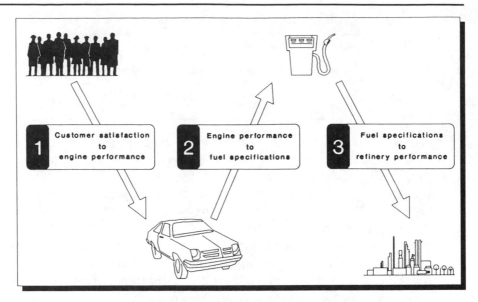

Figure 9.3   Translate: Customer Requirements to Process Performance

Although this example relates to the product and its manufacturing conditions, it is analogous to measurements required in service. As an alternative, this example could have defined the voice of the process in service dimensions rather than along one characteristic of the product itself.

Could the voice of the process in the service dimension be related to measuring the employee selection, training, and compensation criteria for service station attendants? Could it be related to the employees' job satisfaction? Could it be related to the processes for determining the design, location, and hours of operation for the station?

How can the processes that impact on the service characteristics be modeled and measured? Answers to these questions help extend process improvement beyond manufacturing and are offered in Chapter 10.

Step 4: Understand Why

The lack of data increases the difficulty of understanding why a system is performing the way it is. This problem is compounded when the outputs do not appear to be produced by a repetitive system, as is the case for long-term processes, such as research, development, and engi-

Table 9.3: Relating Customer and Process Measures—Product Example

Outcome	Customer survey regarding engine knock	
	67% Pleased 31% Satisfied 2% Dissatisfied	
Output	Customer wants 89.0 octane	Process delivers 89.3 Octane
Process	Feed to reactor A	
	Flow rate = 37,000 barrels day Inlet temperature = 455 degrees F Inlet pressure = 725 psi	

neering. The six-step process improvement model is designed to bridge this gap to assure identification of the specific factors limiting the system's capability.

By defining problems in the context of their process (step 1), identifying all steps in the process (step 2), and measuring performance in objective terms (step 3), the classic tools of statistical analysis and quality can be applied to understand the root causes of the performance gap. Four tools stand out for accomplishing this step: Pareto analysis, cause-and-effect analysis, histograms, and control charts. As with flowcharts (step 2), simplified versions were shown in Figure 9.2, and sources of information are listed at the end of this chapter.

Dr. Deming explains that experience alone teaches nothing and must be applied to knowledge of fundamental principles in order for learning to take place. Steps 2 and 3 of the process improvement model were designed to provide the base of fundamental principles. This is accomplished through flowcharting, modeling, and measuring. Step 4 offers methods to acquire the next level of knowledge and to gain a profound understanding of the process.

> Never have so many
> worked so hard
> to accomplish so little.

Why are people with good intentions often frustrated in their efforts and seem to accomplish precious little that is of long-term benefit? Why do problems recur for no apparent reason? Why do things go from bad to worse?

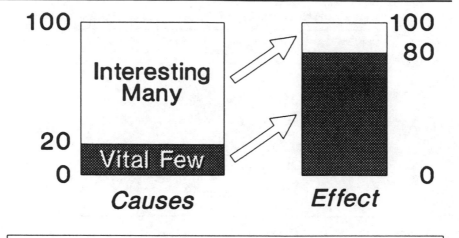

Figure 9.4   Pareto Principle

Answering three basic questions can help build a fundamental understanding of the process in order to take effective and efficient steps toward permanent improvement:

4.1 *Have we distinguished the vital few from the trivial many?* Joseph M. Juran believes that a fundamental law of nature dictates that 80 percent of the problems are the result of 20 percent of the causes. One key to improvement is to identify those crucial 20 percent and focus attention on them. Juran named this concept, which represents a maldistribution of quality losses, in honor of Vilfredo Pareto, a nineteenth century Italian economist.[2] (Pareto found that a large share of the wealth was owned by relatively few people—a maldistribution of wealth.) The Pareto analysis is a method for categorizing and recategorizing causes until the vital few are found. Juran's hypothesis is shown graphically in Figure 9.4.

4.2 *Have we diagnosed the root causes?* Kaoru Ishikawa suggests that the first signs of a problem are its symptoms, not its causes. Actions taken on symptoms cannot be permanently effective. It is necessary to understand and act on the underlying root causes. Cause-and-

Table 9.4: Diagnose and Act on Root Causes

Level	Observation	Action	Outcome
Symptom	Car does not start	Call tow truck	$25 bill for jump start
Cause	Dead battery	Recharge by driving	Arrive at work (late)
Cause	Broken fan belt	Call tow truck (again)	$50 bill for jump start and belt replacement
Root cause	Inadequate preventive maintenance	Implement manufacturer's recommended service	Problem eliminated

effect diagrams, fishbone charts, and Ishikawa diagrams are synonyms for a basic tool that can be used to help differentiate among symptoms, causes, and root causes. An example showing the differences among these levels is provided in Table 9.4.

4.3 *Do we understand the sources of variation?* Another contribution of Dr. Deming is his simplification of the concept of variation. He explains that all variation is caused and that the causes can be classified. Common causes are inherent within the system and yield random variation within predictable bounds. Special causes are assignable to specific reasons or events and result in sporadic variation that defies prediction.

Taking correct action to control variation requires knowing its type, since appropriate actions differ according to the type of variation. Common causes can only be solved by addressing the underlying system. On the other hand, special causes are addressed by eliminating their specific, identifiable source. Control charts help to distinguish between common and special causes of variation.

After the special causes are identified, the remaining inherent variation is attributable to the common causes. The capability of the process is defined by comparing this range of variation to the specifications or customer requirements. Capability can be calculated and can be visualized by plotting the data as a histogram. Figure 9.5 shows the difference between two processes—one that is capable of satisfying the designated requirement and another that is not.

Understanding variation and process capability are the preferred first activities in step 4. However, when outputs are intangible and not frequently repeated, data for this analysis might not be available. In

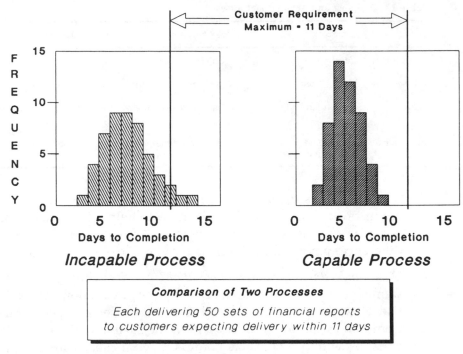

Figure 9.5   Recognizing Process Capability

these cases, the questions posed in step 4 will need to be answered in parallel or in an iterative way.

Step 5: Develop and Test Ideas

Is it pudding yet?
No.
There's no such thing as instant pudding.

Does this process seem complex? Difficult? Never-ending? We know of no shortcuts. If it were simple, quick, and easy, answers would have been widely known and applied before the 1990s. But fear not; progress is in sight. The first four steps built the foundation for understanding the critical dimensions of the process. They assured knowing *what* the processes are, measuring *how well* they are performing, and understanding *why* they are performing the way they are. These steps led to identifying the underlying causes of the principal problem. Developing ideas for improvement begins with step 5.

Ideas for improvement must address the root causes of the problem. Step 5 is the point at which development of new ideas and potential solutions should be encouraged. What are new and different ways to design and operate the process to eliminate the root causes?

A complementary approach for developing improvements is through experimentation. Design and conduct experiments to test the hypotheses developed in step 4. Also, design experiments to test the ideas developed in step 5 before implementing them.

When tests fail to produce the desired results, determine the cause. Was the test valid? Was the improvement idea effective? Were you mistaken about the root causes of the problem? Were measurements inaccurate or taken on the wrong parameters? Was the process completely identified? Were the customer's requirements misunderstood? Recycle back to the appropriate step on the process improvement road map.

Step 6: Implement Solutions and Evaluate

The sixth step begins by planning and implementing the improvements identified and verified in step 5. Step 6 continues to measure and evaluate the effectiveness of the improved process. But these activities represent only one side of this step.

The other side is to evaluate the six-step process itself and to acknowledge and celebrate the contributions of those who participated in this increment of process improvement. It makes no difference whether this was the work of an individual or, as is more likely, a team effort. Reward the contributors for the result achieved as well as for their discipline in applying the six-step model. A worksheet detailing application of the six steps is provided as Figure 9.6.

Finally, return to step 1 to begin the next increment in the ongoing process of continuous improvement.

Is This the Only Approach to Process Improvement?

The six-step process serves as a universal road map to process improvement. It provides a systematic approach to build a fundamental understanding of customers' requirements, process capabilities, and the causes for gaps between them. A road map differs from a prescription. People who are unfamiliar with the route use a road map as a guide for getting from point A to point B. On the other hand, a prescription specifies requirements that must always be followed.

❶ Define Problem

- [ ] Identify output
- [ ] Identify customers
- [ ] Define requirements
- [ ] Identify processes
- [ ] Identify process owner

❷ Identify and Document Process

- [ ] Flowchart
- [ ] Model
- [ ] Identify participants

❸ Measure Performance

- [ ] Customer satisfaction
- [ ] Customer requirements
- [ ] Output delivered
- [ ] Process parameters
- [ ] Cost of quality

❹ Understand Why

- [ ] Distinguish major areas
- [ ] Diagnose root causes

Understand variation
- [ ] Common causes
- [ ] Special causes
- [ ] Capability

❺ Develop and Test Ideas

- [ ] Develop new ideas
- [ ] Experiment
- [ ] Test ideas to address root causes

❻ Implement Solutions and Evaluate

- [ ] Plan improvements
- [ ] Implement system changes
- [ ] Document system changes
- [ ] Evaluate system performance
- [ ] Evaluate six steps
- [ ] Reward participants
- [ ] Recycle to step 1

Figure 9.6   Process Improvement Checklist

The six-step road map guides application of a fundamental improvement strategy known by any of four names: P-D-C-A, plan-do-check-act, the Shewhart cycle, or the Deming cycle. The "plan" phase is guided by the first four steps along the road map. These steps help clarify problems and develop hypotheses as to their causes. Step 5 covers the "do" and "check" phases by testing the previously developed hypotheses. Step 6 completes the cycle ("act") by implementing improvements to the process.

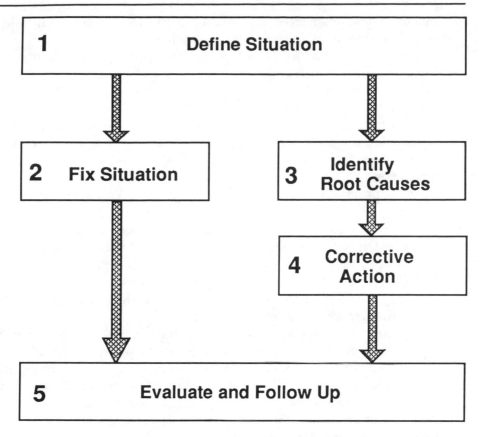

Figure 9.7 Philip Crosby Associates' Method for Eliminating Nonconformances. *Source*: Adapted from concepts by Philip Crosby Associates, Inc.

Numerous alternative guides for P-D-C-A are available, and several organizations have customized the six-step model for their own use. Some have modified the terminology to incorporate their own jargon. Some have reduced the number of steps by combining elements, and others have increased the number of steps by separating elements. The following are examples of two other improvement processes, including explanations of their relationship to the six-step road map.

Figure 9.7 shows the five steps involved in the process for eliminating nonconformances taught by Philip Crosby Associates. It begins by defining the situation (our step 1). Crosby then outlines two parallel paths. One fixes the current situation, and essentially "extinguishes the fire," while the "fire-prevention system" is being developed and installed. The other identifies the root causes (our step 4) and implements corrective action, evaluates, and follows up (our step 6).

Crosby's method has found widespread application in manufacturing operations, and the six-step road map presented in this chapter offers specific complementary features to extend application beyond manufacturing. For example, the first four steps along the road map assure understanding the full spectrum of customer expectations, translating them into process specifications, and applying classic quality tools to understand the underlying causes of gaps between requirements and actual performance. Explicit statement of these steps has been needed when improving intangible outputs or undocumented business processes.

As an added enhancement, the six-step road map suggests testing new ideas in step 5 before implementing them. If followed blindly, the Crosby approach permits skipping the "do" and "check" phases of P-D-C-A. The resultant approach then looks like plan-act-plan-act. Testing is explicitly included in the six-step road map to draw attention to this potentially wasteful shortcut.

Figure 9.8 shows the quality improvement process used throughout Xerox Corporation. It served as the starting point for the development of our six-step model. When combined with its problem-solving model, the Xerox approach closely parallels the six steps. Recognizing Xerox's heritage as a manufacturing company, the six-step model was designed to bridge the gaps between manufacturing and nonmanufacturing applications.

Summary

Systematic process improvement relies on building a fundamental understanding of customers' requirements, process capability, and the causes for gaps between them. Hypotheses are developed and tested, and improvement gained through the continuous cycle of plan-do-check-act. This systematic approach bears striking contrast to the classic short cut of problem detection and subsequent solving, an approach resembling plan-act-plan-act.

The six-step road map was developed as a universal guide for systematic improvement. It can be used to improve manufacturing as well as nonmanufacturing processes, and helps assure application of the plan-do-check-act strategy.

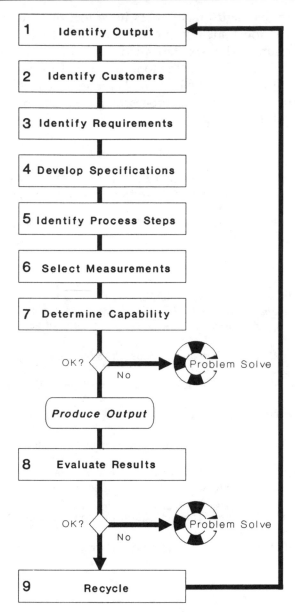

Figure 9.8 Xerox's Quality Improvement Process. *Source*: Irving J. DeToro, "Strategic Planning for Quality at Xerox," *Quality Progress* 20, no. 4 (1987): 19.

Many quality improvement practitioners have focused merely on the application of basic tools such as flowcharts, control charts, and cause-and-effect diagrams. The six-step road map offers a robust approach to improvement, and places the tools in their proper perspective. Although they are valuable, the basic tools are merely techniques to help make the performance of work processes visible and by themselves are of relatively little benefit.

Notes

1. W. Edwards Deming. Statement at seminar, Methods for Management of Productivity and Quality, George Washington University, Alexandria, Va., January 19–22, 1988.

2. John T. Burr, "The Tools of Quality Part IV: Pareto Charts," *Quality Progress* 23, no. 11 (1990): 59.

References

Crosby, P. B. *Quality Is Free.* New York: Mentor, 1979.

Deming, W. E. *Out of the Crisis.* Cambridge, Mass.: MIT CAES, 1986.

DeToro, I. J. "Strategic Planning for Quality at Xerox." *Quality Progress* 20, no. 4 (1987): 16–20.

Gunter, B. "A Perspective on Taguchi Methods." *Quality Progress* 20, no. 6 (1987): 44–52.

Ishikawa, K. *Guide to Quality Control.* Tokyo: Asian Productivity Organization, 1982.

Memory Jogger. Lawrence, Mass.: Growth Opportunity Alliance of Greater Lawrence, 1985.

Nolan, T. W., and Provost, L. P. "Understanding Variation." *Quality Progress* 23, no. 5 (1990): 70–78.

Oakland, J. S. *Statistical Process Control.* New York: Wiley, 1986.

Scherkenbach, W. W. *The Deming Route to Quality and Productivity.* Rockville, Md.: CEEPress, 1987.

Scholtes, P. R., et al. *The Team Handbook.* Madison, Wis.: Joiner Associates, 1988.

Tribus, M. "Deming's Way." *Mechanical Engineering* (Jan. 1988): 26–29.

10 *Measuring Performance*

In God we trust. All others bring data.

One element of total quality management is to base decisions on data, not opinions, and this chapter provides a framework for defining the parameters that are needed to measure performance. Clarifying which parameters can and should be measured will help in the systematic and continuous improvement of all products, services, and processes. This chapter is designed for anyone who has stated: "I believe in the concepts of total quality management but can't apply them because my work can't be measured."

Dr. W. Edwards Deming identified seven deadly diseases that plague Western industry, and one is "Management by use only of visible figures, with little or no consideration of figures that are unknown or unknowable."[1] The visible measures are frequently the short-term financial ones. But what about customer satisfaction or employee morale or community impact? Are these not factors that should also be monitored? If improving customer satisfaction leads to increased sales and profits, why not measure satisfaction and use these data in making business decisions?

One cure for this deadly disease is to make visible the key measures that were previously hidden. A two-part framework for measurement is offered as an antidote. One part establishes three levels of measures: the first one for controlling operations within the process, the second for measuring the outputs delivered, and the third for quantifying the outcomes. The second part of the framework defines four dimensions of results: products and services delivered to the users and customers, financial return for shareholders, job satisfaction for employees, and social impact upon the community.

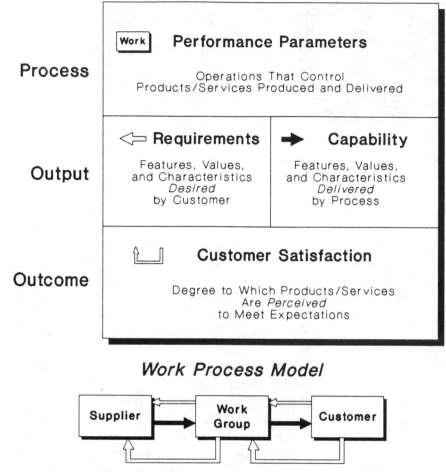

Figure 10.1   Measure at Three Levels

Measure at Three Levels

The use of measurement is pervasive in systematic process improvement. Although measurement was introduced in the third step of the process improvement model (refer to Chapter 9), various measures are used in all steps. Four types of measures were introduced, and they represent three distinct levels: process, output, and outcome. The relationship between the four types of measures and the three levels is shown in Figure 10.1. These measures are described below, along with their application within the six-step process improvement model.

Process

1 *Performance parameters:* Measure each step/activity in the process and the characteristics of inputs delivered by suppliers that control the desired output characteristics. Identify the behaviors that govern each step, and use these measures to control operations and to predict the outputs before they are produced or delivered. Performance parameters are analyzed in steps 4 and 5.

Output

2 *Requirements:* Define the specific features, values, characteristics, and attributes desired by customers for each product and service. These measures represent the voice of the customer and are used in step 1 along the six-step road map. Requirements and expectations must then be translated into product/service specifications.

3 *Capability:* In direct correspondence to every specific feature, value, characteristic, and attribute desired by customers, measure its level, value, or presence in each product and service actually delivered by the process. These measures represent the voice of the process and define what the process has delivered. Process capability is measured in step 3 and tested in step 5.

Outcome

4 *Customer satisfaction:* This is the highest level of measurement and represents the ultimate desired result. Measure how well each product and service satisfies the needs and expectations of the customer, and recognize that these measures are based on vague, idiosyncratic perceptions. Outcomes are beyond the direct control of the supplier and rely on the customer's expectations and actions. These measures often trigger process improvement initiatives (step 1) and can also be used to evaluate the results achieved (step 6).

Example: Measuring R&D at Three Levels

The application of meaningful measurements to corporate research and development has been a subject of debate for decades. Application of measures at three levels can help to remedy this situation.

Measurements at the process level are used routinely by scientists and engineers to perform their tasks. Process measures are represented by data in their day-to-day activities and experiments. These are the measures taken within the projects themselves, whether they be technical, administrative, or financial.

Outputs from the research process include technical reports, patents, publications, and presentations. These outputs can be measured, but as with process measures, these indicators are rarely of interest to the customers. These uninspired customers include corporate directors as well as managers and technical staff of the manufacturing divisions who apply the results of the research. Although these customers are interested in the *content* of the output from R&D, their operations are hardly impacted by the *counting* or measurement of these outputs.

The factor that has been missing from these measures is the bottom-line impact—measurement at the outcome level. How can the ultimate desired objective of corporate research functions be described? The objective is for the users of the technical discoveries to be "happy customers." These users represent the corporate profit centers or the manufacturing divisions, and they are made happy through increased profits. Measuring research against this ultimate objective is fraught with problems and usually avoided.

British Petroleum (BP) is one organization that is bucking the trend and has been measuring R&D performance at the outcome level.[2] As director of research, John Cadogan uses these data in the preparation of an annual "balance sheet" for the board of directors. Cadogan initiated the process in 1985 and included records for the three previous years. The value of R&D is calculated by dividing the financial benefit attributed to research for a given year by the research budget.

BP's measure of R&D outcome is based on the judgment of its business center managers. They are asked to quantify how much of their annual profits are attributable to research. Researchers develop a listing of their projects that are being implemented in each business center. Managers use the respective listings to prepare their responses.

Although many shortcomings of BP's approach could be cited, it offers two distinct benefits. First, Cadogan's system is designed to be quick and simple. It discourages "overworking the numbers." Second, the system directly asks the customers to indicate their perception of the value of specific research projects to their own operations. The impact of errors in estimating the value of R&D is minimized through this approach, since, after all, the ultimate objective is to satisfy the customer, and it is the customers' perceptions that are being measured.

Measure in Four Dimensions

In addition to the output actually delivered to the end customer and the resultant outcome, each process generates by-products and outcomes for other "customers." One is financial return for the shareholders. Another is job satisfaction for the employees. The third by-product is the social impact on the community.

The three levels of measures were described in Figure 10.1 with respect to the actual output, but they also apply to each by-product. Satisfaction and desired characteristics of these by-products are defined by their respective "customers." These, in turn, represent three additional sets of specifications against which process performance can be measured.

As shown in Table 10.1, performance parameters can be defined in four dimensions. Each dimension corresponds to the output or outcome desired by its respective customer: the end user, the shareholder, the employee, or the community.

Antidote to a Deadly Disease

Four dimensions of performance measures applied at three levels are offered as an antidote to the deadly disease of running a company on visible figures alone. Deming explains in *Out of the Crisis* that this disease is the result of a management fixation on counting the money.[3] In essence, Western companies have focused on themselves and the financial markets rather than on their customers, employees, or the community.

Organizations moving toward focusing on the customer can facilitate their transformation by defining and using measures indicative of customer satisfaction. Similarly, organizations striving for total involvement of their work force need to pay attention to the parameters that directly relate to improving employees' satisfaction with their jobs.

It should be obvious that a balanced approach is needed. None of the dimensions can be ignored. To the extent that the shareholders' objectives, the customers' requirements, the employees' needs, and the community's expectations all overlap with each other, the easier the task becomes. Figure 10.2 shows the relationship among these measures. Long-term success can be assured by selecting and leading a balanced attack to improve systematically in all dimensions.

Table 10.1: Four Dimensions of Measures

Dimension	Focus	Example Measures	
1. Actual product or service	End user or customer	• Specific features/characteristics and attributes defined by customers	
		• Customer satisfaction	
2. Financial return	Shareholder	• Costs	• Profits
		• Prices	• Throughput
		• Sales volume	• Waste
		• Productivity	• Efficiency
		• Cost of quality	
		• Capital utilization	
		• Return on investment	
3. Job satisfaction	Employees	• Specific needs and values defined by employees	
		• Employee satisfaction	
4. Social impact	Community	• Regulatory compliance	
		• Atmospheric emissions	
		• Liquid discharge	
		• Waste disposal and recycling	
		• Grants and contributions	
		• Presentations and publications	
		• Taxes and fines	

Example of a Balanced Approach at SAS

Jan Carlzon offers an excellent example of the importance of selecting appropriate measures in his book *Moments of Truth*. [4] As CEO of SAS (Scandinavian Airlines System), Carlzon helped move his company toward being one that would focus on satisfying the customers' needs through an empowered work force. He presents an example of how SAS air cargo operations redefined their measurements to accomplish this vision.

What Are Your Values?
Where Is Your Focus?
Are They Consistent?

If This Is Your Focus . . .	. . . Then This Is Who You Need to Please	. . . and These Are Key Measures
Customer	Customers	✓ Customer satisfaction ✓ Output characteristics defined by customers
Shareholder	Bosses Owners Financial analysts	✓ Financial indicators + Costs, sales, and profits + Cost of quality ✓ Goals and objectives defined by management
Employee	Employees	✓ Employee satisfaction ✓ Factors contributing to job satisfaction
Community	Government agents Social services Professional societies Academia The press	✓ Regulatory compliance ✓ Factors impacting on society

Figure 10.2   Measure in Four Dimensions

SAS had historically measured the performance of its air cargo division by the amount of freight it carried and how well it used available capacity in the cargo holds of the aircraft. The logic had seemed flawless. Efficiency and profitability for a commercial airline are improved by filling the "empty bellies" of passenger planes with air freight.

However, in order to focus on the customers' needs and facilitate decision making at the working level, these measures were inadequate.

How important was SAS profitability to its cargo customers? How did these historic measures help employees to do their jobs? Were other measures more important?

What mattered most to the customers was what SAS termed "precision": prompt delivery to specified locations. Furthermore, the cargo customers defined prompt as "next day." Recognizing this as the voice of the customer, SAS ran an experiment to measure the voice of the process in the corresponding dimension of "precision."

This experiment was conducted in spite of the fact that SAS had thought it was doing very well. After all, the cargo division had reported that only a small percentage of shipments did not arrive on time. As a test, SAS sent one hundred packages to various locations throughout Europe. However, the test showed that instead of arriving the next day, the average arrival time was four days later.

As a result of this test, SAS recognized that it was not measuring the correct parameters. It was measuring a by-product for the shareholders instead of measuring how the process was performing in relation to the real customers' expectations. The customers' requirement for next-day delivery was beyond the capability of the existing system. Even worse, SAS had been oblivious to this gap.

In a related example, Carlzon explains how process performance parameters were defined for baggage handlers. At SAS, historic measures had been defined in terms of the amount of cargo and the documentation attached to it. As long as volume remained at high levels and the documentation remained attached to the shipments, SAS had considered performance to be fine. In fact, Carlzon explains that new records were being set constantly. Unfortunately, these records were self-serving for the organization and were being established in spite of late deliveries and unhappy customers.

SAS empowered its cargo handlers to define more appropriate measures. Known as the QualiCargo system, these data compare the various cargo terminals with each other and are published monthly. The following QualiCargo data are collected to demonstrate process performance against the criteria of greatest interest to the customers:

- Length of time to answer the telephone
- Conformance to promised deadlines
- Arrival of cargo on the intended plane
- Length of time from landing to availability

SAS improved its cargo-handling system and reduced late shipments from 20 percent to 8 percent. Furthermore, this success did not require adding staff or forcing the existing staff to work harder. Instead, the accurate system of measurement identified previously unrecognized problems and led to procedural changes and reallocation of resources. SAS combined financial information with data on performance relative to customer requirements provided by QualiCargo. These measurements enabled the cargo handlers to understand what was important to the customers and profitable to SAS.

QualiCargo was one of many SAS initiatives to help focus on satisfying the customers' needs through an empowered work force. Now all employees at SAS cargo know that "precision" is important to the customers and that "precision" is important to SAS because this is what the customers pay for. Furthermore, the employees know exactly what components comprise "precision," and they know that top priorities are answering telephones, booking shipments, receiving them, forwarding them along with their documentation, receiving them at the other end, reconciling cargo, preparing for customer pickup, and informing customers when their shipments are ready.

This new insight also affected how the cargo division approaches its daily operations. Supervisors no longer need to direct the activities of the baggage handlers and schedule coffee breaks and work shifts. Instead, everyone knows what to do, when to do it, and why it is important.

Hints for Measurement

W. H. Davidow and B. Uttal provide excellent guidance on the subject of measurement in their book *Total Customer Service*. After examining hundreds of process and output measures, they concluded that even the best sets of measures will result in suboptimization unless they are balanced against frequent measures of customer satisfaction.[5] They go on to explain that employees will perform exactly as the measures tell them to, regardless of the original intent of the measures. Furthermore, the measures may only serve the needs of the shareholders and ignore the ultimate customers, employees, and community. At best, measures provide an imperfect representation of the customers' expectations. Even if they are reasonably accurate and complete, they will drift out of alignment because expectations change in response to advertising, competition, and experience.

Table 10.2: Comparing Measurement Guidelines

Essential Variables of Measurement Systems[a]	Tools for Implementing Measurement Systems[b]
1. Simplicity of presentation (few and understandable)	1. Programs have strong support from top management
2. Visibility	2. Programs are developed through the inclusion of employees who will be measured
3. Involvement of all concerned	3. Programs include measures that employees and managers need to do their jobs
4. Undistorted collection of primary information throughout the operations area	4. Managers demonstrate the impact of measures through linkage to the compensation and reward systems
5. Straightforward measurement of what's important	
6. Achievement of an overall feeling of urgency and perpetual improvement	

[a]Tom Peters, *Thriving on Chaos* (New York: Knopf, 1987), 585–593.
[b]W. H. Davidow and B. Uttal, *Total Customer Service* (New York: Harper & Row, 1989), 202–204.

Davidow and Uttal offer four tools for implementing measurement systems. Table 10.2 lists these along with six essential variables offered by Tom Peters in his book *Thriving on Chaos*.

These tools and ingredients can be combined with the concepts in this chapter to yield the following guidelines for measuring performance at each level:

- *Process:* These parameters will be defined by the employees to control, improve, and optimize the performance of their work processes consistent with all desired output characteristics. These measures will not be used to assess the performance of the employees and need not be reported to managers, shareholders, customers, or the community except to the extent that these people can offer ideas and help in identifying which parameters to measure, how to collect and analyze the data, or how to improve the process.

- *Output:* These parameters are defined by the respective customers (end users, shareholders, employees, or community) and characterize the product/service required and expected. The focus of an organization's attention can be adjusted in relation to how much visibility, reward, and attention is devoted to output measures in each dimension. Output measures will be tested continuously against outcomes to assure that they remain consistent with customers' ever-changing expectations.

■ *Outcome:* These parameters determine the ultimate success or failure of the organization. Everyone should understand how his or her process and output measures relate to outcomes, and selected key measures should be displayed conspicuously. Since outcomes are beyond the control of individual employees, it may be unfair to base individual compensation and reward on these measures. Instead, these measures might more appropriately be tied to whole teams or organizations. Customer satisfaction often represents the key outcome measure.

One Final Caution on Measurement

In addition to selecting the correct parameters to measure, it is also important to establish a system for collecting the correct data. A classic story from World War II illustrates this point.

Suffering tremendous losses of its four-engine Lancaster bombers, the Royal Air Force set up a program to measure their vulnerability to enemy antiaircraft fire. By examining patterns of where the planes were being hit, the RAF would be able to design the most effective countermeasures. Spotters observed the fleets returning to their bases in England and recorded the location of damage on large scale-drawings of the planes.

With great interest, the investigators observed a random pattern of damage over the entire fuselage. Furthermore, the density of gunfire on the wings was significantly lower. The absence of damage to the wings suggested that adding armor plating to the fuselage would be an effective solution. It would be unnecessary to protect the wings, since they did not seem to be vulnerable to gunfire.

Fortunately, before adding the burden of heavy armor to the fuselage, the error in the RAF's data-collection method was recognized. What was needed instead was to measure the damage to the planes that were shot down, not to the ones that were returning safely.

Measuring Performance in Your Organization

How is performance measured in your organization? When you report results to your boss, how much time do you spend on measures relating to the process? Outputs? Outcomes? On which dimension do you focus? On organizational needs? Customer satisfaction? Employee satisfaction? Community impact? When you discuss key business results with those reporting directly to you, how much time and interest do you allocate to each dimension?

How are you collecting performance data? Are you analyzing your successfully delivered outputs alone without examining and understanding the defective ones? Are you analyzing desired output characteristics and satisfaction from happy customers? What about the unhappy customers who are not returning or the ones who have always purchased goods and services from your competitors?

Or is the situation even worse? Is yours one of the organizations that doesn't even have measures of customer satisfaction or process performance or employee satisfaction or community impact?

Two worksheets are provided here to help you employ measurements. Figure 10.3 can be used to establish measures in all four dimensions. As an alternative, Figure 10.4 can be used to define the full set of measures in each dimension in greater detail.

Summary

Many organizations are driven by performance measurement. The absence of meaningful goals and measures can lead to useless meandering. Perhaps even worse, use of the wrong measures can drive organizations in the wrong direction. To overcome these problems, this chapter offers a two-part measurement framework. One part establishes three distinct levels of measures: the first for controlling operations within the process, the second for assessing the outputs delivered, and the third for quantifying the outcomes achieved. The second part of the framework defines the perspectives of four basic stakeholders: customers, employees, shareholders, and the community at large.

Underlying these frameworks is a performance measurement paradigm that is provided as a summary of measurement theory:

1 Every product and service can be characterized by a set of performance measures.
2 Your job begins by understanding your customers and identifying the set of characteristics that fully define their needs.

Complete This Worksheet for Each Product or Service

Dimensions

LEVEL	Product or Service	Financial Return	Job Satisfaction	Impact on Society
Output/Outcome / **Customer**	**End Users**	**Shareholders**	**Employees**	**Community**
Outcome Level of Customer Satisfaction				
Output Characteristics/Attributes/Values Desired by Customers				
Characteristics/Attributes/Values Delivered by Process				
Process Performance Parameters				

Figure 10.3 Measurement Matrix

✓ Define the product/service to be improved.

✓ **List** the customers for [a]
   this product/service.

✓ **Identify** the performance
   characteristics required
   and expected by these customers. [b]

✓ **Translate** each characteristic desired by customers into
   corresponding specifications for the product/service, and
   indicate their absence, presence, or value in comparison
   to the customers' expectations.

✓ After documenting the operation
   of the process (flowchart), list
   the measures internal to the process
   that control the performance of the
   product/service against the
   specifications.

a   Customers are the "users" and "buyers" of your outputs.
    Alternatively, this same analysis can be completed for other
    spheres of influence by replacing "customer" with
    "employee," "owner," or "community."

b   As a minimum, characterize how customers would define
    faster, better, and cheaper.

Figure 10.4   Worksheet for Getting Started

3 You must next translate these customer-driven characteristics into process measures and learn the performance level that your process is capable of delivering for each characteristic.
4 You should then determine how satisfied customers are with performance at the current level, and the relative importance customers place on changing the level of each characteristic.

Notes

1. W. E. Deming, *Out of the Crisis* (Cambridge, Mass.: MIT CAES, 1986), 98.

2. D. Fishlock, "When Research Is Seen to Make a Profit," *The Financial Times*, London (Aug. 17, 1988), 12, sec. 19.

3. Deming, *Out of the Crisis*, 97–125.

4. J. Carlzon, *Moments of Truth* (New York: Ballinger, 1987), 107–112.

5. W. H. Davidow and B. Uttal, *Total Customer Service* (New York: Harper & Row, 1989), 201.

11

Example Applications

If you always do what you always did,
You'll always get what you always got.

The literature is filled with success stories, and their publication satisfies a number of objectives for both readers and authors. Published examples pinpoint improvement opportunities for readers and explain how others achieved success. These examples also provide a forum from which authors can showcase their own accomplishments.

Rather than repeat different versions of the same types of examples available everywhere, this chapter's main thrust divulges difficulties encountered when attempting to shortcut a systematic improvement process. This chapter describes several quality activities that did not achieve their objectives, so that we can learn from others' mistakes. A checklist of common pitfalls is featured, and examples are offered for clarification. One example of success is included for balance.

Table 11.1 offers a checklist of common pitfalls to avoid. The process improvement road map presented in Chapter 9 might be armor-plated but cannot be expected to survive a nuclear attack. Through its development and application, a number of teams failed to achieve their goals because they stumbled over fatal (but avoidable) hazards. Although numerous problems will be encountered along the six steps of the road map, those included in the checklist impact the early steps and often cause irreparable damage. In reading the examples that follow, note which pitfalls are involved.

Example 1: Provide Employee Day Care Center

Company ABC provides financial services across the mid-Atlantic states. Corporate headquarters and three of ABC's sixteen operating

Table 11.1: Checklist of Common Pitfalls to Process Improvement

❑ *Tampering:* Is the project targeted at one specific nonconformance or incident when the underlying process is incapable of achieving the required results?

❑ *Incomplete ownership:* Have all stakeholders been identified and included in the project as appropriate, or have some been missed: process owner, participating employees, customers, suppliers?

❑ *Lack of expertise:* Is a team of novices being asked to address an issue normally within the domain of acknowledged experts, specialists, or consultants?

❑ *Imposed solution:* Is a "quality action team" being used as a disguise to implement a solution predetermined by management without understanding the fundamental underlying causes?

❑ *Constraints:* Is the project artifically constrained by expectations established before the underlying causes have been identified (e.g., technical expertise, data, cost, schedule)?

❑ *World hunger:* Is the objective so broad, the situation so deeply ingrained in your culture, or ownership so diffuse that the current level of competence in quality improvement is unlikely to be successful?

divisions are located in a suburban New Jersey community. One of these divisions initiated total quality management in 1992, and one of its early quality action teams identified and documented the benefits of building an on-site day care center for employees' preschool children.

The benefits of offering day care tied directly to one of the company's stated core values: provide equal opportunity for all employees. The proposed day care center also included financial credits through fees paid by employees who chose to use the center.

The quality action team began its project by surveying ABC employees to estimate expected usage. Follow-up interviews defined interest in alternative features of the center and clarified demand sensitivity to fee structures. Not only did the team find stong interest, but it also sensed employee pride in such an initiative.

Space was identified in an unused portion of the building, and a conceptual design was prepared. Costs were estimated to be $65,000 for modifications, equipment, and furnishings. Ongoing operating expenses for labor, insurance, utilities, and maintenance were to be covered through user fees. These fees would also repay the capital improvements within five years and afterward return a small "profit."

Since the plan impacted on physical facilities, company policy required a review by headquarters. Concerned about the appearance of expenditures that were unrelated to ABC's core business lines and about establishing a precedent that might be followed by other divisions, headquarters rejected the proposal. The quality action team members were demoralized, and the first nail was hammered into the coffin being prepared for total quality management at the division.

What Happened in Example 1?

The quality action team's proposal to build and maintain an on-site day care center may have been an excellent idea that could improve the well-being of the work force. The involvement of a diverse group of employees working toward a common goal had merits, and their analysis was sound.

Unfortunately, the team did not have the authority required for implementing this project. Headquarters representation was needed for complete ownership. If all of the stakeholders had been identified and included in the project from its inception, this example would probably have been a success story.

Even worse, management could have bailed the team out from this pitfall if it had wanted to demonstrate its unflinching commitment to its new total quality management process. Instead of looking for excuses to thwart action, management could have approved the center on the basis of its being a pilot, which could not be duplicated at other divisions until firsthand experience was gained.

Example 2: Improve Help Desk Performance

The help desk represents one of several resources that Trent McComas provides to support users of information systems in one division of Exxon Company, U.S.A. His spring 1989 survey of three hundred users defined their level of satisfaction with services offered by his internal support organization and identified improvement opportunities. Responses to the survey, coupled with an analysis of the performance capabilities of the help desk work process, yielded an understanding of its limitations.

Through minor equipment modifications and staff reassignment, the identified limitations were removed. These changes simultaneously improved the quality of service as perceived by the users and improved the efficiency, productivity, and cost-effectiveness of McComas's operations. Extensive measurement of process performance helped to clarify the changes needed and quantify their impact. McComas offers the following comparison of performance before and after these changes:

Customers' Viewpoint

- *Simplified access to help:* Rather than having to select from a five-page list of phone numbers, users merely needed to dial a single phone extension: H-E-L-P.

- *Increased user satisfaction with help desk support:* The spring 1989 survey of users showed their average satisfaction to be 3.3 out of a possible 5.0. This score was similar to the level achieved by most other services included in the same survey. By early 1990, McComas began receiving unsolicited *compliments* for the help desk, praising the responsiveness, competence, and courtesy.

- *Increased usage:* Whereas the average user called the help desk once per year in 1988, demand by these same customers increased to three calls per month by late 1989.

Manager's Viewpoint

- *Increased efficiency:* The help desk operator handled one call per business day during 1988. This capability increased to sixty calls per day by late 1989 for the same staffing level.

- *Reduced cost:* Total operating costs were reduced, and responding to the average call cost less than $4 in 1990, as compared to $260 each in 1988.

- *Customer feedback:* In addition to showing greater customer satisfaction with the performance of the help desk, this function was also able to serve as a mechanism for listening to the voice of the customer for services offered throughout McComas's operations.

What Happened in Example 2?

The improvements made in the performance of the help desk demonstrate how costs can be reduced and quality improved simultaneously. Decisions were based on understanding both the customers' requirements and the process capability. This understanding was built through gathering and analyzing appropriate data. Action steps addressed the fundamental causes of the observed limitations. Customers, management, and employees all shared in the benefits.

Example 3: Improve Performance Appraisal System

The Acme Financial Services Company (AFSC) employs six hundred people, has sales of $75 million per year, and formally kicked off its continuous improvement process in 1987. Consistent erosion of market share precipitated this initiative as an alternative to staff reductions or possible bankruptcy.

In developing its strategy for continuous improvement, AFSC was able to take advantage of its major supplier, a well-known, international *Fortune* 100 computer manufacturer that began quality management in the early 1980s. Elements of the supplier's strategy were incorporated in AFSC's approach to continuous improvement.

AFSC identified its key systems and established objective measures of performance through interviews with selected customers. Recognizing that its employees are the customers for the systems that create the work environment, an employee opinion survey was designed to measure the performance of these systems.

The employee opinion survey was conducted annually, and the first year, 1987, formed the baseline. Analysis of the 1988 data confirmed that employees were dissatisfied with the performance of their supervisors and managers. Problems included weakness in team building, coaching, delegating, and mentoring.

The human resources manager, Don Beggin, faced a dual challenge: improve the systems that govern supervision and foster implementation of the continuous improvement process. Beggin recognized the excellent reputation for quality management enjoyed by its major supplier and investigated the performance appraisal system it used for supervisors and managers. Beggin liked the supplier's approach and in 1989 formed a quality action team of key employees to implement the supplier's appraisal system in AFSC.

What Happened in Example 3?

There seems to be little value in explaining how Beggin's quality action team marched through each step of the process improvement road map. Readers would be amazed at how the team was able to collect and analyze data to support the implementation of the new appraisal system.

It is entirely possible that supervisors' weaknesses in team building, coaching, delegating, and mentoring were caused by the old appraisal system. It is also possible that the proposed new system would eliminate the root causes of these problems. Unfortunately, it is unlikely that Beggin was lucky enough to have guessed right regarding both the causes and the best solution.

In essence, Beggin jumped from the first step of the process improvement process (define the problem) to the last step (implement improvement). Instead of chartering a team to implement his predetermined solution, Beggin needed to proceed through each step in sequence. He needed to identify all of the systems impacting on supervisors' performance, identify likely causes for deficiencies, and then check his assumptions and hypotheses. Next, solutions would be developed and evaluated—and, yes, a new performance appraisal system might be part of the improvement plan.

As a footnote to this example, some readers may question why Beggin was trying to improve the performance appraisal system when, instead, he should have been working to eliminate it. Dr. W. Edwards Deming identifies performance appraisal as one of seven deadly diseases that plague industry (see Chapter 2 for a listing of these deadly diseases). Perhaps if Beggin had lead his team through the process improvement road map, the root causes of performance problems would have been revealed.

Example 4: Eliminate Unplanned System Downtime

Acme Financial Services Company (AFSC) halted a prolonged sales decline in 1986 by landing a major new account. By 1988, attrition of other clients resulted in this new account's representing over one-third of AFSC's business. In measuring performance, however, it was clear that this key client was dissatisfied with AFSC's service, and the major source of irritation resulted from unplanned downtime of the mainframe computer operated by AFSC on the client's behalf.

In its effort to win this new account, AFSC had assured uninterrupted mainframe availability, with mutual agreement required for planned outages. This promise was made in spite of prior experience. Unplanned mainframe outages totaled six, three, four, and two incidents in 1982–1985, respectively.

A quarterly newsletter represented one element in AFSC's strategy to communicate with customers. The following excerpts relate the story behind this example:

AFSC Newsletter—April 1988 (Special Edition)

AFSC apologizes to its users for the six-hour system failure experienced on March 20. We regret the inconvenience it caused, stand behind our promise of uninterrupted service, and remind all users of the exceptional level of reliability provided over the preceding year. The last outage was October 4, 1987, and resulted from the massive power failure experienced throughout northern New Jersey caused by Hurricane Edward.

Clark Shannon, customer services manager, has chartered a quality action team to identify and permanently eliminate causes of the March incident. Members include representatives from AFSC's major customers, systems specialists, console operators, and operations supervisors. The names of members and their affiliation are . . .

AFSC Newsletter—October 1988 (Lead Article)

Service on the AFSC mainframe was interrupted for nearly three hours on July 19, and we apologize to our users. Customer services manager Clark Shannon reports that a quality action team has been chartered to eliminate its causes.

Shannon is pleased to report that AFSC management is reviewing the seventeen recommendations issued by the team that investigated the March 1988 incident. Implementation of these improvements, combined with the findings of the new team, should assure the utmost reliability in the future. Shannon announced that three members of the March team are providing their expertise and experience to the current team.

AFSC Newsletter—April 1989 (Page 4)

AFSC regrets the service interruption experienced by its mainframe users on November 7. Clark Shannon, customer services manager, is leading a blue-ribbon team to investigate causes and . . .

Epilogue

Mark Malone resigned from AFSC in February 1989. A respected console operator with five years of experience, Malone was frustrated by the inaction of his management. He had been an enthusiastic supporter of the company's continuous improvement process, attended all available training programs, and was a member of both the March and July quality action teams. Through hard work and long hours, the March team identified a number of causes contributing to the incident and presented a seventeen-point corrective action plan to management. A parallel approach by the July team yielded similar results and reiterated more than half the earlier recommendations. Malone's biggest disappointment was that fewer than one-third of the proposed items had been approved by the end of 1988.

What Happened in Example 4?

Efforts described in this example to reduce downtime on the computer represent a frustrating but frequently repeated pattern. AFSC had promised its newest customer a service that was beyond its capability to deliver. For one reason or another, service on AFSC's computer system is interrupted unexpectedly a few times every year. These interruptions can be expected to continue in future years until a fundamental change is introduced.

Shannon's attack on each incident in isolation would be characterized by W. Edwards Deming as tampering. Instead, AFSC needs to examine its computer system in its entirety.

Example 5: Accelerate Health Insurance Payments

Roger Phillips, employee benefits manager, is responsible for his company's health care contract with Big Rock Insurance. In 1992, he attended quality awareness training with his company's management team. Among a number of concepts and techniques learned, three found direct and immediate application to Phillips' work with Big Rock:

1 *A belief in consistent conformance to the customer's requirements and a philosophy of accepting no defects.* His company's contract with Big Rock stated that all valid claims will be paid within two weeks of receipt. Phillips had heard a number of complaints about slow payments, reviewed the records, and recognized that each and every late payment was unacceptable to the affected employee. This situation needed to be improved.

2 *Reliance on measurement.* Phillips did not need to work on the basis of vague opinions; he could work from a position of strength with facts and data. In the course Phillips attended, he learned to record the monthly data received from Big Rock on what was referred to as a nonconformance chart. His data are shown in Figure 11.1. Big Rock

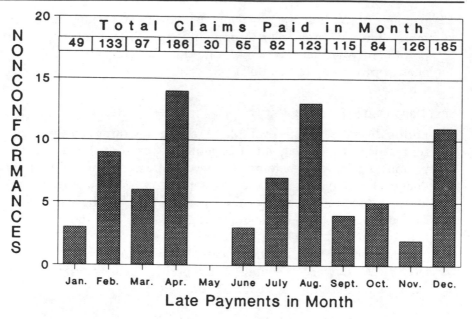

Total Claims Paid in Month											
49	133	97	186	30	65	82	123	115	84	126	185

Figure 11.1   Big Rock Performance Trend for 1992

had been late in paying valid insurance claims seventy-four times in 1992 (6 percent of all claims filed), with incidents nearly every month.

3 *A process to eliminate nonconformances through prevention.* The cause for each and every late payment must be determined and corrected, so that the situation would not recur.

Armed with his new knowledge, data, and the courage of his convictions, Phillips attended the annual contract review meeting with Big Rock in January 1993 prepared to improve Big Rock's performance. Phillips explained his concepts of quality, reminded Big Rock of its contractual agreements, and showed that approximately 6 percent of the past year's 1,275 claims were paid late. As a direct result of this meeting, Big Rock agreed that in 1993, it would investigate the cause of every late payment and prepare a quarterly report on action required to prevent recurrence.

It was estimated that one additional person would be needed on Big Rock's staff during 1993 to coordinate this extra effort. Since this was not covered within the scope of the contract, premiums would have to be adjusted upward. Recognizing the potential payback in improved claims

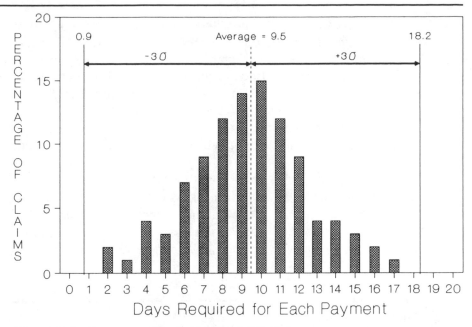

Figure 11.2   Frequency Distribution for 1,275 Claims

processing, Phillips gladly agreed. The meeting attendees also agreed that some of the corrective actions might increase costs and would need to be reviewed for their impact on premiums prior to implementation.

What Happened in Example 5?

Phillips' valiant attempts were doomed to failure. True, he was right in not accepting late payments on behalf of his company's employees. True, he was working with data rather than opinions. True, he was looking to improve the process so that causes for late payments would be eliminated permanently. Unfortunately, the reality of the situation was not revealed through his nonconformance chart.

As an alternative view of the process, refer to Figure 11.2, which shows a histogram of the time required to process all claims for 1992. During this period, claim-processing time averaged about 9.5 days. The data had a standard deviation of 2.9 days. Adding three standard deviations to the average suggests that nearly all claims should be payable in less than 18.2 days. The problem faced in this case was that the insurer had committed to deliver checks within 14 days, a specification that is not supported by the actual performance of the process.

Various reasons might be cited for each incident of payment's stretching beyond fourteen days, but the bottom line was that Big Rock's claims-processing system was simply incapable of consistently delivering checks within the specified period. The data in Figure 11.2 show that the system used during 1992 might be appropriate for paying within eighteen days, but not within fourteen days. Phillips' plan to address the cause of each nonconformance as a specific incident is an example of tampering. Instead, the claims-paying system needs to be examined in its entirety.

The capability of this process is about 0.5 and compares poorly to minimum acceptable values for process capability, often quoted as 1.0, 1.33, or even 2.0. For readers unfamiliar with this measure, a brief explanation is offered at the end of this chapter. Detailed information on calculation procedures and applications can be found in several of the references listed at the end of Chapter 9.

Applications Summary

If experience and hindsight are so wonderful, why are mistakes from the past repeated, repeated, and repeated? Table 11.2 lists the cases from this chapter and the major pitfalls encountered.

Table 11.2: Example Applications and Their Pitfalls

Example	Pitfall
1. Employee day care center	Incomplete ownership
2. Help desk	Success!!!
3. Performance appraisal	Imposed solution
4. Unplanned computer downtime	Tampering
5. Insurance payments	Tampering

Addendum: Process Capability for Insurance Payments

A process capability index compares the variation expected of an output characteristic to the corresponding customer's specifications. In other words, it compares the process control limits (voice of the process) to the tolerance between the specifications (voice of the customer).

Further, the capability index is normally calculated for stable processes (refer to step 4 in the process improvement road map presented in Chapter 9). That is, capability is determined for processes with variation in performance resulting only from common, random causes. Special, assignable causes have been identified and eliminated. Correctly calculated capability indices offer excellent measures against which the results of quality improvement efforts can be gauged.

In the case of paying medical insurance claims (example 5), the specification sets the maximum time for payment as fourteen days. Since no minimum time is specified, the capability index merely compares the observed variation in actual delivery time to the difference between the average and the fourteen-day contractual maximum. The calculation is shown as follows:

Output Data (Days)

Customer Specification
Maximum: 14.0

Process Delivery Calculated
Average: 9.5
Sigma: 2.9 (standard deviation)

Calculated Capability Index

Available tolerance = (Customer specification − process average)
= (14 − 9.5) = 4.5 days

Expected variation = (3 × sigma)
= (3 × 2.9) = 8.7 days

Capability index = (Available tolerance/expected variation)
= (4.5/8.7) = 0.5

Improving Capability

Four options are available to improve the capability of this process:

A Increase customer specification
B Reduce process average
C Reduce expected variation
D Combinations of A, B, and C

As a first approach, consider option A: increase customer specification. Performance in 1992 met the 14-day standard for all but about 6 percent of the claims (74 failures out of a total of 1,275 claims). The maximum estimated delivery time is calculated to be 18.2 days. This is the upper control limit for the process and is calculated as the average delivery time plus 3 sigma.

Table 11.3: Process Capability Comparison

Capability Index	Standard Deviations above Average	Resultant Specification (Days)
1.00	3	18.2
1.33	4	21.1
2.00	6	32.9

Note: Average = 9.5
Standard deviation = 2.9.

If the specification were increased to be identical to the eighteen day-upper control limit, the capability index would equal 1.0. This same process might be expected to fail to meet this relaxed standard about 0.3 percent of the time (997 successes for each 1,000 claims). Note that for 1992, all payments were made in less than eighteen days.

Although it is usually impossible to "manage the customer's expectations," there are situations when option A (changing the specification) is appropriate. Table 11.3 compares the maximum allowable number of days for paying valid claims that could be specified in the contract for various capability indices for the process in place during 1992. As the number of days specified in the contract is increased (high capability index for the same process performance), the likelihood of late payments is reduced.

Options B and C are usually preferred over option A because they actually yield process improvements. Instead of raising the specification from fourteen days to the eighteen-day maximum delivery time expected for the process, options B and C would achieve a capability of 1.0 by improving the process such that maximum delivery would be expected to be less than fourteen days. With option B, this would be achieved by reducing the average by four days. Option C would accomplish this objective by reducing the expected variation above the average by the same four days.

Figure 11.3 and Table 11.4 compare the base case process to each option. Option B would be impossible to achieve. If the variation in the process remained unchanged as suggested in this option, some checks would need to be delivered before the claim was even submitted in order to reduce the average payment time to the required five days. Clearly, the key to successfully improving this process is to improve its reliability and thereby reduce its variation.

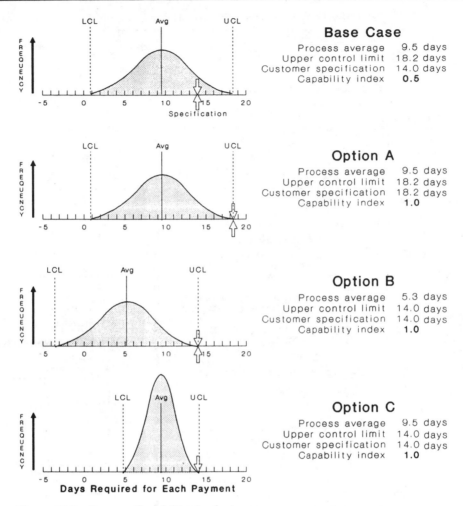

Base Case

Process average	9.5 days
Upper control limit	18.2 days
Customer specification	14.0 days
Capability index	**0.5**

Option A

Process average	9.5 days
Upper control limit	18.2 days
Customer specification	18.2 days
Capability index	**1.0**

Option B

Process average	5.3 days
Upper control limit	14.0 days
Customer specification	14.0 days
Capability index	**1.0**

Option C

Process average	9.5 days
Upper control limit	14.0 days
Customer specification	14.0 days
Capability index	**1.0**

Figure 11.3 Process Capability Analysis

Option D combines gains available through each of the above-described options. Use of option D would increase the available tolerance (manage the customers' expectations for later payments) *and* improve the process (reduce the time actually required for paying valid claims). Motorola drives the performance of its entire organization through this approach, which is shown graphically in Figure 11.4.

An inaugural winner of the United States Malcolm Baldrige National Quality Award, Motorola began its pursuit of "Six Sigma"

Table 11.4: Options Yielding a Process Capability Index of 1.0

Option →	Base Case	A	B	C
		Increase	*Reduce*	*Reduce*
	Capability	*customer*	*process*	*process*
	0.5	*specification*	*average*	*variation*
Process average	9.5	9.5	5.3	9.5
Standard deviation	2.9	2.9	2.9	1.5
Upper control limit	18.2	18.2	14.0	14.0
Customer specification	14.0	18.2	14.0	14.0

Defining Capability

Capability Index (Cp) quantifies the ability of a product or service characteristic to satisfy the customer's need.

Numerator = The Tolerance, or Range of Acceptable Variation

Denominator = The Variation Actually Delivered

Driving Everyone Towards Improvement

Historical approach treated quality improvement as the responsibility of manufacturing

Total Quality Management mobilizes the entire organization - for example:

Marketing, design, and engineering improve quality by increasing the numerator

Manufacturing, delivery, and service improve quality by reducing the denominator

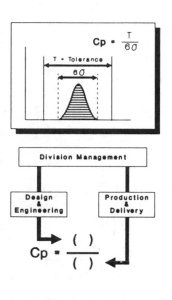

Figure 11.4   Building Process Capability. *Source*: W. Smith, Motorola. Address to the Exxon Corporation Total Quality Assurance Conference, Houston, TX., April 1990.

quality standards in everything it did, both manufacturing and nonmanufacturing operations. Its Six Sigma goal translates into 3.4 defects per million opportunities, which is equivalent to 99.9997 percent perfect. Six Sigma equates to a process capability index of 2.0. Readers might be interested in referring back to Table 11.3 to see the impact that this degree of quality has on the specification of insurance payments for example 5.

IV Total Involvement

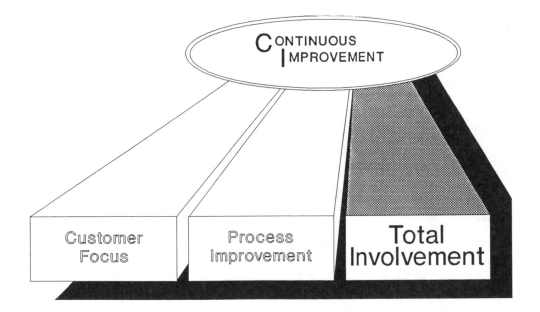

CONTINUOUS IMPROVEMENT

Customer Focus

Process Improvement

Total Involvement

12 *Leadership*

... In fact, to our knowledge, *every* successful quality revolution
has included the participation of upper management.
We know of NO EXCEPTIONS.

—Dr. J. M. Juran[1]

Total involvement forms the third and final core concept of Total Quality Management (TQM). Through it, the idea of winning loyal customers is mirrored into the organization, to build loyal employees and loyal suppliers. Total involvement aligns and integrates the efforts of everyone: managers, workers, and suppliers. This chapter describes the transformation of managers into leaders and their role in championing TQM. Chapter 13 describes steps that can be taken to empower teams of employees, and Chapter 14 explains how to integrate suppliers as partners in a mutually beneficial relationship.

The elements and characteristics of leadership have been described and defined many times in many ways. Our intention is to discuss leadership as it applies to the understanding and implementation of TQM. In this regard, leadership has specific implications for the senior managers embarking on a quality journey. This chapter describes these implications and suggests actions that senior managers can take to enhance the likelihood of success. The relationship among these actions is shown graphically in Figure 12.1.

What Is Leadership for TQM?

When implementing TQM, several fundamental activities must be accomplished by the senior management team. These senior managers bear ultimate responsibility for the success of the organization and, by virtue of their positions, have the authority to set direction, establish policy, allocate resources, and select the markets in which the firm will

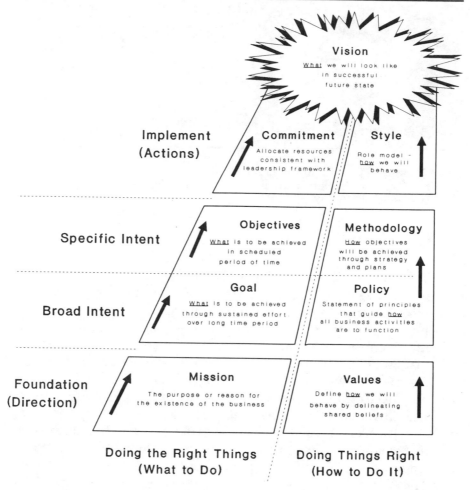

Vision
What we will look like
in successful
future state

Implement (Actions)

Commitment
Allocate resources
consistent with
leadership framework

Style
Role model -
how we will
behave

Specific Intent

Objectives
What is to be achieved
in scheduled
period of time

Methodology
How objectives
will be achieved
through strategy
and plans

Broad Intent

Goal
What is to be achieved
through sustained effort
over long time period

Policy
Statement of principles
that guide how
all business activities
are to function

Foundation (Direction)

Mission
The purpose or reason for
the existence of the business

Values
Define how we will
behave by delineating
shared beliefs

**Doing the Right Things
(What to Do)**

**Doing Things Right
(How to Do It)**

Figure 12.1   Leadership Framework

participate. These individuals are responsible to their customers, their employees, and ultimately their shareholders for the success of the enterprise.

TQM requires skills in both leadership and management. The difference between these two skill sets is stated succinctly by Warren Bennis:

> Leaders are people who do the right thing; managers are people who do things right. . . . Americans (and probably those in much of the

Figure 12.2   Quality Management. *Source*: Adapted from discussions with A. M. Lopez, 1988.

rest of the world) are underled and overmanaged. They do not pay enough attention to doing the right things, while paying too much attention to doing things right.[2]

Further clarification of the distinction between management and leadership is offered in Figure 12.2. To implement TQM, managing to get results will share center stage with leading to improve systems. The old roles of planning, organizing, directing, coordinating, and controlling will be diminished. In their place, we will find leaders who vision, align, empower, coach, and care.

Continuous improvement of all products, services, and processes is accelerated if everyone challenges the status quo every day. Leaders can set the stage for this challenge by developing answers to six fundamental questions:

1 Why do we exist; what is our purpose? (*mission*)
2 What will we look like in the future? What do we want to become? (*vision*)

3 What do we believe in, and what do we want everyone to abide by? *(values)*

4 What guidance will we provide to the many individuals in our organization as to how they should provide products and services to our customers? *(policy)*

5 What are the long- and short-term accomplishments that will enable us to fulfill our mission and attain our vision? *(goals and objectives)*

6 How are we going to move toward our vision and accomplish our goals and objectives? *(methodology)*

Answers to the first three of these questions form the cornerstones of the leadership framework. The mission defines *why* the organization exists. The vision shows *what* the organization wants to create, and the core values explain *how* we want to act. Answers to the remaining three questions fill in the details and build on these cornerstones.

These questions, while seeming simple and obvious, are enormously complex and difficult to answer, especially when an organization's traditional products and services are buffeted by new technologies, by competent and aggressive competitors, or by changes in customers' expectations. Nonetheless, failure to respond to each of these questions renders an organization incapable of understanding and meeting its customers' demands, unable to allocate its resources effectively and efficiently, and incapable of capitalizing on the talents of its people.

Why Do We Exist?

The question of why we exist is answered in the organization's *mission statement*. This statement is comprehensive, easy to understand, usually one paragraph in length, and describes why an organization was created and its primary function. The mission provides a clear statement of purpose to all employees as they perform their daily tasks. The following mission statements are offered as examples to illustrate answers to the question "Why do we exist?"

Ford Motor Company is a worldwide leader in automotive and automotive-related products and services as well as in newer industries such as aerospace, communications, and financial services. Our mission is to improve continually our products and services to meet our customer's needs, allowing us to prosper as a business and to provide a reasonable return to our shareholders, the owners of our business.

—*Ford Motor Company*[3]

[Imperial Oil] is a responsible and efficient developer of the country's natural resources and supplies a wide range of quality products and services, primarily under the ESSO brand.

—*Imperial Oil, Ltd.*[4]

To meet customers' transportation and distribution needs by being the best at moving their goods on time, safely, and damage-free.

—*Canadian National Railways*[5]

These statements, when published and disseminated to employees throughout the organization and widely communicated to customers and the public at large, commit an organization internally and externally to a specific purpose. A well-articulated mission statement also guides employees as to how they should manage their activities and sets a level of expectation among customers as to what they should get from this organization.

What Type of Organization Do We Want to Become?

The *vision* provides a description of what the organization will evolve into in the future and, like the mission statement, provides continuous guidance to employees at every level as to how they should manage their respective responsibilities. Usually, the vision is drafted as soon as the mission statement is completed and is developed through the same collaborative process.

The vision need not be described in precise financial or market terms. Rather, the intent is to provide a broad description of what an organization can become if everyone's efforts are focused and successful. The vision is less a dream, less a soft expectation of what is desirable, than a realistic picture of what is possible. The vision states what the organization wants to become and where it wants to go. This direction may be based on data regarding what is being achieved by others and what is possible for this organization.

Any of three flaws can be fatal to the process for building an inspirational vision: (1) failure to have a genuine vision—one that is important, challenging, and at the same time realistic; (2) failure to communicate the vision; (3) failure to rally everyone's genuine support. In his book *The Fifth Discipline*, Peter Senge summarizes these fatal flaws as follows:

If any one idea about leadership has inspired organizations for thousands of years, it's the capacity to hold a shared picture of the future we seek to create. One is hard pressed to think of any organization that has sustained some measure of greatness in the absence of goals, values, and missions that become deeply shared throughout the organization. IBM had "service;" Polaroid had instant photography; Ford had public transportation for the masses, and Apple had computing power for the masses. Though radically different in content and kind, all these organizations managed to bind people together around a common identity and sense of destiny.

When there is a genuine vision (as opposed to the all-too-familiar "vision statement"), people excel and learn, not because they are told to, but because they want to. But too many leaders have personal visions that never get translated into shared visions that galvanize an organization. All too often, a company's shared vision has revolved around the charisma of a leader, or around a crisis that galvanizes everyone temporarily. But, given the choice, most people opt for pursuing a lofty goal, not only in times of crisis but at all times. What has been lacking is a discipline for translating individual vision into shared vision—not a "cookbook" but a set of principles and guiding practices. . . .

A vision is truly shared when you and I have a similar picture and are committed to one another having it, not just to each of us, individually, having it. When people truly share a vision they are connected, bound together by a common aspiration. Personal visions derive their power from an individual's deep caring for the vision. Shared visions derive their power from a common caring. In fact, we have come to believe that one of the reasons people seek to build shared visions is their desire to be connected in an important undertaking. . . .

Visions that are truly shared take time to emerge. They grow as a by-product of interactions of individual visions. Experience suggests that visions that are genuinely shared require ongoing conversation where individuals not only feel free to express their dreams, but learn how to listen to each others' dreams. Out of this listening, new insights into what is possible gradually emerge.[6]

Tom Peters urges: "Develop and live an enabling and empowering vision. Ensure that the vision is at once (1) specific enough to act as a 'tie breaker' (e.g., quality is more important than volume) and (2) general enough to leave room for the taking of bold initiatives in today's ever-changing environment."[7] To help in this endeavor, examine the following examples and the eight traits of effective vision statements offered in Table 12.1.

Table 12.1: Develop an Enabling and Empowering Vision

1. Effective visions are inspiring.

   Steve Jobs, at Apple, wanted no less than to start a revolution in the way the average person processed information. Fred Smith, founder of Federal Express, had a vision of truly reliable mail service. The Nordstrom family seeks to create "an experience" with its stores. These leaders were not simply engaged in "market creation," as important as that is. They were engaged in a crusade and asked employees, customers, and suppliers to join them.

2. Effective visions are clear and challenging—and involve excellence.

   The visions various leaders conveyed seemed to bring about a confidence on the part of employees, a confidence that instilled in them a belief that they were capable of performing the necessary acts. These leaders were challengers, not coddlers.

3. Effective visions make sense in the marketplace and, by stressing flexibility and execution, stand the test of time.

   The vision is paradoxical: it is relatively *stable*—focusing on superior quality and service, for instance; but it is *dynamic*, in that it underscores constant improvement. The vision positions the company by defining how the company makes itself distinctly different from all its competitors.

4. Effective visions must be stable but constantly challenged—and changed at the margin.

   The vision must act as a compass in a wild and stormy sea, and like a compass, it loses its value if it's not adjusted to take account of its surroundings.

5. Effective visions are beacons and controls when all else is up for grabs.

   To turn the vision into a beacon, leaders at all levels must model behaviors consistent with the vision at all times.

6. Effective visions are aimed at empowering our own people first, customers second.

7. Effective visions prepare for the future but honor the past.

8. Effective visions are lived in details, not broad strokes.

   A vision is concise, encompassing, a picture of sustaining excellence in a major market.

Source: Adapted from Tom Peters, *Thriving on Chaos* (New York: Knopf, 1987), 486–49.

As we accomplish our mission, CN Rail will be a long term business success by being:
- Close to our customer
- First in service
- First in quality
- First in safety
- Environmentally responsible
- Cost competitive and financially sound
- A challenging place to work

—Canadian National Railways[8]

During the next decade, we want to become the best managed electric utility in the Unted States and an excellent company overall and be recognized as such.

—Florida Power & Light Company[9]

In order to position themselves to be more competitive and more focused on customers' needs, Florida Power & Light Company sharpened their vision in 1991 to be more specific and more tangible:

We will be the preferred provider of safe, reliable, and cost-effective products and services that satisfy the electricity-related needs of all customer segments.

—Florida Power & Light Company, 1991[10]

What's Important to Us?

Every organization operates with some behaviors being understood without ever being explicitly stated. But why leave these things unstated if they are important to running the business? Why not provide clear definitions of those important things, so everyone has a clear sense of the *values* of the organization?

But be careful. State your true shared values, not a set of ideals that look good on posters and wallet-size laminated cards. In fact, if stated values are inconsistent with realities, their posting will be a hindrance and will reveal the hypocrisy of the leadership team. Values cannot merely be proclaimed; they need to be lived convincingly. The following is an example of a credible set of corporate values:

People: Our people are the source of our strength. They provide our corporate intelligence and determine our reputation and vitality. Involvement and teamwork are our core human values.
Products: Our products are the end result of our efforts, and they should be the best in serving customers worldwide. As our products are viewed, so are we viewed.
Profits: Profits are the ultimate measure of how efficiently we provide customers with the best products for their needs. Profits are required to survive and grow.

—Ford Motor Company[11]

Table 12.2: Elements of Quality Policy

Element	Example Statement
Importance of quality	Quality is first among equals
Quality competitiveness	Best in class
Customer relations	Meet customer's needs
Internal customers	Quality extends to all segments
Work force involvement	Our policy is to provide 40 hours of quality training annually to every employee
Quality improvement	We will continuously improve our services

How Do We Want Everyone to Work?

Organizations consist of many different individuals with many different opinions. The "quality level" for the production and delivery of goods and services should not be left for everyone to determine individually. Instead, provide a *written quality policy* and consider the elements listed in Table 12.2 and in the following example policy.

> Xerox is a quality company. Quality is the basic business principle for Xerox. Quality means providing our external and internal customers with innovative products and services that fully satisfy their requirements. Quality is the job of every employee.
>
> —*Xerox Corporation*[12]

What Do We Have to Do?

Leaders must next move from the broad direction provided by mission, vision, value, and policy statements to declare what must actually be accomplished. Unless these statements are translated into measurable performance targets, they will be little more than nice sets of words. *Goals* cover the organization's broad intent by defining what is to be attained through sustained effort over the long term. By contrast, *objectives* define what is to be achieved in a specified period of time.

The following are example goals for one company whose vision was presented earlier in this chapter. Consider how these goals contribute toward that vision, how progress toward the goals might be measured, and how the goals might challenge the organization.

1. Improve customer satisfaction with sales and service quality:
   a. by reducing customer complaints to be among the lowest in the electric utility industry,
   b. by having adequate capacity to meet the needs of existing and future customers, and
   c. by having service unavailability to be among the lowest in the industry.
2. Strengthen effectiveness in nuclear plant operation and regulatory performance:
   a. by achieving nuclear plant availability to be among the highest in the industry, and
   b. by improving nuclear safety through the achievement of reduced automatic plant shutdowns . . . to be among the lowest in the industry.
3. Improve utilization of resources to stabilize costs:
   a. by improving quality,
   b. by maintaining stable and reasonable prices, as compared to the CPI, while maintaining a fair rate of return for stockholders, and
   c. by securing the safety of our employees and community.

   —*Florida Power & Light Company*[13]

Clear-cut, measurable objectives help spur everyone in the right direction and serve as mileposts against which progress can be gauged. Five criteria (listed below) help in framing effective objectives. In their book *Strategy Formulation and Implementation*, A. A. Thompson and A. J. Strickland present example objective statements that illustrate use of these criteria (see Table 12.3).

1 Objectives should be definitive and specific.
2 Objectives should describe accomplishments or results, not activities or behaviors.
3 Objectives should be measurable (quantifiable).
4 Objectives should delineate a time frame or deadline.
5 Objectives should be challenging yet achievable (they should be within the control of the responsible business unit and not rely on what might be accomplished by other organizations).

Table 12.3: Stating Objectives: "Good" versus "Bad" Examples

Poor: Our objective is to Maximize Profits.

Remarks: How much is "maximum"? The statement is not subject to measurement. What criterion or yardstick will management use to determine if and when actual profits are equal to maximum profits? No deadline is specified.

Better: Our total profit target in 1988 is $1 million.

Poor: Our objective is to increase sales revenue and unit volume.

Remarks: How much? Also, because the statement relates to two topics, it may be inconsistent. Increasing unit volume may require a price cut; and if demand is price inelastic, sales revenue would fall as unit volume rises. No time-frame for achievement is indicated.

Better: Our objective this calendar year is to increase sales revenues from $30 million to $35 million; we expect this will be accomplished by selling 1 million units at an average price of $35.

Poor: Our objective in 1989 is to boost advertising expenditures by 15%.

Remarks: Advertising is an activity, not a result. The real objective is what result the extra advertising is intended to produce.

Better: Our objective is to boost our market share from 8 percent to 10 percent in 1989 with the help of a 15 percent increase in advertising expenditures.

Poor: Our objective is to be a pioneer in research and development and become the technology leader in the industry.

Remarks: Very sweeping and ambitious especially if the industry is one with a wide range of technological frontiers.

Better: During the 1980s our objective is to continue as a leader in introducing new technologies and new devices that will allow buyers of electrically powered equipment to conserve energy usage.

Poor: Our objective is to be the most profitable company in our industry.

Remarks: Not specific enough; by what measures of profit—total dollars or earnings per share or unit profit margin or return on equity investment, or all of these? Also, because the objective concerns how well other companies will perform, the objective, while challenging, may not be achievable.

Better: We will strive to lead the industry in rate of return on equity investment by earning 25 percent aftertax return on equity investment in 1989.

Source: A. A. Thompson and A. J. Strickland, *Strategy Formulation and Implementation,* 4th ed. (Homewood, Ill.: Irwin, 1989), 31.

How Are We Going to Accomplish These Objectives?

Having established *what* is to be achieved through a sustained effort over a specific period of time, the next step is to determine *how* these objectives are to be achieved. This is accomplished through development of strategies and plans for specific courses of action: *who* does *what* by *when*.

One element of the strategy is the adoption of TQM as a comprehensive management system to achieve objectives by assuring that all work is performed in a systematic, integrated, consistent manner. The installation of TQM becomes the work of senior management, and its pursuit of TQM is a prime example of its leadership.

How Do We Develop These Statements?

Statements of mission, vision, values, policy, and objectives developed behind closed doors by a single executive or by just a few top-level managers in isolation serve a useful purpose but are limited in impact. In this case, the key advantage of developing these statements is quickly lost once the task is completed.

The advantage of securing ownership, commitment, and involvement will accrue to organizations that use a collaborative process to forge these key statements. Furthermore, the benefits will last for an extended period of time. A senior manager who either establishes a new vision or reaffirms an existing mission by involving others in a participative manner garners ownership and commitment from all those who were involved in the process. Table 12.4 offers guidelines on how to develop your organization's key statements.

Three notes of caution: First, managers are often more preoccupied with completing the task of formulating these statements and moving on to new activity than they are with using this exercise as a means of securing support from key managers, employees, and impacted departments. Be aware of the "task"-oriented mentality, and recognize the value of the "process" itself.

Second, using a participative decision-making process to develop fundamental statements does not imply democracy or a need for total consensus. When making a major change in the organization's culture, some individuals invariably disagree with the new direction. Determine which views represent added value and which represent anchors holding the organization to past practices that are inconsistent with the new

Table 12.4: Step-by-Step Guide for Developing Key Statements

1. Look to your prior experiences.

   Your don't come to the table cold. You've been part of the organization (or some organization) for years. What have you learned? What really bugs you? What's been memorable? What seems to have been going on at work when people are really soaring? When they are at each other's throats?

2. Fiddle around, but make haste.

   Make lists. Doodle. Write ideas on index cards. Talk with others—from all walks of life—and seek their advice. Reflect on all such numerous inputs—but move fast.

3. Try some participation.

   After noodling a bit, you might schedule fifteen meetings in the next thirty days with disparate groups—first-line people from each function, first-line supervisors, suppliers, customers, wholesales, community leaders. Chat about your ideas. Seek their list of top-ten irritants, their ten best experiences with the company or function, and keep on scratching away.

4. Clarify over time.

   Perhaps a two- or three-day session with those who report directly to you is in order. Again, swap stories, dreams, precise internal and market assessments; wallow in the data (mainly anecdotes). Ask them to come to the party with lots of data, gathered by doing their own smaller-scale version of what you've been up to. Maybe the result will be a formal declaration, maybe not. Maybe it will be two flip charts' worth of handwritten ideas that everybody sticks up in his or her own office. Perhaps it will eventually be turned over to a printer and circulated to everyone on wallet-size cards and posters alike. But then again, maybe it never will.

5. Remember, listening is basic.

   Leaders must be superb listeners, particularly to those advocating new or different images of the emerging reality. Successful leaders, we have found, are *great askers,* and they do pay attention.

Source: Adapted from Tom Peters, *Thriving on Chaos* (New York: Knopf, 1987), 490–492.

vision. "An unconscious conspiracy in contemporary society prevents leaders—no matter what their original vision—from making changes. Within any organization, an entrenched bureaucracy with a commitment to the status quo undermines the unwary leader."[14]

Third, having stated that participation is important, be careful not to cross the fine line that separates participation from abdication. Senior management is responsible for the direction of the organization and for developing the enabling strategies. Participation is one way to accomplish this task, but ultimate responsibility for deciding which course to take cannot be delegated. This caution will be further explained in Chapter 13.

Other Elements of Leadership

The last two elements of the leadership framework cover management's actions in day-to-day activities. Commitment relates to *what* is done by managers themselves and in the allocation of resources. Style relates to *how* they do things.

Commitment

Although there are many additional examples that illustrate leadership in the installation of TQM, one that remains as significant as the process of forging key statements is the demonstration of *commitment* by senior managers. The demonstration of commitment takes many forms and is evidenced by what managers *do* as well as by what they say.

The first opportunity to demonstrate commitment (or reveal the lack of it) is often found in reallocating resources and funding additional staff to implement the extensive training that is required to equip all employees with the skills and knowledge needed to pursue TQM. Will the resources be provided? Will funds be made available from the redirection of traditional training programs?

Equally important are senior managers willing to demonstrate commitment by participating in the same training that everyone else will undertake? Will senior managers use the tools, jargon, and processes to pursue continuous improvement? Or will they merely instruct their subordinates to do it?

Are senior managers willing to create structures to support TQM, such as boards and steering committees? And are they willing to participate in these structures? Or are they going to delegate (abdicate) this responsibility?

Are senior managers capable of demonstrating long-term commitment to implement continuous improvement, even when improvement may be viewed as having high start-up costs? Commitment means more than new procedures, policies, directives, letters, and speeches. Employees look for commitment from top management by observing their behaviors and their style.

You should expect that employees will question and test the beliefs you now espouse. How committed are you to the following?

- Maintaining a long-term perspective in the face of short-term pressures
- Providing a focus on meeting customers' needs and being sensitive to the markets in which you participate

- Realizing that some returns are immediate but others will take three to five years of dedication and hard work
- Stressing that improving the process is as important as attaining results and that both must be accomplished
- Allocating resources to support TQM training and implementation
- Instituting compensation, recognition, reward, and promotions based on the criteria that support TQM
- Fostering employee involvement and better relationships across functions and between unions and management
- Building partnerships with suppliers for mutual benefit
- Acting as a role model; " walking the talk" using quality improvement tools and jargon

Style

Life isn't fair. In addition to what you do, how you do it is equally important. Tom Peters offers clear guidance here:

> Understand the power of our subtle actions: Amidst uncertainty, when people are grasping at straws in an effort to understand the topsy-turvy world about them, their symbolic significance is monumental. People in organizations are all boss watchers, especially when external conditions are ambiguous. For better or worse, what you spend your *time* on (not what you sermonize about) will become the organization's preoccupation. Likewise, the proactive use of symbols, such as the sorts of stories you tell people and the people you invite to meetings, sends powerful signals to the organization about what's important. The final confirmation of what really counts around here, when things are changing, is who gets promoted—risk-takers and harbingers of the new, or "the same old crowd."[15]

Plan to lead by example; serve as the role model. Not only become the foremost spokesperson for your own vision, but be a living, walking, talking embodiment. Reallocate how you spend your time. For example, as CEO of his Malcolm-Baldrige-National-Quality-Award-winning company, Roger Milliken devoted fully half his time to quality improvement. To emphasize his priority, the subject of quality was the first agenda item at Milliken's staff meetings.

The printing of cards and slogans is the least important part. If you began with a formal declaration, you are probably doomed. You don't know what it really means, let alone anyone else. You are likely to be

Table 12.5: Attributes of a Leader

- ❏ Creates More Leaders
- ❏ Focuses on Customers
- ❏ Knows When to Coach and When to Judge
- ❏ Removes Obstacles to Joy of Work
- ❏ Understands Variation
- ❏ Works to Improve Systems
- ❏ Creates Trust
- ❏ Forgives Mistakes
- ❏ Listens
- ❏ Improves Continually His/Her Education

continually trapped by a thousand tiny inconsistencies as you wobble toward clarity. That is, some small personnel decision or some small customer decision requires you to do the thinking you should have done before turning on the printing press. Such inconsistencies, after a formal declaration, convict you of hypocrisy and set the process back, perhaps derailing it forever.[16]

So how might ideal behaviors be defined? Two sets of criteria are offered to help define your performance as a leader of TQM. Six guidelines follow, and Table 12.5 lists ten leadership attributes.

1 Leaders base decisions on data. Opinions are interesting, but decisions should be based on what you know, not what you think.
2 Leaders are resources, coaches, facilitators for the individuals with whom they work. Employees who are looking to their leaders for direction, decisions, or approvals don't understand your new role. Have you explained the difference? Is your style consistent with your intent?
3 Leaders are actively involved. They learn new skills along with their employees. Being proficient, leaders are then able to assist others in their pursuit of continuous improvement.
4 Leaders build commitment. They assure that everyone understands the organization's mission, vision, values, and goals. Furthermore,

leaders assure that everyone knows his or her individual role and is eager to contribute.

5 Leaders inspire confidence. They extract the best from everyone and encourage personal development.

6 Leaders say thanks. They do so with every imaginable form of monetary and nonmonetary incentive.

Summary

TQM is a strategic process that is launched from the executive suite and requires both management and leadership skills. This principle, when accepted, sets in motion a series of activities by senior managers that shape the organization's future. These activities cannot be delegated, and the process of *how* things are done is as important as *what* is actually accomplished. That is to say, the right things must be done right.

Leaders will begin by addressing the basic questions about what the organization is and what it is to become. Through a collaborative process, they will secure the cornerstones of the organization's foundation: the mission, vision, and core values. They will galvanize commitment by all to this foundation and provide an environment within which the details can be built. The degree to which these issues are resolved is the extent to which the organization can meet its stated objectives in the short run and its vision in the longer term. Leaders will be unrelenting in their pursuit of the organization's goals.

Finally, make no mistake about the impact of your personal actions. Use your own style to reinforce the crusade toward your vision. On the other hand, if you are not committed to the fundamental statements that you have had printed, laminated, and posted, recognize that your style will betray you and reveal your true beliefs. If this is the case, rip down the false statements, go back to the beginning of this chapter, and start over.

Notes

1. Reprinted by permission of The Juran Institute (Oct. 31, 1990).
2. Warren Bennis, *Why Leaders Can't Lead* (San Francisco: Jossey-Bass, 1990), 18.
3. Reprinted by permission of the Ford Motor Company (June 14, 1991).
4. Imperial Oil, Ltd., *Outline of the Organization* (Toronto: Imperial Oil, Ltd., 1991), A-2.
5. Reprinted by permission of the Canadian National Railways (June 13, 1991).
6. Peter M. Senge, *The Fifth Discipline* (New York: Doubleday, 1990), 9, 206,

217–218. Copyright 1990 by Peter M. Senge. Used by permission of Doubleday, a division of Doubleday Dell Publishing Group, Inc.

7. Tom Peters, *Thriving on Chaos* (New York: Knopf, 1987), 482.

8. Reprinted by permission of the Canadian National Railways (June 13, 1991).

9. *Summary Description of FPL's Quality Improvement Program* (Miami, Florida: Florida Power & Light Company, 1989), 10. Reprinted with permission.

10. Neil De Carlo, Corporate Communications Department, FPL, Miami, Florida, telephone interview with Arthur Tenner, June 28, 1991.

11. Reprinted by permission of the Ford Motor Company (June 14, 1991).

12. Xerox Corporation.

13. *Summary Description of FPL's Quality Improvement Program* (Miami, Florida: Florida Power & Light Company, 1989), 10. Reprinted with permission.

14. Bennis, *Why Leaders Can't Lead*, xii.

15. Peters, *Thriving on Chaos*, 496.

16. Ibid., 492.

13 Empowered Work Force

Every manager knows what must be done. Just issue a directive, a memo, and let's get on with it! If they don't do it, "Take names and kick butts." If you've heard that before, you know that's the way things used to be done, but that approach doesn't work anymore. Why not? What's changed in our work force over the last fifty years? A lot, and this chapter describes those changes as well as the techniques for implementing participative practices to take full advantage of the talents of *all* employees.

Are We Different Today?

Yes, we are very different today. The work force in North America has changed dramatically since the end of World War II. Work used to be a series of simple, manual tasks performed by unskilled laborers, and those tasks could be observed easily. For every ten to twelve workers driving spikes to lay railroad track, one crew chief assured that work progressed smoothly and that everyone contributed his fair share. For every ten crew chiefs, one foreman monitored the performance of the crew chiefs; and for every ten foremen, one superintendent supervised the entire operation.

This hierarchical model, fashioned after the military organization, was necessary because uneducated, unskilled labor toiled with mechanical tools on tasks that had to be observed to assure that work was done, and done correctly. The boss dispatched and allocated tasks and then monitored the work by being physically present to observe directly that all was progressing as required.[1]

Contrast that scene to one in a modern office where an individual sits in front of a computer screen. It's not possible to know, simply through observation, whether the individual is daydreaming or developing answers to the organization's most critical problem. In addition, it is no longer possible to tell who is in charge, since the old hallmarks of physical appearance no longer apply. An administrative aide may dress as well as the CEO, drive a similar car, dine at the same restaurants, and live in the same town. The distinction between blue collar and white collar as well as other signs of social standing are passé.

More important, the education of subordinates may be similar if not superior to that of the manager, especially in highly skilled areas of technology. Organizational distinctions are blurred, and the simple mantle of authority may be insufficient to manage young, competent, highly motivated employees. Most important, those people who are actually doing the work are likely to know far more about it than their managers.

So how does one supervise a large number of educated, competent, motivated employees? The answer is certainly not to issue directives, give speeches, take names, and kick butts.

So What Do We Do Now?

Many U.S. managers learned, during the 1970s and 1980s, about participative practices by visiting Japan or by reading about Japanese management techniques. Many grew certain that employee participation was the answer they needed for improved productivity. There was a great rush to establish quality circles in U.S. plants, with some encouraging initial results. Today, however, there is little to show for all this effort. If participation is the answer, and we tried it without achieving the tremendous benefits we were seeking, where do we go from here?[2]

We regroup, because the concepts of employee participation and high involvement are valid. Early disappointments represent a miss, not a failure! There are many cases in which employees have been successfully empowered to improve their work outputs, and if empowerment works well in some places, we should be able to adapt the concepts to work well everywhere. To do this, we should follow some basic precepts to create an atmosphere that supports teamwork and empowers employees.

What Is Empowerment?

Let's first dispel some myths about one of the more popular buzzwords associated with the subject of quality—*empowerment.* "Our employees are educated, competent, and motivated, so all we need to do is turn them loose to improve quality and productivity. We'll get out of their way; we'll empower them." Have you heard these words or tried this yourself? Success cannot be assured, because this is not empowerment. It's abdication. If we are serious, we will build empowerment in its three requisite dimensions (see Figure 13.1).

The first dimension of empowerment is alignment. All employees need to know the organization's mission, vision, values, policies, objectives, and methodologies (refer back to Chapter 12). Furthermore, the broad direction of the overall organization must be sharpened as the message cascades to define the role of work groups and individuals. "Empowering the individual where there is a relatively low level of alignment worsens the chaos and makes managing the team even more difficult."[3]

Fully aligned employees not only know their role, they are dedicated to supporting it. Leaders have inspired them to contribute to the mutual benefit of the organization and themselves. This dedication is synonymous with commitment, and commitment can neither be bought nor sold. It is earned. The traditional hierarchical organization did not require commitment; its authoritarian style merely needed compliance.

Gaining true alignment requires bridging the subtle gap between compliance and commitment (see Table 13.1). In essence, the difference between compliance and commitment is that people who are committed to the organization's direction truly *want* it. Although empowerment requires commitment, in the near term, leaders may need to settle for compliance and work to move people up the compliance ladder. Commitment cannot be enforced; efforts to do so will, at best, build compliance. All that can be done is to establish an environment that is favorable to the growth of commitment.[4]

The second dimension is capability. Employees must have the ability, skills, and knowledge needed to do their jobs. They must also have the resources needed from the organization: materials, methods, and machines. In our experience, many organizations have over-achieved in this dimension. Selection criteria bring in new hires who are

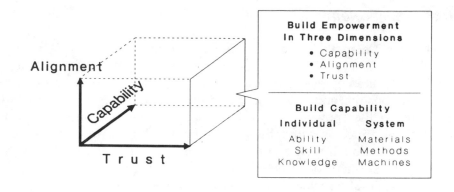

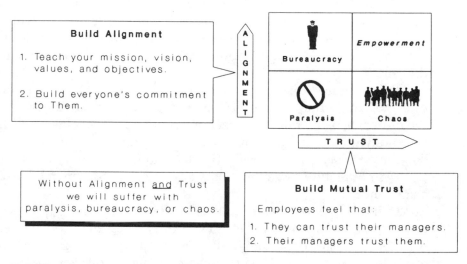

Figure 13.1 Empowerment Matrix. *Source*: Adapted from leadership training materials developed by K.S. Herald-Marlowe, Exxon Research and Engineering Co., 1988.

"overqualified," and investments in facilities, equipment, and training have far outstripped growth in the other two dimensions—trust and alignment.

Mutual trust is the third dimension of empowerment. Once we have developed alignment and capabilities, we are in a position to unleash the power, creativity, and resourcefulness of the work force. This will not happen, however, unless we've also provided this third

Table 13.1: Climbing the Compliance Ladder to Commitment

Commitment:	Wants it. Will make it happen. Creates whatever "laws" (structures) are needed.
Enrollment:	Wants it. Will do whatever can be done within the "spirit of the law."
Genuine compliance:	Sees the benefits. Does everything expected and more. Follows the "letter of the law." "Good soldier."
Formal compliance:	On the whole, sees the benefits. Does what's expected and no more. "Pretty good soldier."
Grudging compliance:	Does not see the benefits but does not want to lose job. Does enough of what's expected because he or she has to but also lets it be known that he or she is not really on board.
Noncompliance:	Does not see the benefits and will not do what's expected. "I won't do it; you can't make me."
Apathy:	Neither for it nor against it. No interest. No energy. "Is it five o'clock yet?"

Source: Adapted from Peter M. Senge, *The Fifth Discipline*

dimension. Employees need to trust management *and* feel that management trusts them. Mutual trust therefore completes the picture required to build an empowered work force.

Don't underestimate the importance of the dimension of trust and the amount of mistrust that may pervade your organization. Warren Bennis explains: "Change occurs in two primary ways: through trust and truth or through dissent and conflict. We have tried dissent and conflict and have not changed but have merely become combative. . . . Positive change requires trust, clarity, and participation."[5]

Empowerment can therefore be seen as the natural consequence of effective leadership. This positive result can be expected as long as "management systems and controls" don't get in the way. In some organizations, policies have been developed to safeguard company interests from a "few rotten apples." You might say that you trust an employee, but do your policies echo your words or betray them?

Use Figure 13.2 as a checklist to clarify how your management systems symbolize the level of trust for your employees that you demonstrate. Do your policies limit their access to financial or physical assets? Is the flow of information denied to anyone? If empowerment relies on alignment, capability, and trust, it is unreasonable to expect employees to feel empowered if they don't feel trusted. It's

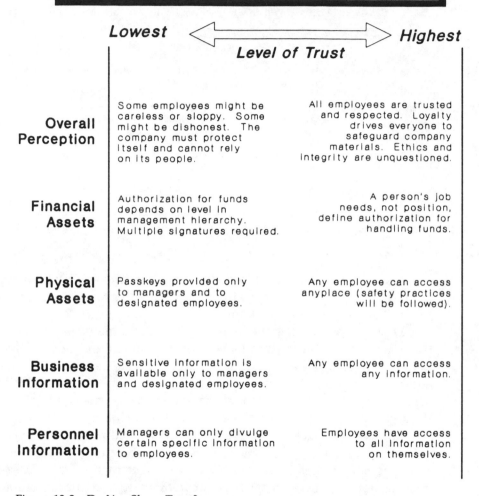

Figure 13.2 Do You Show Trust?

so simple: treat people with the same respect with which you would like to be treated.

We are not implying that you should remove your protective systems. They may very well be needed because you cannot trust all of your employees. The lack of trust may be a product of your selection process, or it may have been created through divisive practices. Instead, our purpose is to direct your attention to questioning your fundamental beliefs and practices.

What Is Teamwork?

Teamwork is a group of individuals working together to reach a common goal. The goal may be to increase market share, to boost customer satisfaction, or to improve overall performance through cooperation and collaboration. Teamwork is at first a sharing of responsibility and eventually a sharing of decision making that impacts the entire organization. Collaboration and teamwork build a new level of capability, a new strength that the organization can harness to increase its customers' satisfaction.

Like empowerment, *teamwork* and *team building* have become popular terms in business circles. But look at their evolution. Before the industrial revolution, a "team" usually consisted of horses, mules, or oxen drawing carts or plows. During the past century, a "work team" might more aptly have been described as a gang or crew.

It is relatively recently that teams have become recognized in industry and discussed in the context of collaboration, cooperation, competition, and sporting events. But even now, the terms are frequently misused. In traditional, hierarchical, autocratic organizations, *teamwork* has often meant compliance, and a *team player* is often a euphemism for a conformist who suppresses his or her own goals for the sake of the organization.[6]

Some managers mistakenly assume that a group cannot be called a high-performing team if it doesn't fit some idealized model of total autonomy and equality. The optimum degree of autonomy, control, interdependence, and collaboration varies for different types of teams.

Different types of tasks demand different types of teams.[7] For instance, consider the differences in decision making, interdependence, and collaboration required to perform the following tasks: driving spikes into miles of railroad tracks, deciding on the guilt or innocence of an alleged criminal, winning a football game, or improving the design of a data-processing system.

Constructing miles of railroad track is an example of an *additive* task, and the accomplishment of the team equals the summation of individual contributions. In this type of task, the team will accomplish more than any individual; however, the contribution of each member is frequently below that of the same individual performing on his or her own. The maximum potential capability of teams performing additive tasks is proportionate to the size of the team, but the actual work accomplished will be less. The key to leading this type of team is to minimize this gap.[8]

A jury deciding on guilt or innocence represents a team performing a *disjunctive* task. Solving problems and making decisions are common disjunctive tasks. In this type of task, the performance of the team will approximate that of the most knowledgeable member. Teams cannot perform beyond their available resources, and optimal performance will be realized through identification and support of the most knowledgeable member.[9] Popular corporate team-building exercises such as "desert survival" and "lunar landing" games provide practice for teams performing disjunctive tasks.

By contrast, playing a football game is a *conjunctive* task. Here, each member must perform his or her task, and the team's capability may be limited by the ability of the *weakest* member, not the strongest.[10]

A quality improvement team working to improve the design of a data-processing system is an example of an *optimizing* task. Here, the goal is to produce some specific, most-preferred outcome. Collaboration and cooperation among members result in the team's performance potentially exceeding the summation of the abilities of all the individuals. Furthermore, this quality improvement team will likely address subtasks that are additive, disjunctive, or conjunctive. The mode of operation of the team should adjust for each subtask.

When forming teams, examine how the type of task will determine the teams' needs for autonomy and collaboration. Also evaluate the stake the members have in the outcome. Is it high—will the outcome impact on members' jobs, pride, or compensation? Or is it low—will the outcome merely impact on others and on members' consciences? Can you do anything to increase members' stake in the outcome if it is low? Although the remainder of this chapter is aimed primarily at teams performing optimizing tasks, the concepts can be applied to all types of teams.

Guidelines for Building Teamwork

Teamwork should be beneficial to all: employees, customers, and the shareholders. The following guidelines are offered to help maximize likelihood of building successful teams:

Management support: Managers are delegating responsibility, not abdicating, when embarking on a participative management process. This requires managers to clarify expectations and boundaries (what's off-limits). Team members need to understand what's important to the manager and to the company. Members need to know the issues that the organization is facing. In short, they need information. A sure way for a nonsupportive manager to kill a team is to withhold information. Another surefire killer is to withhold resources.

Clear charter: Information needed to clarify the direction and scope of a team's effort can be included in its charter. Three essential elements are: (1) a general description of the problem or opportunity to be addressed, (2) the expected outcome, and (3) the boundaries. Teams formed to resolve specific issues will benefit from clear and comprehensive charters. Teams that are "natural work groups" will likely find that their charters are embedded in their mission (description); vision, goals, and objectives (expected outcomes); and core values, policies, strategies, and plans (boundaries).

Benefits for team members: Organizations introduce teamwork to improve work processes and increase customer satisfaction, and to do both of these at substantially lower cost. These benefits are part of the organization's stated objectives. Yet where are the benefits of teamwork for employees stated? "Our employees are our most valuable resource." If this claim is to ring true, then clear statements of how teamwork will benefit employees are needed. Benefits for employees can include improved quality of work life, development of personal skills, rotational job opportunities, and increased ability to make decisions that will influence the direction of the organization. Benefits also include direct, specific, and timely rewards and recognition.

Bias for action: Recommendations must be acted on in a timely manner. Managers should expect that teams are aligned with the organization and that their recommendations will be of value. If recommendations are not accepted, team members are owed an explanation from the highest-level executive. The process of any unsuccessful team should be studied so that future teams will not stumble. What were the root causes of the problem that derailed the team?

Skills: Although participation on most teams is voluntary, individuals may occasionally be drafted because they possess unique skills that are required by the team. Such individuals might be full-fledged team members, or they might merely participate during one phase of the work. Regardless of the role, if expertise is required, get it.

Training: Members need to be skilled in one or several of the disciplined processes used by teams. Problem solving, benchmarking, or process improvement are examples of road maps that teams may follow to reach their destination. Training in these techniques equips everyone on the team with a common core of skills, regardless of dissimilarities in their work experience or education. Training in group dynamics and meeting skills may also be required if members have difficulty working in a group environment.

Facilitators: Even when individuals are trained in team dynamics, support may still be needed, particularly in the early stages. Such assistance can be provided by an "outsider" who acts as a process expert—someone who will focus on the team's *process* and not the content.

Start small: Teams should begin with simple opportunities within their own function and, when successful, branch out to more complex and rewarding cross-functional problems. Cross-functional opportunities are often more challenging and require more effort, expertise, and resources to solve. They also often yield bigger payoffs, but teams should develop some success, expertise, and confidence before tackling more complex issues.

Life cycle: Teams are born, live, and die like natural organisms, and this cycle should be recognized. When the problem is solved, then perhaps the team created to solve that problem should disband. If, however, related opportunities are found, then the team may move from issue to issue. If members are from the same group and are working to improve their normal work processes, then that team should be encouraged to continue.

Celebrate: True teams succeed or fail together. Members of successful teams should be recognized and rewarded. One form of recognition is to present their story to others during publicized events. This not only serves to recognize the contributions of the team but also provides a learning experience for other employees who may be struggling with similar issues. Communication of these successes reinforces the drive to empower individuals. The value of appropriate communications cannot be overstated with regard to fostering teamwork, empowerment, and process improvement.

Criteria for Team Performance

We advocate teamwork to get results. However, the process of building teams provides value by itself. To keep sight of this, six criteria, each of equal weight, are offered for evaluating the performance of teams. Alternatively, results may become paramount, and other criteria may diminish in perceived value. When this occurs, the organization has reverted to the old way of doing things and is not following an approach that has been validated as essential to total quality management (TQM). Evaluate a team's success by considering how well it performs in each of the following areas:

Goals

- Are goals understood and supported by all team members and by management?
- Are goals realistic—ambitious but achievable?
- Are goals within the scope of ownership of the team members or the sponsoring manager?
- Do the goals contribute to the mission, vision, and objectives of the organization?

Roles

- Do all members know and fulfill their responsibilities? Members' responsibilities may include allocating time to team meetings and performing specific roles (taking minutes, for instance) as well as working outside of meetings. Members are also responsible for coaching other members. If one member is not supporting the team, others have the responsibility of asking that individual to leave the team.

Process

- Has a structured, defined, disciplined process been followed by the team in pursuit of its goal? Examples of such processes include problem solving, benchmarking, and the six-step road map for process improvement (see Chapter 9).

Development

- As a result of involvement on the team, have all members learned new concepts, tools, or techniques that they can apply to their own work outside of the team?

Innovation

- Did the team question conventional wisdom and traditional approaches?

- Did the team find new ways to attack old problems?
- Did the team recommend an entirely new approach that both improves customer satisfaction and reduces costs?

Results

- Did the team achieve its goal?
- Does the solution permanently improve the underlying work process? *Note:* Results usually arrive incrementally, and rarely as dramatic breakthroughs. Don't debate which is more important, because both are needed. In our opinion, breakthroughs only come when a lot of incremental improvements have already been achieved and when processes are under control. The danger of looking only for one major breakthrough, and not for the incremental improvements as well, is that you may get neither.

Stages of Team Development

The road to achieving successful, high-performing teams is a bumpy one, with different forms of support required along the way. B. W. Tuckerman's four-stage model serves as a road map to team development and helps to guide the sponsoring manager's role. The four stages defined by Tuckerman are summarized in the following subsections.[11]

Stage 1: Forming

This is the initial stage in which new relationships are formed among team members. A great deal of testing is going on as individuals seek to understand the reason for the team being formed, the scope of responsibility, the legitimacy of the team, why various members were selected, the "doability" of the task, and what the task really is. This initial activity helps the group to orient itself to the work to be done.

In this initial stage, the role of the sponsoring manager is critical to get the team started in a positive and constructive manner. The sponsor must provide complete information, establish a level of trust that enables the group to be open and honest, and explain roles and expectations.

Stage 2: Storming

This second stage is characterized by the interpersonal conflicts that arise among team members while clarifying their tasks, roles, responsibilities, expectations, and organizational issues. This phase is characterized by debate, arguments, conflict, and perhaps hostility and open warfare.

Care must be taken by the sponsoring manager to assure that discussion remains constructive and is directed at the issues and not at individuals, and that all issues are surfaced, debated, and clarified. Managers at this stage will draw on their skills as facilitators. Objective information gathering and decision making will be aided by techniques such as brainstorming, weighted voting, and consensus building. During this second stage, little progress will be made toward the team's goals; instead, energy will be directed toward the team's processes. This stage, however, must be successfully completed before real work can begin.

Stage 3: Norming

This third stage is marked by a coming together of team members. Cohesion is exhibited through a healthy flow of opinions, sharing of personal experience and data, cooperation, and overall good work. At this point, members feel good about their involvement on the team and feel that their work has purpose and value. The group of individuals starts to evolve into an effective team and begins to work together toward achieving its goal.

The sponsoring manager at this point may feel that the team is self-sufficient, fully capable of managing its activities. The role of the manager changes from being a director or referee to being a participant or resource. The manager may even withdraw and allow the team to define its own leaders and administrators.

Stage 4: Performing

This stage is the payoff! Team members are performing their roles. Work is characterized as cooperative and collaborative, and the team's objectives are being achieved. Teams at this stage are mature and self-directing and exhibit a natural sharing of roles and responsibilities. They effectively use systematic processes. They achieve results and bring innovative solutions to the organization.

The sponsoring manager in this phase may well see the makings of an autonomous work team in which recommendations are developed and implemented without prior approval. Here, the manager's role is that of a coach. The manager helps the team improve the process by which it works. The manager no longer needs to allocate and monitor

Table 13.2: Steps of Process Improvement—Degrees of Employee Involvement at Each Step

Process Improvement Step	Low Involvement	Degree of Involvement ——————→	High Involvement
1. Define problem	Manager defines customers, requirements, and necessary processes	Group proposes opportunity; manager approves	Team defines opportunity as next stage in continuous improvement
2. Identify and document process	Manager or staff documents processes	Group works with staff to document processes	Team documents and flowcharts processes
3. Measure performance	Manager collects data but shares little	Manager defines data for group to collect	Team determines what data to collect and gets them
4. Understand why	Manager analyzes data and draws conclusions	Manager suggests causal factors and group confirms	Team analyzes data, determines root causes, and understands variation
5. Develop and test ideas	Manager defines improvements	Manager suggests alternatives for group to evaluate	Team identifies and tests alternative solutions
6. Implement solutions and evaluate	Manager drives implementation and evaluates outcome	Group implements solution and shares evaluation with manager	Team has responsibility and authority to implement solution and track results

Source: Adapted from R. Chappell, Xerox Presentation: Quality Council Meeting, May 1986.

work, since the team is fully capable of doing this itself. The manager works with the team on its process; the team works on providing results.

Stages of Application

Table 13.2 lists how empowered employees can progress through phases of development as a team addresses the need to improve quality or productivity. Using the process improvement road map described in Chapter 9, the matrix displays the evolution, in a micro sense, of the characteristics of a group that is becoming more self-reliant and self-directing in applying the basic quality tools to achieve improvement. The task for managers is to foster this progression among all employees.

Table 13.3: Phases of Employee Involvement

Organizational Phase	Traditional ⟶	Transitional ⟶	High-involvement
Structure	Hierarchical	Less hierarchical	Flat
	Precise job descriptions	Loose job descriptions	No job descriptions
	Functional units	Matrix management	Self-directed teams
Focus	Internal targets	Competition	Customers' needs
	Preservation Costs	Adaptation Quality and productivity	Flexible, responsive Customer satisfaction
	Problem solving Find-and-fix	Product service improvement Detection	Process improvement Prevention
Authority	Top-down command	Special assignments	Consensus
	Inflexible Controlling	Open to challenge Sharing	Seeks challenge Trusting
	Rank and title	Committee	Knowledge
Idea sources	Work measurement	Staff studies	Work teams
	Suggestion systems	Quality circles	Customers and employees
Stake	Apathetic	Compliant	Committed
	No ownership	Some ownership	Full ownership

When employees throughout the organization are trained in the tools and techniques of process improvement, and when managers provide information, coaching, and resources, then an organization begins to take on a different set of characteristics. These are displayed on Table 13.3 for the entire organization and represent the macromodel of an organization whose employees become empowered.

Managers' Responsibilities

Managers should recognize that not every group will become a high-performing, autonomous work team. Yet teams may still make valuable contributions as they progress through the stages of forming, storming, and norming. Team progress is attributable in part to the sponsoring manager's effectiveness in guiding and supporting his or her teams.

Managers must also understand that empowering others and delegating authority requires a great deal of planning and hard work on their part. Often, we hear senior managers announce that they have delegated decision making and responsibility to the "appropriate level." Later, we hear these same senior managers complain that no one has seized this opportunity; nothing has changed. People are still saying, "Tell us what you want us to do; give us a signal."

Building an environment to support empowerment requires teamwork as well as leadership. Guidelines for building teamwork were provided earlier in this chapter, and leadership was discussed in Chapter 12. However, providing both of these ingredients may still not free teams and individuals to make decisions for themselves. If the organization still does not respond, if middle managers are not being supportive, or if teams are not confronting and resolving issues in their areas, then an additional stimulant is needed.

One form of stimulant can be provided by senior managers' fabricating a minicrisis, if a legitimate one does not already exist. This is simply done by increasing the span of control and the responsibilities of managers at all levels. It soon becomes apparent that the traditional ways of managing have to change.

Another stimulant to support change is to drive the organization to meet a new challenge—one that is specific, measurable, and of recognized importance. For example, achieving 100 percent performance on every target should be the new goal. No defects, no errors, 100 percent accurate invoices, every product and service delivered on time, every time, 100 percent customer satisfaction are all targets that will at first appear to be impossible. But setting targets at less than 100 percent may artificially cap performance. More important, stretch targets will signal to everyone that we have to change the way we do business because we cannot achieve these stretch targets by doing the same old thing.

What Opportunities Will Teams Address?

The generation of ideas on which teams would act has historically been in the domain of managers and their supporting staffs of specialists. But what about tapping the reservoir of ideas stored in the minds of those who are closest to the work and closest to the customers? What about tapping the resources who are best positioned to see the reality of day-to-day problems and who will be responsible for implementing improvements?

The empowered work force captures the ideas within the work group. Systems are designed to stimulate the generation, development, and implementation of these ideas. How well is your organization performing in this dimension? How many ideas does every employee contribute each year? How many of these are then implemented?

Toyota serves as a benchmark for employee suggestion systems, and research by Michael A. Cusumano[12] reveals its progress over two decades. By the early 1980s, Toyota was getting about 1.6 million ideas from employees annually. This represented an average of about 30 ideas from *every* employee. Furthermore, about 95 percent were implemented! But the avalanche of employee suggestions did not happen by luck or accident. It was achieved through Toyota's systematic effort.

Cusumano reported that Toyota introduced a suggestion system in 1951, having borrowed this approach from Ford. Toyota, however, let its system lapse in the late 1950s due to low levels of participation. Toyota received an average of only one suggestion per employee annually during the 1950s and 1960s. Performance of the Toyota system at this time was no different from the level attained by typical CYI (coin your idea) programs in North American companies.

Contributions rose dramatically in the 1970s after management combined the suggestion system with quality circle activities (see Figure 13.3). Toyota workers submitted nearly thirty-three suggestions apiece by 1982. Like quality circle attendance, the practice stopped being voluntary after the 1960s; managers set quotas, kept records of who submitted suggestions, and used these data when determining bonuses. Staff superiors also presented awards for suggestions and criticized workers who failed to contribute their share.

Contrasting systems such as Toyota's to the results and practices of typical CYI or "suggestion box" programs yields four simple guidelines for building effective programs:

1 *Align:* Employees who are committed to support the organization's goals are more likely to contribute "good" ideas. Implementing these suggestions not only benefits the organization but reinforces the suggestion-system process.

2 *Implement:* Don't analyze suggestions to death. If in doubt, err on the side of action, not inaction. Accepting people's ideas will encourage them to offer more. Don't expect that all ideas will be perfect; most will require work to fine-tune and develop.

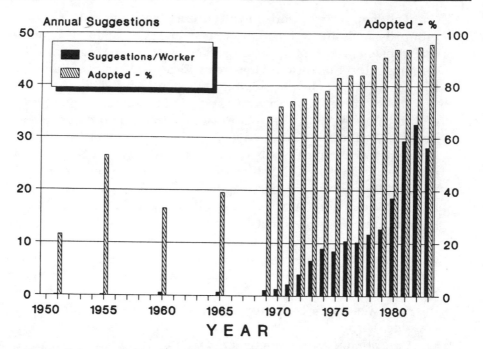

Figure 13.3   Toyota Employee Suggestion System. *Source*: M. A. Cusumano, *The Japanese Auto Industry: Technology and Management at Nissan and Toyota* (Cambridge, Mass.: Harvard University Press, 1985), 359.

3 *Reward:* Contributors can be rewarded in two ways. The first is for people to see that their own ideas are valued; they are acted on and implemented. The second is to receive recognition, awards, and increased compensation. But act quickly; the value of positive feedback diminishes as time increases. Don't get bogged down in complex formulas that take years to account for value and determine the employee's share. Instead, offer some meaningful token immediately, and include longer-term analyses in discussions of performance and calculation of bonuses and compensation.

4 *Count:* Measure the performance of your suggestion system. How many ideas are submitted? How many are implemented? Work to improve the performance of this business process in the same way as you would improve any other. Post performance numbers to bring the system to everyone's attention. But don't let your tracking system slow down the process of generating ideas, rewarding contributors,

and implementing improvements. How would you need to design your system if everyone contributed one idea each week, if 90 percent of the ideas were implemented, if receipt of ideas were acknowledged within twenty-four hours, and if action were initiated within one week?

Summary

In the empowered work force, we will tap the discretionary effort of all employees. Everyone will understand what the organization is trying to accomplish and what his or her role is in this endeavor. Moreover, everyone will be committed to contribute toward these goals. Aligned employees will have the requisite capabilities in an environment built on mutual trust.

Teamwork will be supported. Team members, leaders, and facilitators will understand the factors that contribute to success and will recognize the natural evolution of teams through four basic stages: forming, storming, norming, and performing. The organization's senior members will shift from being commanders and controllers toward becoming coaches and teachers.

Ideas will be generated from all levels and particularly from those who are closest to the work processes and customers. These ideas will be consistent with the organization's needs, and an overwhelming majority will find rapid implementation. Success will feed on success and stimulate a chain reaction benefiting everyone.

Notes

1. Barry A. Stein, "Quality of Work Life in Action: Managing for Effectiveness," American Management Association briefing (1983).

2. *QC Circle Koryo: General Principles of QC Circle* (Tokyo: QC Circle Headquarters, JUSE, 1980).

3. Peter M. Senge, *The Fifth Discipline* (New York: Doubleday, 1990), 235.

4. Ibid., 222.

5. Warren Bennis, *Why Leaders Can't Lead* (San Francisco: Jossey-Bass, 1990), 27.

6. Robert W. Keidel, *Corporate Players* (New York: Wiley, 1988), 11.

7. I. D. Steiner, *Group Process and Productivity* (New York: Academic Press, 1972). Jerry Harbour, "Understanding and Improving Small Group Performance," *Performance & Instruction* (Jan. 1990): 1–7.

8. Harbour, "Small Group Performance."

9. Ibid.

10. Ibid.

11. B. W. Tuckerman, "Development in Small Groups," *Psychological Bulletin* 63 (1965): 384–399.

12. Michael A. Cusumano, *The Japanese Auto Industry: Technology and Management at Nissan and Toyota* (Cambridge, Mass.: Harvard University Press, 1985), 351–359.

References

Aubrey, C. A., and Felkins, P. K. *Teamwork: Involving People in Quality and Productivity Improvement.* Milwaukee: Quality Press, 1988.

DeToro, Irving J. *Doing It Right: Quality through Employee Involvement.* Buffalo, N.Y.: Bearly, Ltd., 1990.

Lee, Chris. "Beyond Teamwork." *Quality Digest* (Aug. 1990): 20–39.

Scholtes, P. R., et al. *The Team Handbook.* Madison, Wis.: Joiner Associates, 1988.

14 Supplier Quality

Build trust through a pattern of success by all parties
to fully and faithfully deliver that which was promised.
—*John Carlisle*

Along with management and employees, suppliers represent the third group of people who must be integrated into the total quality management process. The historical picture of customer-supplier relationships has been one of self-interested adversaries negotiating against each other to maximize their slice of the pie at the expense of the other. A new picture has emerged, however, through the total involvement concept of total quality management. Rather than fighting as adversaries, the approach is to build a mutually beneficial partnership. Joint efforts will improve quality, reduce costs, and increase market share. This, in turn, will yield a larger pie to be shared, and negotiating the size of slices becomes a relatively mundane matter of detail (see Figure 14.1).

The pressure to integrate suppliers into your total quality management process increases as more and more companies apply the concepts. If nothing else, failure to keep pace could result in your company's receiving materials that have been rejected by your competitors.

This chapter summarizes the subject of supplier quality. It lists the benefits expected from correctly selecting suppliers and explains how leading organizations are accomplishing this objective.

Trust: A Requirement for Building Partnerships

Interviews with Japanese corporate purchasing managers offer insight into the philosophy underlying the building of partnerships with suppliers. Westerners frequently stereotype Japanese purchasing meetings as slow, costly dining, drinking, and after-hours extravaganzas. How

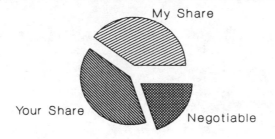

*The historical adversarial view of relationships
drives win-lose negotiations.*

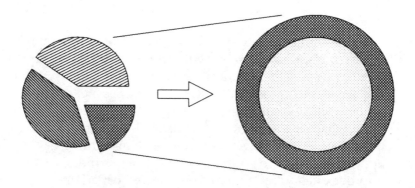

*Total quality management builds partnerships
for mutual gain achieved through improved quality
and reduced costs. This view drives
win-win negotiations.*

Figure 14.1   Building Win-Win Relationships

can this possibly be an effective and efficient purchasing process? Far
from being irrelevant to the business at hand, this process is the one by
which customers and suppliers begin building their relationships. They
develop an understanding of their counterparts as people; they learn
their business requirements and ultimate objectives.

Such deals are consummated by a mere handshake. But why not?
Each party leaves the table knowing he or she has something to gain.
The partnership will strengthen both organizations and help each partner to clobber his or her respective competitors. This success, however,
also depends on one simple but essential ingredient—mutual trust.

Contrast this approach to the typical Western-style purchasing process, which can be characterized as one built on distrust: "I'm looking out for myself, and I know my suppliers are looking out for themselves." In this zero-sum game, we can only maximize our own gains at the expense of others. No wonder we need two levels of bureaucrats to sign agreements in triplicate.

In its ultimate sense, therefore, a true supplier partnership is built on a relationship of mutual trust for mutual gain. How, then, do we accomplish the leap of faith required to trust suppliers? To help get started, John Carlisle (coauthor with Bob Parker of *Beyond Negotiation*) offers an excellent working definition of trust that was presented at the beginning of this chapter. Take small steps. Build trust through a pattern of success. Rather than jumping across the chasm, we can walk across a bridge. Supplier quality systems and certification processes represent this bridge. These systems are being used by quality-award-winning companies to select suppliers with which they will build mutually beneficial partnerships.

What Are Quality Leaders Doing with Suppliers?

Purchasing decisions in Western corporations had historically been based on selecting the lowest-priced qualified bidders. The picture of quality envisioned by many had been that of sampling and inspecting incoming materials. This same picture showed customers keeping their suppliers "on their toes" through frequent competitive, price-sensitive bidding wars. Typical customers and suppliers viewed each other as adversaries: who could outnegotiate the other?

Companies leading the way to quality improvement have changed their purchasing criteria to account for the total cost of the transaction and not merely the listed price. These same companies are also recognizing the value of building long-term relationships with those suppliers that are leaders in their field.

The quality leaders are requiring improved quality from their suppliers and are reducing the number of companies from which they purchase.[1]

- After winning the Malcolm Baldrige National Quality Award in 1988 (refer to Chapter 17), Motorola told thirty-six hundred of its largest suppliers that they, too, must be prepared to compete for the award. Two hundred companies that refused to comply were dropped as suppliers.

- In 1983, Xerox declared quality improvement to be the company's driving principle. Whereas supplier components were 92 percent defect-free in 1982, the comparable figure was 99.97 percent in 1988. Concurrently, Xerox eliminated 90 percent of its suppliers and by 1990 was awarding all business in North America to merely 450 remaining suppliers.

- Ford Motor Company began selecting suppliers on the basis of total quality and expectations for continuous improvement instead of price tag in the 1980s. Ford had fifty thousand suppliers in the 1970s and was reducing its list of qualified vendors to ten thousand by the early 1990s.

Why Reduce the Number of Suppliers?

The pattern of the Motorolas and Xeroxes and Fords is identical. Select suppliers that demonstrate the ability to produce the best products and services now and that are expected to improve faster than their competitors. Build partnerships and interdependence with these select, world-class suppliers.

Building true partnerships, however, has its price. It includes an investment in training and a trust in the sharing of data. Since this level of involvement cannot be spread over an industry, it forces companies to focus on sole suppliers for each desired product or service.

Sole sourcing offers a number of benefits to the customer. It reduces the variation in incoming materials and reduces the administrative costs associated with dealing with multiple sources. It also strengthens the interdependence between customers and suppliers.

With greater dependency on a single supplier, longer-term relationships will be cultivated. Prompt, collaborative problem solving might replace finger pointing and abandonment. Inventory planning and reduction can be managed jointly between the customer and the supplier. Development of future products and services will justify involving key suppliers earlier in the planning stage. Better planning will favor longer-term decision making and help to break down barriers that inhibit joint research and development.

Examining the relationship from the supplier's viewpoint offers additional benefits. Longer-term relationships and higher volumes of business as the sole supplier will lead to greater opportunity for the supplier to improve and refine its processes. A better understanding of the customer's needs will be gained through the stronger relationship. This, in turn, can be converted into an even stronger market position.

The American Supplier Institute serves as an example of mutual benefit. It was established by Ford to help its suppliers learn from new approaches and to improve their quality and productivity.

Supplier Certification at Ford

Several approaches have emerged for selecting key suppliers. Motorola, for example, has used the Malcolm Baldrige National Quality Award as its criterion. Another, more common approach is to employ a recognized set of quality standards, such as the ISO 9000/9004 series (refer to Chapter 17). Finally, some companies are defining their own system for certifying potential and continuing suppliers.

Ford Motor Company's program shows how one organization evaluates its suppliers. Ford's system includes a minimum quality standard (Q101) and two progressive levels of awards (Q1 and TQE). Information on Ford's approach was supplied to us by Joel Berenter of Ford's corporate quality office, and his contributions are appreciated.

Ford developed "Quality System Standard Q-101" to formalize its quality expectations for suppliers as well as for its own manufacturing plants. This manual (first issued in 1964 and periodically updated) includes a "Quality System Survey" that is used to evaluate all current and potential suppliers. A minimum score on this survey is required to be considered a "qualified supplier."

To stimulate supplier improvement, Ford established its "Q1 preferred Quality Supplier Award." To qualify for this award, suppliers must have a System Survey score at least 10 percent higher than the "qualified supplier" minimum. Additionally, the supplier must have had no quality rejections over the prior six months and must be unanimously endorsed by Ford's purchasing, product engineering, quality assistance, and customer plant personnel. As a further incentive to suppliers, Ford has announced that, effective in 1990, all new business will be sourced exclusively to recipients of the Q1 award.

But Ford's program doesn't end there. A "Total Quality Excellence (TQE)" program has been developed to recognize excellence not only in product quality but also in delivery to schedule, technical assistance, and commercial performance.

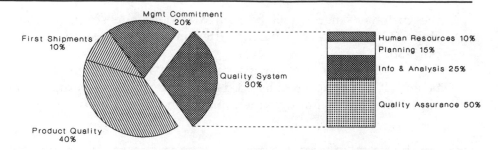

Overall Rating   20 Questions

Figure 14.2 Ford Motor Company Supplier Quality Rating System. *Source*: Adapted from data provided by Ford Motor Company and a letter from N. F. Ehlers, Executive Director, NAAO Production Purchasing to all NAAO Production Purchasing Suppliers, August 28, 1987. Courtesy of the Ford Motor Company.

Ford's supplier quality rating system is the key input for the Q1 award and a major factor in consideration for the TQE award. Its elements are shown in Figure 14.2 and explained in Table 14.1.

Ford's TQE award goes beyond the scope of Q101 and Q1 to recognize excellence in all dimensions that impact on customer satisfaction. In addition to the quality-rating system, TQE also includes engineering, commercial, and delivery criteria.

Engineering activities examined by Ford for TQE include product design, development, testing, and manufacturing engineering. Its evaluation also includes manufacturing processes and support. The clear definition of control points and use of statistical methods weigh heavily in Ford's criteria.

Delivery criteria cover timeliness, reliability, and cost-effectiveness of the supplier's processes for shipping materials to Ford. Among other factors, Ford measures overall performance, supplier responsiveness, and volume of shipments commanding premium freight charges.

Ford evaluates commercial performance of TQE candidates in three categories. Fifty percent of the score is assigned to worldwide cost-competitiveness. Thirty percent of the score is awarded for responsiveness to business issues. This includes timeliness and thoroughness of quotations, performance when launching new parts, and responsiveness to problem-solving situations. The evaluation also covers the supplier's adaptability to a changing environment, including use of long-term

Table 14.1: Ford's Supplier Quality Rating System—Overview

Supplier Quality System (Maximum = 30 Points)

Ford's survey of 20 questions provides a systematic method for suppliers to conduct and document self-evaluations. The survey includes questions relating to human resources management and employee training, quality planning, data analysis, and quality assurance. Consistent with Ford's own approach, statistical methods (Statistical Process Control—SPC) are required. Self-evaluations are followed by audits from Ford.

Management Quality Awareness and Commitment (Maximum = 20 points)

Evaluation criteria include continuous improvement efforts and demonstrated response to quality concerns.

Ongoing Performance (Maximum = 50 Points)

Up to 10 points are awarded for techniques to assure quality in newly developed products, whereas the majority (up to 40 points) are applied to Ford's experience in receiving defect-free material from the supplier.

---

contracts, just-in-time (JIT), statistical methods, and computer-aided design/computer-aided manufacturing. The remaining 20 percent is awarded for such issues as management depth, financial resources, new-part launching experience, and adaptation to changing customer needs.

A Word of Caution on Supplier Involvement

Although the concept of supplier certification and rating systems might appear sound, its application is not immune to pitfalls. Dr. H. J. Bajaria found that flawed application creates costly evaluation guidelines and keeps suppliers busy attending seminars to understand the new procedures. He also found that some suppliers had merely rearranged their paperwork to show compliance with their customer's new standards. The presentation of plaques to some suppliers created a false sense of progress, when their efforts were in fact directed more toward public relations than toward fundamental improvement.[2]

Dr. Bajaria identified four potential problems with supplier quality programs, which true quality improvement leaders strive to avoid:

1 Incompetency in the supplier evaluation process
2 Costly window dressing by suppliers
3 Nonstrategic supplier activity
4 False sense of confidence in suppliers[3]

We suggest that Dr. Bajaria's pitfalls can be avoided by recognizing the forest through the trees. Recall that what we are trying to do is identify suppliers with which we can build mutually beneficial relationships. We are trying to identify world-class suppliers with which we will build an alliance to crush our respective competitors. We each have the potential to gain from our win-win relationship. Above all else, we are looking for partners with which we will build trust through a pattern of success.

Summary

Companies with leading approaches to quality improvement have been working to push their philosophies and techniques "upstream" to their suppliers. Rather than playing contractors off against each other in hopes of squeezing out better workmanship and lower prices, long-term alliances are being forged for mutual benefit. Criteria for selecting suppliers extend beyond the price tag alone and recognize the suppliers' quality, reliability, and future expectations for continuous improvement. Key suppliers are integrated into the planning and design stages of new products and services.

Ford, for example, has developed a comprehensive system for selecting and monitoring suppliers. In 1990, it bought nearly 90 percent of the parts for each of its models under five-year contracts from single sources.

Notes

1. J. Main, "How to Win the Baldrige Award," *Fortune* 121, no. 9 (1990): 101–116.
2. H. J. Bajaria, "Supplier Quality," *ASQC Quality Congress Transactions* (San Francisco, 1990): 324–329.
3. Ibid., 324.

References

Carlisle, J. A., and Parker, R. C. *Beyond Negotiation.* New York: Wiley, 1989.
Deming, W. E. *Out of the Crisis.* Cambridge, Mass.: MIT CAES, 1986.
Port, O., et al. "Deming's Point Four: A Study." *Quality Progress* 21 (1988): 31–35.
———. "A Smarter Way to Manufacture." *Business Week* (Apr. 30, 1990): 110–117.

V Developing the Quality Strategy

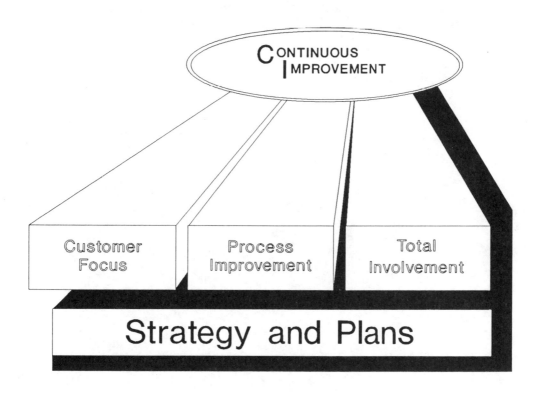

15

Organizational Support

Managers are challenged daily by the demands of the marketplace, so how can they take on the additional task of transforming their organization into a total quality managed company? More specifically, how can they take a structure designed and created to achieve marketing, financial, and production objectives and use that same structure, and the same individuals, to improve their management processes and correct cultural problems? How can a rigid, hierarchical organization whose members are dependent on the organization for their career, promotion, pay, and rewards perform surgery on itself to become the flat, lean organization that it must become in the decade of the 1990s to survive in the international marketplace?

The final chapters of this book provide the remaining pieces of the puzzle to address these critical issues. Chapter 3 introduced six elements to implement total quality management (TQM); some have already been covered, and the remainder will be dealt with in these final chapters. Measurement and leadership were covered in Chapters 10 and 12, respectively. Chapter 15 describes approaches for providing supportive structures, effective communications, and systems for recognizing and rewarding employees. Education and training are the subjects of Chapter 16.

This section, then, should help the reader develop a strategy for implementing TQM. Chapter 17 covers quality standards and systems that can be used to both inspire and evaluate TQM efforts. And Chapter 18 describes the approaches employed by several benchmark organizations with which individual TQM strategies can be compared.

What Do We Have to Do?

Organizations—profit and nonprofit, government and nongovernment alike—are typically based on the classic bureaucracy described by Weber.[1] This organizational design was created to achieve low-risk, routine production by utilizing top-down direction, by requiring rigid job descriptions to take advantage of specialized skills, and by directing the organization through long chains of command. This model served us well as long as workers were unskilled and uneducated and markets were stable. As we discussed earlier, employees have changed: they are better-educated, aware of their rights, and interested in meaningful work. Work itself has changed, in the sense that work is less mechanical and more intellectual, and the traditional management role of assigning and monitoring work is no longer applicable. Markets have changed: competition is competent and intense, competitive pressures are increasing, and barriers to entry into U.S. markets are essentially nonexistent.

Assisting senior management to bring about change means keeping the current structure in place to continue to run the organization and augmenting that existing structure with new, flexible devices that will address the changes required.[2] These devices are task forces, problem-solving teams, quality improvement teams, and other participatory mechanisms that allow individuals to come together in new ways to solve old problems. Organizations that have been struggling to become innovative and responsive to changing market conditions may already have experimented with many forms of this approach. Rosabeth Kanter notes in her book *The Change Masters:*

> The idea behind having a second, or parallel organization only makes explicit what is already implicit in an integrative, innovating company: the capacity to work together cooperatively regardless of field or level to tackle the unknown, the uncertain. In a formal, explicit parallel organization, this is not left to happenstance but is guided—managed—to get the best results for both the company and the people involved.[3]

The effect, then, of a parallel organization is to draw leadership from any individual, from any level—as opposed to the traditional organization, which relies on leadership associated with a job title and position in the organization. Other differences are that participative approaches may include individuals from any and all levels of the organization, who work through much shorter chains of command and who don't expect promotions and rewards for their involvement but rather enjoy the experience, the learning, the ability to contribute in new ways.

Support Structures

An approach that has been successfully used to install TQM is to form a committee of senior managers who have the following responsibilities:

- Ensuring that the organization is focusing on the needs of the marketplace, the needs of the customer.
- Cascading the mission, vision, and values of the organization throughout the organization so that all individuals are aware of their purpose, where they are going, and how they intend to get there.
- Identifying the critical processes that need attention and improvement.
- Identifying the resources, the trade-offs that must be made to fund the TQM activity.
- Reviewing progress and removing barriers that have been identified and brought to the committee for resolution.
- Improving the macroprocesses in which they are involved as senior managers, both to improve the performance of the process and to demonstrate their ability to use the improvement tools on which they have been trained.

These committees are called TQM boards, steering committees, quality improvement teams (Crosby), or quality councils (Juran), and they are usually linked to similar groups in other parts of the organization. "In large companies it is common to establish subcouncils for major organizational segments, such as divisions or functional departments."[4]

When a subcouncil exists, its function may be more specific than that of a steering committee, and its responsibilities may include:

- Assessing processes within the organization and targeting specific processes for improvement.
- Creating improvement teams and activities to address process problems. Usually, individuals associated with a particular process or individuals with the required skills are formed into a team, which will make a joint effort to address the problems.

- Arranging for training of the team members and/or facilitation support.
- Monitoring, directing, reviewing, and supporting the team's efforts so that the recommendations from the team can be accepted and implemented.

The existence of such an arrangement of councils and subcouncils creates a mechanism by which improvement issues can be brought directly to the attention of top organizational leaders, usually in a more direct and supportive manner than may be possible through the traditional organizational structure.

An Example of a Support Structure

An example of the application of a quality support structure is provided by the Fuji Xerox Corporation of Japan. Fuji Xerox (FX) started total quality management in 1976 in an effort to improve its corporate operating performance. The company had been battered by increased competition and lower demand for its products, in large measure resulting from the problems encountered in Japan over the oil crisis of the early 1970s. Suffering from higher prices for energy and raw materials, as well as higher wages, FX saw its profits decrease for the first time.

The company announced a new management strategy called the "New Xerox Movement," which was to be implemented by a committee headed by the vice president, Yotaro Kobayashi. Other members of the committee included senior managing directors who had major responsibility for the daily operations of the company. But as a steering committee, they came together solely to address restructuring the company to support total quality management.

Their goals were to:

1 Assure the product quality level that customers expect.
2 Boost both sales and technical capabilities, to make Fuji Xerox the winner in all business competition.
3 Strive for overall reduction in costs.
4 Encourage more personal creativity.[5]

During the first year, the committee concentrated on educating all managers on the need for a total quality process and the specific goals they wanted to achieve through their New Xerox Movement (NX). Over the next four years, they continued to manage the installation of total quality from the NX committee, and their efforts were rewarded with an increase in revenues, an increase in profits, and the Deming Prize, a coveted prize in Japan for business excellence.

The experience of FX, and its use of a "change committee," is described because the parent company—Xerox Corporation, of Stamford, Connecticut—found itself in a similar market position in 1980. The significant loss of market share and profits by Xerox Corporation due to the increased and effective competition from Japanese copier manufacturers caused the U.S.-based firm to study and then adopt essentially the same approach employed by FX, with strikingly similar results.

Networks as an Extension of a Parallel Organization

Another resource to assist managers in bringing about the installation of TQM is to create a network of quality support people. This network may consist of a "quality officer," who ideally reports to the chief operating officer (COO) and who is responsible for helping the senior managers first understand and then install a TQM process. This role of quality officer may then be replicated for each major function and each major facility until a network of full- and part-time employees is dedicated to supporting quality in their respective business units.

These managers help keep quality issues in the forefront by arranging quality training for the business unit and by constantly advocating the use of quality tools and processes. Senior managers who create such networks then have two ways to influence their subordinates and bring about meaningful change. The first is through the traditional formal reporting structure, and the other is informally through the quality network. This network is different from, and should not be confused with, the informal organization described by social scientists.

The senior quality officer can also privately assist other senior managers to increase their understanding of the requirements of managing in a total quality management process and can work with the business-unit quality managers to overcome functional and local barriers. This double-pronged approach allows the COO flexibility in changing "the way things work around here." Quality managers also support the drive toward employee involvement by assisting problem-solving teams, task forces, and quality improvement teams; by arranging specialized training and benchmarking studies; and by removing existing barriers.

Other Supporting Elements

Two other important activities that senior managers often fail to appreciate are the use of effective communications to strategically disseminate information throughout their organizations, and the recognition of those individuals who are successfully applying the concept of Total Quality Management.

Communications

The organization embarking on the installation of TQM should recognize that everyone is looking for signals, for the true meaning of what's going on in the organization. "What does TQM really mean, and how will I be impacted?" "What's expected of me in an organization shifting to a management philosophy based on the principles of TQM?"

To answer these questions, communications techniques must be developed to both inform and instruct everyone in the practices, processes, and approaches that are required for TQM to be successful. Traditional organizational communication mechanisms such as newsletters, communications meetings, or videos of the CEO reporting on the state of the business may be appropriate, or they may be inappropriate. If the credibility of the communication vehicle is neutral to good, existing publications, meetings, or videos can be used. If employees view the company rag or annual "all-hands" employee meetings as irrelevant to their work, concerns, or interests, then additional communication techniques have to be developed.

Xerox Corporation, for example, uses an annual quality fair, "Teamwork Day," as a means of demonstrating that teams throughout the company have applied improvement tools and resolved problems or improved processes successfully. This day was originally designed in 1984 to communicate to the doubters, the cynics within Xerox, that the TQM approaches being pushed by the top of the house did indeed improve processes and resolve problems to the benefit of everyone—the company, the employee, and the customer. Individuals attending Teamwork Days at Xerox, or similar events at Corning, couldn't help but be impressed by the accomplishments of their fellow employees. More recently, Teamwork Day at Xerox has served the additional purpose of providing recognition to successful teams, since they must compete to participate in the event.

Recognition and Reward

Once individuals and/or teams have successfully applied the tools of TQM and have secured results through process improvement, these employees must be sought out and identified as role models. In the early stages of implementing TQM, individuals may be unsure of what is expected from them, and they may be unsure of how to proceed in order to implement TQM in their area of responsibility. Recognizing and rewarding exemplary performance helps to clarify expectations.

During the first twelve to eighteen months, you may want to shower the organization with small awards that can be earned by participating in training, joining teams, or serving on task forces. As implementation progresses, you should begin to differentiate between passive participants and those who are committed to the concepts of TQM, actively supporting participation, and getting results. Adjust your existing performance and compensation systems to support the cultural changes needed. Add new, meaningful awards and recognition programs as further encouragement and end the shower of trivial awards.

Managers determine who gets promoted, who gets special publicity, and who is singled out for special attention. The point is to encourage managers to support those who demonstrate the desired performance. In some organizations, promotions are limited to those who demonstrate competence in using the tools of TQM and serve as role models for the organization.

Senior managers who are committed to TQM go to great lengths to provide recognition to employees who demonstrate similar convictions. That's why CEOs will travel to a distant office or plant to thank a quality improvement team for removing a barrier to performance.

Recognize and reward managers who demonstrate their own commitment to TQM. Who are the managers in your organization who focus their employees' attention on serving customers? Who is operating as an effective "process owner" and systemically improving key business systems? Who is creating teams around process issues and following the leadership framework presented in Chapter 12? Who is serving as a role model, coach, and mentor?

Recognize and reward teams that meet the performance criteria presented in Chapter 13. A team that did a superior job of articulating its goals, securing participation, following a process, and achieving innovative results is a team that must be recognized, and possibly rewarded, if others are going to follow.

Summary

Senior managers must think about and develop mechanisms that can be put in place to support the installation of TQM. The introduction of TQM can be facilitated by the use of steering committees, boards, or councils and the addition of quality managers and specialists. These resources help the line organization accept change as its members go about their normal tasks and provide excellent developmental positions for employees who are being groomed for greater responsibility.

In addition, communicate to everyone all the elements of a TQM strategy as well the successes and difficulties of installing and working with such a strategy. Employees must know what the organization really wants. At first, they need to be recognized for participating; later, when they achieve success, they need to be rewarded for such success.

Notes

1. Max Weber, *The Theory of Social and Economic Organization* (New York: Free Press, 1947).

2. E. C. Miller, "The Parallel Organization at General Motors," *Personnel* (1978), 56.

3. Rosabeth Moss Kanter, *The Change Masters: Innovation for Productivity in the American Corporation* (New York: Simon & Schuster, 1982), 359.

4. J. M. Juran, *Juran's Quality Control Handbook*, 4th ed. (New York: McGraw-Hill, 1988), 22.8.

5. *Fuji Xerox: The First 20 Years, 1962–1982* (Tokyo: Fuji Xerox Co., Ltd., 1983), 224.

16 Training and Education

> Managers had better assume that the skills, knowledge and tools they have to master and apply fifteen years hence are going to be different and new. . . .
>
> And only they themselves can take responsibility for the necessary learning, and for directing themselves.
>
> —*Peter E. Drucker*

All of the experts agree, extensive training for everyone is required to implement the concepts of total quality management (TQM) and begin building the required skills. Why have some quality initiatives failed even when they have included the best training programs available?

This chapter helps managers to understand the array of skills and knowledge that are generally found to be needed when implementing total quality management and offers guidance on how to satisfy these needs. The chapter begins by clarifying why training, although often a necessary ingredient in the performance improvement process, may by itself be insufficient. It then offers an overview of the areas of skills and knowledge most frequently found to require augmentation in the corporate classroom. The bulk of the chapter focuses on the companywide training needs encountered when first introducing total quality management into an organization. It offers a practical guide on which subjects to cover and how to deliver them.

Why Training Can't Cure Every Problem

We have consulted with a number of well-respected and well-meaning organizations that have encountered an annoying recurrent problem: excellent training programs have been delivered to fully qualified employees without yielding performance improvement on the job.

Table 16.1: When Training Isn't Enough

Assumed Root Cause	Reality
1. *Customer service* training is offered to improve the interface between front-line employees and customers. Employees do not know how to be courteous and responsive to customers' needs.	Management systems focus attention internally or on the boss instead of on the customers.
2. *Creative problem-solving* workshops provide methods and jargon that employees can use to stimulate new ideas. Employees do not know how to think creatively by themselves or in groups.	Management resists change and studies employees' ideas to death. Resources are reserved to promote management's projects.
3. *Team-building* workshops are used to foster more effective interactions among groups of employees. Employees do not know how to interact effectively as members of a team.	Management systems promote internal competition and individual accomplishment and preserve organizational boundaries.
4. *Quality awareness* training is given to all employees to teach the importance of eliminating nonconforming outputs. Employees do not know why they must "Do it right the first time."	Systems are incapable of producing and delivering the required products and services.
5. *Introduction to statistics* teaches fundamentals of data analysis and use of seven basic tools. Employees do not know how to collect and analyze data and apply results to improve their products and services.	Employees lack the required analytical skills, and management systems stifle their application.

Why? The answer should come as no surprise. Training programs should not be expected to provide positive impact when they are delivered as "the wrong solution to the right problem."

Table 16.1 lists five commonly delivered training programs that often yield disappointing results. In the cases studied, the training programs were well-designed, effectively delivered, and genuinely needed. Unfortunately, the shortcomings in employee skills and knowledge that were addressed by each program represented only one among several root causes of the targeted performance deficiencies.

Hindsight is so wonderfully powerful. The full set of root causes represented by the realities listed in Table 16.1 were ultimately identified and addressed by organizations working with us. However, the frustration and the waste of time and resources could have been avoided if this analysis had preceded rather than followed the training programs. A classic approach to understanding performance improvement needs is offered by Dr. Tom Gilbert and summarized in his book *Human Competence* (shown in the References list at the end of the chapter).

As pictured in Figure 16.1, the analysis begins by determining both the *desired* and the *current* performance levels. The next step is to define the discrepancy between these two levels. Next, the root causes for these gaps are determined. (Readers might be interested in referring back to the first four steps in the six-step process improvement model presented in Chapter 9 for details of an analogous approach.)

The performance deficiency identified in the third step of Gilbert's approach can represent the gap between desired and current performance at any level. That is, it can be viewed at the level of the individual employee, a group of employees, or an entire organization. Furthermore, Gilbert is careful to define desired performance as exemplary rather than as normally expected or as minimum standard. The pursuit of exemplary performance drives continuous improvement and helps to avoid the trap of settling for mediocrity.

As listed below, and expanded in Figure 16.1, Gilbert's behavior engineering model establishes six categories of potential causes for performance deficiencies. Three of these categories cover the system or environment to support desired behavior, and three cover the individual's repertory of behaviors. This model is offered by Gilbert as a diagnostic tool.

1 Data
2 Resources
3 Incentives and rewards
4 Skills and knowledge
5 Capacities
6 Motives

Only one of these six categories—skills and knowledge—represents a deficiency that can be solved through education or training. In spite of the poor odds (one-to-six), many companies find it less painful to throw training at their employees than to analyze the underlying causes of their performance deficiencies.

Steps

1. Determine desired performance.
2. Identify current performance.
3. Determine performance deficiency.
4. Determine cause of deficiency.

Desired   Current   Deficiency

	Information	Instruments	Motivation
System	*Data* Inadequate: • Procedures • Performance criteria • Performance feedback	*Resources* Insufficient: • Materials • Equipment • Number of people • Organization	*Incentives and Rewards* Insufficient positive or negative consequences
Individual	*Skills & Knowledge* Inadequate training or education	*Capacities* Inadequate personnel selection Poor job match	*Motives* Lack of interest Fear of failure

Six Potential Causes of Deficiencies, with Only One Type Cured by Training

Figure 16.1 Improving Human Performance. *Source:* T. F. Gilbert, *Human Competence* (New York: McGraw-Hill, 1978), 86–93.

Table 16.2: Behavior Model for Creating Incompetence

Information	Instruments	Motivation
System Supports		
Data	*Resources*	*Incentives*
1. Don't let people know how well they are performing.	1. Provide resources without ever consulting with the people who use them.	1. Make sure that poor performers get paid as will as good ones.
2. Give people misleading information about their performance.	2. Provide inadequate resources.	2. See that good performance gets punished.
3. Hide from people what is expected of them.		3. Don't make use of nonmonetary incentives.
4. Give people little or no guidance about how well to perform.		
Individual Behaviors		
Knowledge	*Capacity*	*Motives*
1. Leaving training to chance.	1. Schedule work for times when people are not at their best.	1. Design the job so that it has no future.
2. Put training in the hands of supervisors who are not trained as instructors.	2. Select people for tasks they have intrinsic difficulties in performing.	2. Avoid arranging working conditions that employees would find pleasant.
3. Make training unnecessarily difficult.		3. Give pep talks rather than incentives to promote performance in punishing situations.
4. Make training irrelevant to the employee's purpose.		

Source: Adapted from T. F. Gilbert, *Human Competence* (New York: McGraw-Hill, 1978), 87.

Although Dr. Gilbert's book was published in the 1970s, many organizations are still plagued in the 1990s by fundamental performance deficiencies (Table 16.2). Table 16.3 offers a simplified worksheet for analyzing which of these fundamental causes are present in any particular situation. In actual practice, the six questions in Table 16.3 would be expanded and would refer to the specific circumstances under analysis. Figure 16.2 displays how various solutions to the identified deficiencies might appear in the form of a cause-and-effect (fishbone) diagram.

To avoid the pitfall of throwing the wrong solution at the right problem, use the following plan *before* investing in training programs:

1 Determine the performance desired of your employees in measurable terms. Focus on outputs and accomplishments, and include internal measures of actions and behaviors only to the extent needed to analyze causes.
2 Determine employees' current performance in the same terms as defined in step 1.
3 Determine the specific differences between steps 1 and 2.
4 Determine the root causes for each specific deficiency. Consider expanding the questions presented in the Performance Improvement Worksheet (Table 16.3) to diagnose categories of causes for each deficiency.
5 Identify solutions to the root causes, and implement the *full* set of solutions. Recognize that education and training may be *one* element within the set. As a general guide, if the performance gap can be described by a phrase such as "Employees do not know *how* to do something," then training is a likely solution. On the other hand, if the gap can be described by a phrase such as "Employees do not know *what* to do or *why*," then the intervention will likely include elements beyond the classroom.

How Are We Going to Get Started?

Implementing total quality management requires specific sets of capabilities and competence for various groups of employees. These, in turn, rely on various levels of skills and knowledge. Education and training are needed to bridge the gaps between the skills that people currently possess and those that are required.

The remainder of this chapter defines the subjects that usually need to be taught when introducing total quality management and describes

Table 16.3: Performance Improvement Worksheet

	Questions	Yes	No
Data	1. Do employees know how well they are performing against standards?	❏	❏
Resources	2. Do they have the methods, machines, materials, and conditions needed?	❏	❏
Incentives	3. Are their incentives contingent on how well they perform?	❏	❏
Knowledge	4. Do they know enough to do their job as well as the exemplary performer?	❏	❏
Capacity	5. Do they have the intelligence and physical ability to perform as well as the exemplary performer?	❏	❏
Motives	6. Are they willing to work for the available incentives?	❏	❏

Source: Adapted from T. F. Gilbert, *Human Competence* (New York: McGraw-Hill, 1978), 93.

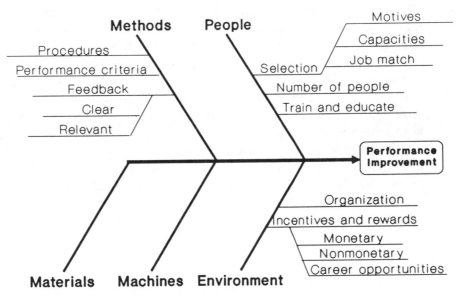

Figure 16.2   Improving Deficient Performance

how successful organizations have implemented these initial training programs. The chapter also provides guidance on the types of training often needed to supplement the initial orientation. Training required by quality improvement specialists is beyond the scope of this chapter. Similarly, this chapter does not cover the array of management training often needed to build a new work environment.

Core Curriculum

Although specific training needs of organizations vary significantly, the authors have found three types of courses to be universally needed. First is an education program that introduces the concepts of Total Quality Management within the business environment of the organization—it is commonly referred to as orientation or "awareness." Second is a skills-building course that enables employees to apply the basic quality improvement tools to their work: it is often called process improvement, problem solving, or quality tools. Third is a climate setting course that helps clarify new roles and expectations in a more supportive and participative environment: this type of course is commonly referred to as participative management, facilitator training, or "leadership workshop."

Orientation

The education program introducing total quality management should assure that all employees have full knowledge in several key areas. First, all employees need to understand the organization's mission, vision, values, and objectives. Employees also need to know their role in contributing to the organization. Next, orientation sessions should explain the background and concepts of TQM, the state of the business, and why the organization is investing in TQM. Before leaving orientation, employees should know both what is expected of them and what they can expect from TQM.

In organizations with large numbers of employees, orientation may be accomplished through a series of briefings (under two hours). These presentations are usually conducted by managers, as opposed to trainers. This approach affords the opportunity for senior managers to bring their message directly to all levels of employees in decentralized organizations and to display their commitment to TQM.

Process Improvement

Process improvement integrates three sets of skills and knowledge: job knowledge, team skills, and process analysis (see Figure 16.3). The

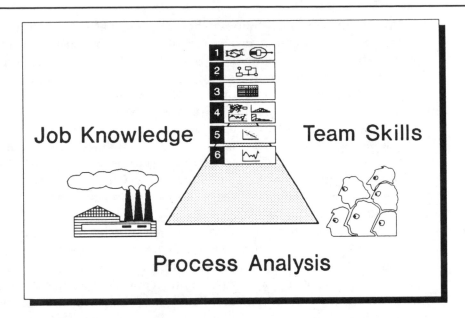

Process Improvement Integrates Three Sets of Skills

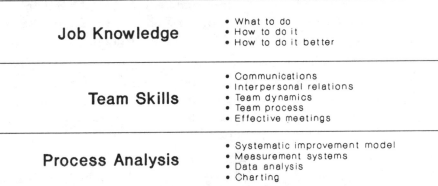

Job Knowledge	• What to do • How to do it • How to do it better
Team Skills	• Communications • Interpersonal relations • Team dynamics • Team process • Effective meetings
Process Analysis	• Systematic improvement model • Measurement systems • Data analysis • Charting

Figure 16.3   Process Improvement Building Blocks

design of process improvement training depends on the needs of the organization—the difference between employees' current capabilities in these three areas and the level of proficiency needed. Although it is desirable for everyone to be highly skilled in all three dimensions, compromises are often made in the early stages. One start-up strategy is to build familiarity and "entry-level" skills for all employees and assure the availability of quality improvement and teamwork specialists who have expertise in their respective disciplines.

Process improvement training should enable participants to begin applying the tools of quality improvement to their work as soon as they return to their jobs. Sessions usually run in the range of one to four days. They often begin by reviewing the teachings of orientation: the components, elements, and principles of TQM, including the need to refocus attention on customers. Training is provided on techniques for identifying internal and external customers and on how to build an understanding of their expectations. This is followed by teaching employees how to apply a systematic process improvement model and use the basic quality improvement tools (see Chapter 9). The role, approaches, and dynamics of quality improvement teams are taught as well (refer to Chapter 13).

Training needs to be followed by application of newly acquired skills, or the investment in training will be lost. Therefore, process improvement training must conclude with the identification of quality improvement projects. Work on these projects will continue when the employees return to the workplace. Four criteria help in the selection of initial projects:

1 *Importance:* The task is important to either the business unit, employees, or both. Successful completion will yield a *measurable* and clearly visible improvement for the organization.

2 *Doability:* The task is not overly complex and can be worked on by the unit's members without the need to involve others outside of the department. Employees working on the project have the necessary skills, resources, and abilities to complete the project successfully in a reasonable period of time (usually less than six months).

3 *Energizing:* The project is of inherent interest to all team members, and they have a stake in its outcome. It has a high probability for success, is challenging yet manageable, and when successfully completed will improve morale and working conditions as well as business performance. Team members are interested in putting forth the required effort.

4 *Ownership:* The process owner (see Chapter 8) is sponsoring the improvement effort or is a member of the team. Others who have a stake in the outcome of the project, but are not directly involved, are kept informed by the team.

Successfully completed projects should be shared with subsequent classes as examples of how results can be achieved through the application of the quality improvement tools and techniques. Some organizations have team members handle the presentations rather than instructors. This approach builds credibility for process improvement training and affords an opportunity to recognize team members' contributions.

Participative Management

Managers and supervisors need to be trained in how to lead the building of a new work environment—one that is less autocratic and directive, and more supportive and participative (see Chapter 12). For many managers, this change is dramatic, unsettling, and threatening. They need to understand how the new approach will help them to achieve their objectives and those of the organization.

Middle managers and first-line supervisors need education and training to enable them to make the transition to a new management style. They must understand the need to manage differently, and they must be provided with the skills to do so. Middle managers and supervisors are usually "victims" of a change in management processes, since they are not always informed and supported by senior managers during this change process. Management training needed to implement TQM is a subject unto itself and beyond the scope of this chapter.

Additional Training—As Required

A number of other training modules need to be available and ready to support individual requirements. A brief overview of commonly needed supplementary courses follows.

Problem solving: This course complements the process improvement training delivered in the core curriculum. It guides individuals or teams through a disciplined process to assure that problems are solved completely. This course provides techniques that can be applied to problems, or specific deviations from what is normal, in a process that is under control.

Statistical process control: Like problem solving, this course builds on the approaches to analyzing data that were introduced in process improvement training. The statistical process control (SPC) course introduces the use of statistics as the foundation for collecting, analyzing, and using data for making decisions. Although SPC training is often included in the core curriculum of manufacturing organizations, experience has shown that this approach is usually premature and wasteful in the service sector. It makes little sense to introduce SPC to people who are still struggling to identify who their customers are and have not yet established measurement systems.

Benchmarking: Benchmarking helps individuals and teams to seek out, understand, and adopt superior work practices (refer to Chapter 7 for more information on benchmarking). Training in the subject stimulates employees to accept the superior level of performance as their own target. This training builds the skills needed for identifying gaps in performance and helps to motivate participants to close those gaps and become the benchmark.

Other courses: Other courses are needed to develop specific skills, as required. In some organizations, the climate for teamwork and collaboration is so poor that individuals need training in business-meeting and interpersonal skills. These and other specialized requirements can be addressed through commercially available seminars and customized courses.

How Do We Deliver Training?

Delivery of the core curriculum should begin with the senior managers (CEO, COO, etc.) and cascade down throughout the organization, with each manager attending twice, first as a participant and then as a coteacher.

Managers and their direct reports participate in training as teams of natural work groups. This approach allows them to discuss their own unit's mission, improvement opportunities, and any barriers that might impede their progress. Some organizations have formalized this approach, with business units using this initial "start-up meeting" as a forum to define issues that must be addressed to assure the successful introduction of TQM. Some organizations combine the start-up meeting with orientation.

Involving managers as coteachers offers four benefits:

1 The managers' learning of concepts and techniques through participation in the first session is reinforced when they prepare to explain them to their subordinates in a subsequent training session.

2 The managers' commitment to the subject is demonstrated to their employees through their role as coteachers. (Note that their lack of commitment will be equally visible.)

3 Individuals returning to their workplace will expect to find the supportive, encouraging, reinforcing environment that their managers described in the training session.

4 The managers will have the opportunity to directly address the questions that invariably arise during the introduction of TQM.

Managers will need to be prepared to answer the following typical questions:

- What is the organization's definition of quality?
- What is the extent of management's commitment to TQM? What level of resources, staffing, trainers, quality specialists, consultants, and class time is the organization prepared to allocate?
- How important is quality relative to budget and schedule?
- What does the organization want to accomplish with this strategy, and what mileposts or goals have been selected to measure progress?
- What is management's role in implementing TQM, and what problems or opportunities have senior managers identified to address themselves?
- How will the organization recognize and reward those who actively support TQM, and what are the consequences to individuals who do not support this process?
- What will happen to employees whose jobs are eliminated through efficiency and productivity improvements?
- Will we be expected to improve our work processes in addition to doing the work already assigned to us?
- What's different about management's commitment to TQM as compared to prior "flavor of the month" campaigns?

Although designated as coteachers, managers need not deliver the entire curriculum of TQM courses. A logical demarcation of roles has managers deliver the educational portions to provide knowledge to their employees and trainers cover the skill-building topics. By splitting classroom responsibilities as shown in Table 16.4, sessions are enriched by being more of a management intervention than a simple training exercise.

Training Deployment

Training can be cascaded in several different ways. One method is to saturate the entire organization with training at every level in every

Table 16.4: Division of Classroom Responsibilities

Type of Instruction	Leader	Topics
Provide knowledge	Manager	Mission
		Vision
		Goals
		Concepts of TQM
		Management's role
		Improvement opportunities
Build skills	Trainer	Process improvement
		Problem solving
		Statistical process control
		Benchmarking
		Interpersonal/meeting skills
		Cost of quality

department until everyone is trained. This may be a viable approach in a small organization, especially if there is a disciplined effort to apply the newly acquired skills to real work once training is completed.

A different approach may be needed in larger organizations, especially if employees view managers as adversaries instead of partners. In this case, training should cascade down from senior managers to their headquarters staff. From this point on, it may be advisable to concentrate training in a vertical slice through designated functional areas. For example, this would start with a functional senior manager (vice president of customer service) and his or her staff, then one of the regional organizations (northeast regional service), then one district within that region (New York district service office).

This vertical-slice approach has several advantages, the least of which is that it conserves resources. The bigger advantage is that this approach allows the organization to apply process improvement techniques more quickly to long-standing problems and secure some measure of success. These successes allow the balance of training to proceed with the full knowledge that there is something valuable to be gained. The incentive has been provided to proceed with training in every other part of the organization.

Another advantage of the vertical-slice approach is that it permits training to proceed at a natural pace without enforcing a "lockstep" race. Units that begin training first can be self-selected, where interest already exists among the leaders.

Senior Managers' Application of Process Improvement

Senior managers are more often than not customers for the outputs of others, not producers in the traditional sense. Therefore, senior managers struggle to apply process improvement training to their own complex work. There will be few examples of the successful application of quality improvement tools by executives that can be used in training. Nonetheless, every effort must be made to apply improvement techniques at every level if TQM is to be spread throughout the organization.

Many problems that reach senior managers may have been addressed previously by others but not solved because they either affect the entire organization, exceed everyone's authority level, or represent some political or career risk. This complexity means that these issues cannot be expected to be resolved in a short period of time, and success is anything but assured. Clearly, these types of problems don't satisfy the criteria for the selection of initial improvement projects.

So what is an executive to do in this dilemma? Defer embarking on the improvement process or select a project likely to fail? Neither is a good choice. A third alternative is to select a problem that is workable—like getting to meetings on time or improving the executive's interactions with his or her secretary. Unfortunately, this approach is only marginally better, since most employees laugh at the "trivia" the bosses are working on in comparison to their compensation level.

If senior managers cannot identify projects that satisfy the criteria for selecting initial projects, why not consider a different approach? Instead of trying to force-fit one of their own problems to the rigors of process improvement, they can act productively in their role as process owners. Identify a key business process for which they are responsible, sponsor a team to improve it, and participate as an *active* member.

Training Hints

1 Since most of the initial activity in implementing TQM is training-related, some managers will be tempted to complete the core training immediately, so everyone can get back to regular work and so that they can be seen to be supportive of the TQM initiative. When this occurs, the crush of training does not allow management adequate time to assure that the skills learned in class are applied to real work.

2 If training is cascaded without evidence that it is being applied, subsequent classes should be delayed and resources diverted to starting other quality improvement activities. Completing training is not the objective. Rather, it is a means of equipping people with new tools to solve old problems. If this is not the case, if employees are not applying their new tools after completing training, if quality improvement projects are not under way, do not proceed with training until the underlying problems preventing application are confronted and resolved.

3 Individuals and teams usually need skilled facilitation support from quality specialists the first few times they apply the tools and techniques they have been taught. The classroom experience provides theory and limited practice on applications. Employees who are novices in process improvement will easily get derailed. If support is not readily available, or if the techniques are used improperly, individuals will become frustrated and report their experience as evidence that the improvement process does not apply to their work. They will be reluctant to try again.

4 Trainers often make ideal facilitators, and using trainers as facilitators offers them the opportunity to practice what they teach. This practical experience will make them better instructors and provide them with real examples to bring into their classrooms. If trainers provide facilitation support, this additional work load must be included when calculating the number of trainers needed to satisfy training demand.

5 Build self-sufficiency, even though it might be tempting to rely entirely on one of the numerous TQM training and consulting firms. They can be excellent resources to start the initial training process, and their generic training materials can certainly be purchased. But the details should be tailored to fit the specific needs and culture of

the organization in which the training will be applied. Internal trainers should be developed quickly through train-the-trainer programs, so that the organization can become self-sufficient as soon as possible. Building internal capability strengthens the organization and serves as an example of management commitment to TQM.

6 The ideal class size is twelve to fifteen participants. Larger classes reduce the instructor's ability to respond to everyone's questions. Larger classes also require additional subgroups for exercises, or subgroup sizes must be increased. Such larger sessions tend to become communications events, not training classes, and skills cannot be developed effectively in such an environment.

Summary

Education and training are tactics in a larger strategy for implementing TQM. They provide individuals with *knowledge* of what is being pursued, the rationale for the pursuit, and the *skills* they need in order to achieve quality improvement. However, training requires such a large commitment of resources and people that it can appear to be the total strategy for securing quality improvement. When this occurs, the improvement process usually comes to a halt when training is completed, and employees go back to doing exactly what they were doing before.

Define the skills, knowledge, and behaviors desired within your organization and compare them to current performance. Provide education and training to bridge the identified gaps, *and* reinforce application on the job. Although this might sound straightforward, logical, and obvious, many leading organizations have managed to pursue either of two less desirable alternatives. One is to question the value of training without knowing the cost of ignorance and decide that training is too expensive and that people can do without it. The other is to hide behind the facade of massive training—throw time, money, and people at training courses but don't require that the new skills and knowledge be applied on the job.

Help managers lead the transformation of the organization by serving as classroom trainers. Give them the opportunity to perform in their new role as coaches and mentors. Let them practice what they preach and preach what they practice.

References

Aubrey, C. A., and Felkins, P. K. *Teamwork: Involving People in Quality and Productivity Improvement.* Milwaukee, Wis.: Quality Press, 1988.

Gilbert, T. F. *Human Competence.* New York: McGraw-Hill, 1978.

Juran, J. M., and Gryna, F. M. *Juran's Quality Control Handbook,* 4th ed. New York: McGraw-Hill, 1988.

Nilson, C. *Training Program Workbook and Kit.* Englewood Cliffs, N.J.: Prentice-Hall, 1989.

17 Quality Management Systems

Most quality programs fail for one of two reasons:
They have system without passion,
or passion without system.

—*Tom Peters*[1]

Total quality management rests first and foremost on the fundamental beliefs, values, and convictions of its leaders. It requires an unflinching pursuit of long-term customer satisfaction through the systematic improvement of all products, services, and processes. Total quality management relies on soft concepts like leadership, respect, trust, and intrinsic motivation. It relies on principles that are impossible to measure.

With these caveats in mind, this chapter introduces quality management systems. These systems provide frameworks within which to measure and audit the performance of an organization along its endless quest to improve quality. Although these frameworks can supplement management's commitment to quality improvement, they cannot replace it.

A quality management system integrates all elements required by an organization to continuously improve customer satisfaction through better products, services, and processes. There is no universal prescription, but a number of benchmarks are available that provide operational definitions of total quality management. These benchmarks include recognized standards such as the International Organization for Standardization Series 9000/9004, British Standards Institute BS5750, and ANSI/ASQC Q90/Q94. Frameworks are also provided by national awards such as the Deming Prize and the Baldridge Award.

The major standards and awards all share a core of common features but exhibit differences in their relative emphasis on specific elements. Without implying judgment as to the superiority of any one over another, this chapter features the evaluation criteria of the United States' Malcolm Baldrige National Quality Award and the ISO 9004-2 standard for service organizations. This chapter also offers a brief comparison among other major standards and awards. Readers can use these criteria as a benchmark for the design or evaluation of their own systems.

Malcolm Baldrige National Quality Award

The Malcolm Baldrige National Quality Award is based on a three-stage review process: (1) evaluation of a written examination; (2) site visits to applicant companies scoring high on the written examination; and (3) final judging of overall results.

The written examination plays a central role in the award process. The examination criteria not only provide the primary basis for assessing award applications but also represent a specific value system for total quality management. These criteria establish a codified picture of a total quality management system and enable the award to serve three purposes:

1 Promote quality awareness
2 Recognize quality achievements of U.S. businesses
3 Publicize successful quality strategies

The examination covers seven categories in four main elements. Leadership by senior executives is the first element and the driving force behind quality improvement. The improvement system is the second element and includes four categories: information and analysis, strategic quality planning, human resource development and management, and management of process quality. Quality and operational results form the third element and include measurable improvements derived from analysis of customers' requirements and expectations. Customer focus and satisfaction is the fourth element and ultimate goal of the process.

If a total quality management system is pictured as a process whose output is the improvement of products and services, then the four main elements of the Baldrige Award parallel the three levels of measurement explained in Chapter 10. Scores for the elements of leadership and system represent measures at the process level. The third element, results from quality assurance, corresponds to the output level. The fourth element, customer satisfaction, represents the ultimate desired goal, and its scoring is the key measure at the outcome level.

The definition and weighting of individual diagnostic indicators within each category project the value system for total quality management as defined by the Malcolm Baldrige National Quality Award Consortium. In the spirit of continuous improvement, the consortium reviews and updates the indicators annually. Table 17.1 lists the set of indicators within each category that were used in 1993. Their respective weighting in the 1,000-point scoring system and the relationship among the elements and categories are shown in Figure 17.1.

Within each category, the scoring system is based on three factors: approach, deployment, and results. *Approach* refers to the methods used to achieve the purposes addressed in the examination item. *Deployment* refers to the extent to which the approaches are applied to all relevant areas. *Results* refers to the outcomes and effects in achieving the purposes stated and implied in the examination item.

Named in honor of former Commerce Department Secretary Malcolm Baldrige, the National Quality Award was created by the U.S. Congress in 1987. The examination process is administered by a consortium formed by the American Society for Quality Control and the American Productivity and Quality Center. As many as six awards can be made annually, two each for manufacturing, service, and small business. Details on the program are available from the National Institute of Standards and Technology (formerly known as the National Bureau of Standards), Gaithersburg, Maryland 20899; (301) 975-2036.

The Deming Prize

Instituted in December 1950 by the Union of Japanese Scientists and Engineers, the Deming Prize is coveted as the highest form of industrial recognition in Japan. It was established in recognition and appreciation of W. Edwards Deming's achievements in the introduction and development of statistical quality control. The award was also established to promote statistical quality control in Japan.

Two major types of awards are made annually. The first is for excellence in research in the theory or application of statistical quality control. The second is for organizations that have achieved notable results through the application of statistical quality control. This second award is further subdivided into awards for corporations and small enterprises.

The Baldrige Award was established as an attempt to achieve the same results in the United States as the Deming Prize has achieved in

Table 17.1: Malcolm Baldrige National Quality Award—Examination Categories and Point Values

1993 EXAMINATION ITEMS AND POINT VALUES

1993 Examination Categories/Items	Point Values
1.0 Leadership	**95**
1.1 Senior Executive Leadership	45
1.2 Management for Quality	25
1.3 Public Responsibility and Corporate Citizenship	25
2.0 Information and Analysis	**75**
2.1 Scope and Management of Quality and Performance Data and Information	15
2.2 Competitive Comparisons and Benchmarking	20
2.3 Analysis and Uses of Company-Level Data	40
3.0 Strategic Quality Planning	**60**
3.1 Strategic Quality and Company Performance Planning Process	35
3.2 Quality and Performance Plans	25
4.0 Human Resource Development and Management	**150**
4.1 Human Resource Planning and Management	20
4.2 Employee Involvement	40
4.3 Employee Education and Training	40
4.4 Employee Performance and Recognition	25
4.5 Employee Well-Being and Satisfaction	25
5.0 Management of Process Quality	**140**
5.1 Design and Introduction of Quality Products and Services	40
5.2 Process Management: Product and Service Production and Delivery Processes	35
5.3 Process Management: Business Processes and Support Services	30
5.4 Supplier Quality	20
5.5 Quality Assessment	15
6.0 Quality and Operational Results	**180**
6.1 Product and Service Quality Results	70
6.2 Company Operational Results	50
6.3 Business Process and Support Service Results	25
6.4 Supplier Quality Results	35
7.0 Customer Focus and Satisfaction	**300**
7.1 Customer Expectations: Current and Future	35
7.2 Customer Relationship Management	65
7.3 Commitment to Customers	15
7.4 Customer Satisfaction Determination	30
7.5 Customer Satisfaction Results	85
7.6 Customer Satisfaction Comparison	70
TOTAL POINTS	**1000**

Source: 1993 Application Guidelines—Malcolm Baldrige National Quality Award (Gaithersburg, Md.: National Institute of Standards and Technology, 1993), 15.

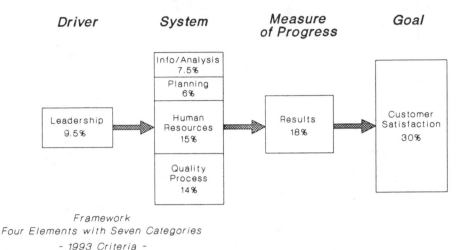

| Driver | System | Measure of Progress | Goal |

Framework
Four Elements with Seven Categories
- 1993 Criteria -

Figure 17.1   Malcolm Baldrige Award Examination. *Source:* National Institute of Standards and Technology.

Japan. As such, both awards share a large degree of commonality. Both seek total involvement throughout the organization—from top to bottom and along the customer-supplier chain. Both seek systems to assure and continuously improve the quality of products and services. However, the emphasis and approach of each award is different.

Unlike the Baldrige Award, which is aimed at the improvement of quality management, the Deming Prize focuses on the application of statistical quality control. The emphasis of the Deming Prize reflects Deming's approach and his strong following among the Japanese. The respect shown for this award by the Japanese attests to their belief in the strength of statistical methods.

The Baldrige Award places greater emphasis on customers than does the Deming Prize. For example, scoring for the Baldrige examination includes measures of customer satisfaction and the role of customers in the information analysis and quality assurance systems. By contrast, the Deming Prize criteria focus on the process used to apply statistical quality control.

The Deming Prize guidelines are less detailed and specific than those for the Baldrige Award. As a result, the Deming Prize evaluation is more dependent on the qualifications, capability, and interpretation of the judges.[2] The Fuji-Xerox translation of evaluation criteria for the Deming Prize for the application of statistical quality control is shown in Table 17.2.

Table 17.2: The Deming Prize for Applications—Evaluation Checkpoints

1. Policy

Policy Toward Product Quality, Business in General
Content of Policy
Communication of Policy Throughout Company
Short Term, Long Term Planning and Their Relationships
Method for Establishing Policy
Utilization of Statistical Methods
Monitoring of Policy Achievement

2. Management of Organization

Clarity of Boundaries of Responsibility
Contact and Communication Between Departments
Utilization of Staff
Monitoring and Auditing of Quality Control
Appropriateness of Functional Boundaries
Personnel Activities as a Whole
QC Circle Activities

3. Education

Plan and Actual Educational Activities
Level of Consciousness Toward Quality, Management, and Quality Control
Propagation of Education About Statistical Concepts and Methods
Results/Achievement
Educational Sources from Outside the Company
QC Circle Activities
Number of Proposals for Improvement

4. Information Gathering

Information Gathering from Outside the Company
Speed of Information Communication
Communication of Information Between Departments
Processing of Information (Statistical Analysis)

5. Analysis

Selection of Major Problem Themes
Utilization and Application of Statistics
Analysis of Quality and Process
Analysis Method
Specialized Techniques
Application of Analytical Results

Total Quality Management

6. Standardization

Standardization System
Actual Rate of Adherence to Established Standards
Application of Statistics
Application of Standards
Stabilization and Revision of Standards
Content of Standards
Effects Upon Technology

7. Control

System for Cost and Quality Control of Products
Application and Utilization of Statistical Methods
Actual Achievement of Control Activities
Aggressive Submittal of Improvement Proposals
Control Points and Items
QC Circle Activities
Control Conditions

8. Quality Assurance

New Product Development Method
Improvement of Control Process
Inspection
Monitoring and Auditing Quality Assurance System
Product Quality Evaluation, Auditing
Analysis of Product Development/Reliability/Design
Product Safety
Capacity of Process
Control of Equipment Ordering/Procurement/Service
Application and Utilization of Statistical Methods
Condition of Quality Assurance
Inspection

9. Results

Projection of Results
Results Not Quantitatively Measurable
Actual Achievement of Results versus Projections
Quantitative Results for:
 • Product Quality
 • Profit
 • General Working Environment
 • Cost
 • Safety

10. Future Planning

Clarity and Understanding of Current Status
Planning for Future Operations
Measures for Solving Problem Areas
Long Term Planning

Source: Guidebook to the Deming Prize and Nippon Quality Control Prize, trans. Fuji-Xerox, Ltd. (Tokyo: Fuji-Xerox, Ltd., 1982), 48–53.

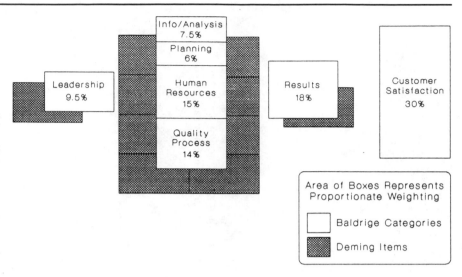

Figure 17.2   Comparing the Baldrige Award and the Deming Prize

Figure 17.2 maps the ten items in the Deming Prize evaluation against the seven categories of the Baldrige Award. The nearly 10 percent awarded for leadership in the Baldrige Award overlaps the policy item in the Deming Prize. However, the weighting assigned to the evaluation of the quality improvement system is substantially different. Whereas the Baldrige Award assigns about 42 percent of the score to the four included categories, 80 percent of the Deming Prize items fit under this heading. The Baldrige Award assigns 18 percent to results, which is nearly double the weighting of this same item in the Deming Prize.

The measurement of outcome shows the greatest difference between these two awards. The Baldrige Award assigns 30 percent to the evaluation of customer satisfaction, but the Deming Prize has no corresponding item. This contrast invites comment on W. Edwards Deming's position on the measurement of outcomes. Anyone who has attended one of Dr. Deming's seminars on managing quality improvement should remember how Deming scorns U.S. management for "managing outcomes." Deming compares this approach to driving a car by watching where the road has been through the rearview mirror.

Consistent with Deming's teachings, the Japanese prize bearing his name devotes nine of its ten examination items to measuring the process of quality improvement, one to results, and none to outcomes. (Information on competing for the Deming Prize is available from the Union of Japanese Scientists and Engineers, 5–10–11 Sondagaya-Ku, Tokyo 151, Japan.)

ISO 9004-2 for Service Organizations

The International Organization for Standardization has developed a series of standards for total quality management. ISO 9000 provides guidelines for their selection and use. ISO 9001 covers *product* design, development, production, installation, and servicing. ISO 9002 covers production and installation, and ISO 9003 covers final inspection and testing. ISO 9004 includes all elements of standards 9001–9003. ISO 9004-2 was developed for application to *services* and builds on the principles of 9004.

ISO 9004-2 was drafted to provide service organizations with a systematic approach to quality management. Its underlying intention is to assure that the stated and implied needs of customers are both understood and met. The evaluation criteria within the standard cover the full spectrum of operations—from marketing, through service design and delivery, to the analysis of service provided to the customer. In addition to normally expected elements such as management responsibility and the structure of an organization's quality system, criteria include the human interactions with customers, the importance of customers' perceptions, and the motivation and development of personnel.

The concepts and principles of the standard are intended to be applicable to all forms of services. This includes services provided to ultimate end users as well as to staff who are internal to an organization. Application is intended both for pure services and for services performed in conjunction with the manufacture and supply of products. Table 17.3 lists the evaluation criteria.

Further information can be obtained directly from the standards or from supporting organizations. As shown in Table 17.4, the ISO series directly corresponds to other recognized international standards.

Summary

Quality awards and standards provide a useful framework for defining the elements of a total quality management system. They also establish a system of measures against which progress can be gauged. However, it may not be possible to codify and quantify the subjective underlying beliefs and culture of an organization that are ultimately required in the never-ending quest for long-term customer satisfaction. These ingredients may elude the boundaries of such frameworks.

Table 17.3: ISO Standard 9004-2 for Service Organizations—Evaluation Criteria

Quality System Principles

Management Responsibility

Quality Policy
Quality Objectives
Quality Responsibility and Authority
Management Review

Quality System Structure

Service Quality Loop
Quality Documentation and Records
Internal Quality Audits

Personnel and Material Resources

Personnel
  • Training and Development
  • Communications
Material Resources

Interface with Customers

Quality System Operational Elements

Marketing Process

Quality in Market Research and Analysis
Supplier Obligations
Service Brief
Service Management
Quality in Advertising

Service Delivery Process

Supplier's Assessment of Service Quality
Customer's Assessment of Service Quality
Service Status
Corrective Action for Nonconforming Service
  • Responsibilities
  • Identification and Corrective Action
Measurement System Control

Service Performance and Analysis

General
Data Collection and Analysis
  • Statistical Methods
Service Quality Improvement

Design Process

General
Design Responsibilities
Service Specification
  • Service Delivery Specification
  • Service Delivery Procedures
  • Handling, Storage, Identification,
    Packaging and Traceability
Quality Control
Design Review
Validation of Service Specification
    and Service Delivery Specification
Design Change Control

Source: "Quality Management and Quality System Elements, Part 2: Guidelines for Services," (Draft), International Organization for Standardization, Geneva, Switzerland (1990) : 8–27.

Recognition of these limitations is perhaps best expressed by C. W. Reimann, director of the Malcolm Baldrige National Quality Award, as reported in a 1990 article in *Fortune*. Stripping away the numerical criteria, he distills the core of the award to eight critical factors for which the Baldrige examiners look:

A plan to keep improving all operations continuously.

A system for measuring these improvements accurately.

A strategic plan based on benchmarks that compare the company's performance with the world's best.

A close partnership with suppliers and customers that feeds information back into operations.

Table 17.4: Equivalency among Quality Standards

ISO Standard	British Standard BS 5750	ANSI/ASQC
9000	Part 0, Sec. 0.1	Q90
9001	Part 1	Q91
9002	Part 2	Q92
9003	Part 3	Q93
9004	Part 0, Sec. 0.2	Q94

Source: British Standards Institute, 2 Park St., London W1A 2BS; American Society for Quality Control, 310 West Wisconsin Ave., Milwaukee, Wis. 53203.

A deep understanding of the customers so that their wants can be translated into products [and services].

A long-lasting relationship with customers, going beyond the delivery of the product to include sales, service, and ease of maintenance.

A focus on preventing mistakes rather than merely correcting them.

A commitment to improving the quality that runs from the top of the organization to the bottom.[3]

Notes

1. T. Peters, *Thriving on Chaos* (New York: Knopf, 1987), 74.
2. D. Bush and K. Dooley, "The Deming Prize and Baldrige Award: How They Compare," *Quality Progress* 22, no. 1 (1989): 28–30.
3. J. Main, "How to Win the Baldrige Award," *Fortune* 121, no. 9 (1990): 101–116.

References

DeCarlo, N. J., and Sterett, W. K. "History of the Malcolm Baldrige National Quality Awards." *Quality Progress* 23, no. 3 (1990): 21–27.

Koyanagi, Kenichi. *The Deming Prize.* Tokyo: Union of Japanese Scientists and Engineers, 1960.

Reimann, C. W. "The Baldrige Award: Leading the Way in Quality Initiatives." *Quality Progress* 22, no. 7 (1989): 35–39.

———. "Reagan Lauds First Baldrige Award Winners." *Quality Progress* 22, no. 1 (1989): 25–27.

18 Sample Strategies

This chapter showcases total quality management (TQM) strategies employed by two companies that are recognized leaders in its implementation. In one case, this leadership led to the achievement of the Malcolm Baldrige National Quality Award. The objective of this chapter is to help service leaders attain an equivalent world-class level of quality as quickly and effectively as possible.

The chapter begins by outlining a sequence of five stages of quality maturity, which are shown in Figure 18.1. Research by Roger Williams and Boudewijn Bertsch of Erasmus University in Rotterdam revealed that only about 150 companies *in the world* had reached the highest stages of maturity by the late 1980s.[1] Recognition of these stages and the impediments to progressing through them helps managers differentiate between strategies that are worthy of emulation and those that are merely interesting. Organizations that have successfully progressed to the highest stages serve as benchmarks of total quality management.

We used four criteria to select company strategies for this chapter. First, results of the strategy demonstrate a capability to propel the company to the highest stages of quality maturity. Second, the strategy reinforces and demonstrates the teachings of this book. Third, the candidate is either a service company or a manufacturer that has extended systematic quality improvement beyond production. Fourth, we were able to offer insights not readily available to others.

Readers can easily obtain additional information on the successful strategies of Deming and Baldrige winners such as Florida Power and Light, Federal Express, Motorola, and Milliken. Therefore, these strategies are not repeated here.

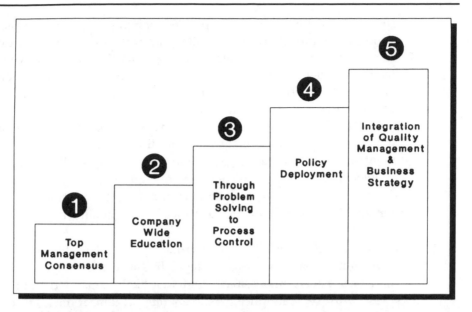

Figure 18.1 Stages of Quality Maturity. *Source*: R. Williams and B. Bertsch, *Stages in the Management of Quality Improvement Programmes* (Rotterdam, Netherlands: Erasmus University Department of Business and Organisation, Strategic Quality Institute, 1989), 4.

Five Stages of Quality Maturity

Through their research on companies in Europe, the United States, and the Far East, Roger Williams and Bod Bertsch identified five stages of growth toward quality maturity. Their sequence of stages helps to identify when major difficulties can be expected to arise in the journey toward world-class quality.

Stage 1: The first stage, top management consensus, is reached when top management wholeheartedly embraces quality management as the appropriate means to improve productivity, achieve customer satisfaction, and thereby enhance performance in the marketplace.

Stage 2: The second stage, companywide education, focuses on the companywide educational process through which everyone learns to use the fundamental concepts of total quality management and problem-solving methods, such as the seven statistical tools and the plan-do-check-act cycle.

Stage 3: In the third stage, the problem-solving tools are applied to problems within departments, allowing participants to build experience and refine their problem-solving skills. Quality improvement teams or circles are formed, and by the end of this stage, a high degree of error prevention through control of the basic manufacturing (and service) processes may be attained.

Stage 4: The fourth stage is very different. It is a major step forward. It involves the management and coordination of quality improvement across the entire organization. Thus, it typically deals with problems across functions, departments, and even company boundaries. It requires the strong commitment of top management, a clear-cut quality policy, and the identification of quality break-through projects.

Stage 5: The fifth stage is characterized by the integration of quality management and business strategy. In the earlier stages, integration was usually impossible. TQM was likely separated from business with separate meetings, separate organizational structure, and separate performance measures. The ultimate aim is for TQM and the business strategy to merge and contribute to long-term success.[2]

Overcoming Barriers

Williams and Bertsch suggest that world-class quality can only be achieved when an organization is well advanced into stage 4. They equate this to the level of Deming Prize and Baldrige Award recipients. Their research shows that the transition between stages 3 and 4 poses major problems and that only perhaps 150 companies in the world achieved this level by the late 1980s. Progressing to stage 5 is also difficult, and the researchers feel that perhaps only seven or eight companies (all Japanese) had reached this stage.[3]

The five stages identified by Williams and Bertsch overlap and are cumulative. For example, consensus does not stop after a company makes the transition to stage 2; rather, it deepens as the company grows toward quality maturity. Similarly, education does not stop after stage 2. Education is an ongoing activity that includes refresher courses and the regular introduction of new tools and techniques.

Strategies that have successfully propelled companies through the first three stages are worthy of investigation. This chapter describes the implementation of TQM by companies that are at or near stage 4.

Banc One Corporation

The Ohio-based Banc One Corporation grew to be the nation's tenth largest bank holding company by 1992, and grew to be among the most profitable in its industry. As explained by its chairman and chief executive officer, John B. McCoy, TQM plays a vital role in Banc One's quest of: "Striving to be the 'best of the best.'"

Charles A. Aubrey II helped shape Banc One's approach to TQM as vice president and chief quality officer through 1991. His time and effort in sharing this experience with us is greatly appreciated.

Leadership

TQM at Banc One began with the determination and leadership of the senior management team. Their shared belief and values relative to quality improvement are articulated through the combination of six key documents (see Table 18.1 and Figure 18.2):

1 Mission statement
2 Precepts of quality
3 Banc One quality goal
4 Banc One quality policy
5 Quality definition
6 Quality characteristics

Quality Improves Project by Project

How is the leaders' quest for quality improvement at Banc One conducted? It is accomplished on a project-by-project basis through the TQM process shown in Figure 18.3. This never-ending process links seven vital steps: planning, training, leading, determining customer requirements, measuring, improving, and rewarding.

The effectiveness of this approach is attributed to five strategic elements: organizational structure, annual quality plans, quality improvement process, communications, training, and reward/recognition. The following overview of each element is intended to provide readers with an understanding of the strategy underlying Banc One's success.

Organizational Structure: Upper managers steer Banc One's quality improvement process through the quality council. This group has six responsibilities:

Table 18.1: Banc One Mission Statement

We Believe . . . Enterprise and the opportunities created by individual choice are the corner-stones of our "Uncommon Partnership." They produce the greatest value for the customer and the greatest stimulant to business. Those core values provide the best plan for delivering true satisfaction for every customer and the most desirable return for investors.

Precepts . . . Based on this belief, the Board of Directors of BANC ONE CORPORATION adopted these precepts as the official guideline for the commitment and performance of our people.

One   We believe in creating an atmosphere in which our people working together:

- care about what they do

- utilize their own abilities to make the right decision

- focus on customers and uncover innovative ways to service their changing financial needs

- promptly respond to problems and customer concerns in a professional sensitive manner.

Two   We believe in conducting our business:

- with uncompromising honesty, fairness and integrity

- to achieve superior financial performance for our shareholders

- to identify, develop, retain, and provide equal opportunity for all people who demonstrate the willingness and ability to perform and grow

- with an unflinching focus on providing a quality of services that ensures customer satisfaction.

Three   We believe management should base decisions on:

- maintaining a balance between the needs of our customers, employees and share-holders

- the need to support the social, cultural and economical programs which enchance the quality of life in our communities

- providing creative leadership to the direction and success of the financial industry

- expanding the geographic influence and customer service opportunities of the orga-nization as enterprise and prudence permits.

We believe commitment to performance and a focus on the quality of customer service are essential to success. We believe in the everlasting process of building a great bank.

Source: C. A. Aubrey II et al., *Quality of Customer Service Handbook* (Columbus, Ohio: Banc One Corporation, 1988), 1.

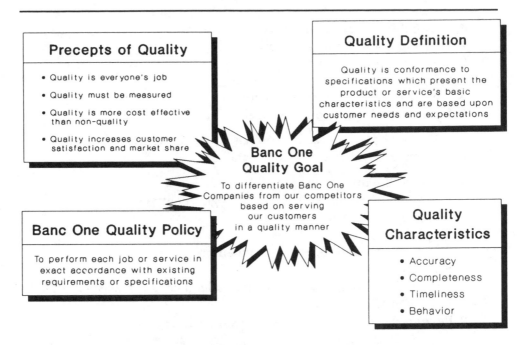

Figure 18.2 Quality at Banc One. *Source*: C. A. Aubrey II et al., *Quality of Customer Service Handbook* (Columbus, Ohio: Banc One Corporation, 1988), 2–4.

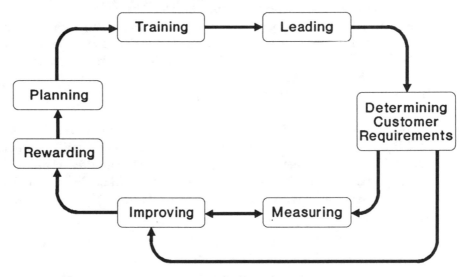

Figure 18.3 Banc One Corporation–Total Quality Management. *Source*: Charles A. Aubrey II, *Total Quality Management* (Columbus, Ohio: Banc One Corporation, 1990). Permission granted by Banc One Corporation, Columbus, Ohio.

1 Set guidelines for the improvement process.
2 Seek out and authorize projects.
3 Authorize projects to begin.
4 Select project leaders.
5 Approve implementation of solutions.
6 Develop and approve the annual quality plan.

Furthermore, the leadership has explicitly defined eight tasks for upper managers that are nondelegatable:

1 Serve on the quality council.
2 Approve and communicate the strategic quality goals.
3 Allocate the needed resources.
4 Review progress.
5 Communicate and recognize team efforts.
6 Serve on project teams.
7 Revise the reward system to put adequate emphasis on quality improvement.
8 Enlarge the scope of business goals to include goals for quality.

Projects are implemented through quality improvement teams (QIT). Collectively, the members of a QIT should possess five characteristics. The team requires membership of the people who have the organizational *authority* to bring about change. The team includes people who can *influence* the speed and direction of the change and also have *knowledge* of the details of the problem. The QIT is composed of people who have the ability to work with others as a team and *facilitate* progress. Finally, the QIT includes a *leader* who has the time and ability to focus on the content of the problem.

Annual Quality Plans: Banc One has developed a planning process for application by each department of its banking affiliates. Worksheets are provided for use by each unit to articulate specific quality improvement goals and annual action plans. In addition to a worksheet for calculating the costs associated with poor service (cost of quality), plans encompass five key areas:

1 *Leadership:* Goals and action plans identify the activities to be engaged in and the actions to be taken by all levels of management and staff in order to provide leadership of the quality improvement process.
2 *Human resources utilization:* Activities are identified to utilize people and maximize their effectiveness and thoroughness in quality man-

agement and quality improvement. Included are activities to assure the highest motivation and contribution of individuals by effective hiring, training, provision of objectives or expectations, feedback, and reward.

3 *Information and analysis:* Annual plans delineate activities to collect, analyze, and use data on product/service performance and trends for quality improvement and control purposes.

4 *Quality assurance of products and services:* Goals and plans are defined for assuring the highest quality of service delivery through measurable, verifiable results of quality control (consistent service delivery) and quality improvement efforts. The emphasis is on systems and processes that minimize quality problems; provide for continuous, real-time quality performance measurement; and feedback for control and continuous improvement.

5 *Customer satisfaction:* Goals and plans are prepared for activities to assess and assure customer satisfaction and the resulting quality performance in terms of quality trends and level of customer satisfaction. Results are obtained through direct communications with customers (mail, telephone, and focus groups), or third parties, in order to improve quality and develop quantitative evidence of improvement from the customers' perspective.

Quality Improvement Process: But how is quality actually improved? Referring back to Banc One's TQM process, shown in Figure 18.3, we see a step called "Improving." Improvement is achieved by QIT projects. QITs handle their projects through teamwork and by applying Banc One's systematic improvement process, called IDEA:

Identification and selection of project/problem
Data collection
Evaluate data to determine solution(s)
Act on the evaluation by solution testing and selling

Communications: Banc One uses a number of communications vehicles, including its own internal quality newsletters. It has also established its quality management information and control system (QMICS). This is a mainframe-based system that is networked through on-line terminals or PCs and used by all Banc One affiliates to manage and control measurement data on selected products, services, or processes.

Specific measures are determined by affiliate management based on customer feedback regarding product/service priorities and expectations. The system generates monthly reports detailing a measure's standard, its degree of importance, and a comparison between individual affiliate performance and the standard. These monthly reports are used by management to identify quality problems or potential problems related to customer service.

The project tracking report is a subsystem of QMICS. It includes data and information on projects completed by QITs, and monthly reports enable affiliates to review projects completed by other affiliates. Communication of ideas and projects throughout the corporation enhances each affiliate's ability to identify potential new projects. Data in this system include:

- Project name
- Project description
- Benefits to customers, employees, community, shareholders
- Impact on accuracy, completeness, timeliness, behavior
- Cost/revenue impact
- Implementation date
- QIT members

Training: Skills and knowledge of employees are built through an extensive training curriculum. During the six-year period from 1986 to 1991, the corporation offered an average of 2,700 quality training classes annually. The following are examples of widely deployed courses:

Customer First Teams: This program of eight one-hour modules provides teams of front-line employees with basic training in the tools and techniques they need in order to address problems that have direct and immediate impact on customer satisfaction. Assignments within each module provide teams with the opportunity to work on current problems. Topics covered include:

- Questions and answers (introductions and definitions)
- Case study and problem prevention techniques
- Brainstorming
- Data-collecting techniques
- Data-collection formats plus graphs
- Decision analysis using Pareto analysis

- Basic cause-and-effect problem analysis
- Management presentation (data analysis and recommendations)

First Impressions: This process is designed to communicate service expectations to all associates and assess performance regardless of their positions. The process has been evolving since 1986, and substantial improvements were incorporated through information revealed by the 1988 customer opinion survey. Initial training is followed by the use of a mystery shopper (see Chapter 7 for the role of mystery shoppers). Banc One uses professional shoppers, customers, and employees as mystery shoppers. Training is conducted in three to four hours and includes videotaping of the employees' performance.

Beyond Customer Satisfaction: This training package is designed to address issues relative to customer interactions for front-line employees and for internal support groups. Its six modules can be delivered separately or in a two-day session. The program is augmented by three leadership modules for managers and supervisors. The nine modules are:

1 Make Service Your Competitive Edge
2 Building a Customer Information System
3 Create a Story for Your Customer
4 Learning to See Mistakes as Opportunities
5 Involve Everyone in Measuring Service
6 On Becoming a Better Customer
7 From Cop to Coach: The Leader's Changing Role
8 Beyond Empowerment: Create Front-line Ownership
9 Holding People Accountable

Managing the Quality of Customer Service: This seminar is designed for all executives, managers, and supervisors, to ensure that Banc One affiliates know how to differentiate themselves from their competitors based on superior quality. This two-day course covers the fundamentals of quality, how to measure and improve quality, the essentials for team members, participative management, leading the quality effort, and the key techniques used in the quality improvement process.

Quality Improvement Team Leader and Facilitator Training: This one-day course is designed for QIT facilitators and leaders. It covers leading projects, leading teams, getting started, finding projects, forming teams, holding effective meetings, project management, and introducing change into organizations.

Reward/Recognition:

Message from the Chairman

The degree to which we care about our customers, show concern for our employees and perform for our shareholders are the standards by which we are measured.

Over the years our caring attitude, quality of customer service and performance have set us apart from our competition.

That's why we set aside time to salute affiliates and employees who have demonstrated continuous outstanding performance by delivering the highest quality customer service.

—John B. McCoy, chairman, Banc One Corporation

Banc One presented over fifteen thousand awards to its employees in 1990 in recognition to their contributions to quality improvement. "We Care" awards represent the core of its recognition program. The process begins by supervisors at affiliate banks nominating employees who demonstrate extraordinary commitment to customer service. Plaques are awarded in the presence of coworkers, and affiliate recipients are automatically nominated for the annual corporate "We Care" award. The corporate recipient is recognized at the annual awards banquet and included in the corporation's annual report.

The annual awards banquet also provides a forum for presenting "Best of the Best" improvement team awards, branch office awards, and the chairman's "Quality of Customer Service" awards. Objectives of this latter award are to (1) recognize quality excellence, (2) promote greater quality awareness, and (3) publicize effective quality strategies. Criteria for selecting the affiliate to receive the chairman's award parallel the Malcolm Baldrige National Quality Award (see Chapter 17):

Category	Weight
Leadership	10%
Strategic quality planning	10
Human resources utilization	10
Information and analysis	20
Quality assurance	25
Customer satisfaction	25

Results Achieved by Banc One

So what has Banc One gained from all this effort? For one thing, it has increased the skills, knowledge, and capabilities of its 38,000

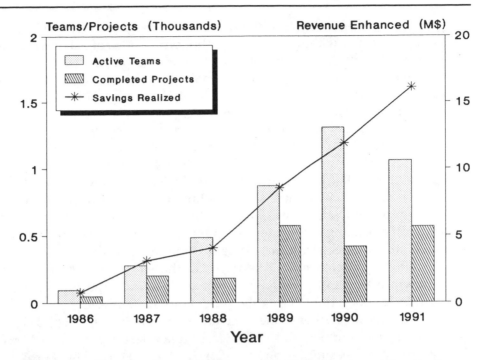

Figure 18.4   Banc One Corporation–Annual Quality Improvement Results. *Source*: Charles A. Aubrey II, *Summary Report on Banc One Corporation Quality Improvement* (Columbus, Ohio: Banc One Corporation, 1990 and correspondence from L. R. Wente, March 1993). Permission granted from Banc One Corporation, Columbus, Ohio.

employees. In addition to learning through formal training programs, the bank's personnel gain vital information through customer and employee surveys and through participation on QITs. In the six-year period beginning in 1986, during which corporate-wide activities were tracked, an average of 138,000 customers and 11,400 employees were surveyed annually.

On average, 540 QITs were in operation each year from 1986 through 1991 (see Figure 18.4). They completed 330 projects annually. The average project yielded savings/revenue enhancements of about $22,000, which totals over $7 million annually.

Xerox Corporation

In 1959, the Haloid Corporation of Rochester, New York (renamed Xerox in 1961), introduced a revolutionary new product, the 914 xerographic copier.[4] The effort strained the resources of the small Haloid Corporation, and many within the company thought the idea of making a copier costing $29,500 was sheer folly. Competitive copiers, based on a wet chemical process available from Kodak and others, sold for less than $300. Industry experts and consultants all discouraged the idea of marketing such a costly device as the 914.

Yet Haloid had little choice. Its core business of manufacturing large, specialized cameras and archival photographic paper was in a slow decline, and the firm was desperate to find new products. Haloid stumbled on the invention of Chester Carlson, a New York attorney, when Haloid's chief scientist, Dr. John Desssuer, read an article in a journal about Carlson's invention of dry printing. Haloid invested considerable resources in the development of xerography, so much so that an inability to recover its investment would have bankrupted the firm. Haloid had offered to sell the rights to the technology to other well-known corporations, and they had all declined the opportunity. Haloid had little choice but to bring the product to market itself.

To ease the burden of the high initial purchase price, Joseph Wilson, son of the founder, devised a lease plan fashioned after AT&T's approach of leasing its phones. The rest is history! The Xerox 914 Copier, reputed to cost less than $4,000 to manufacture, returned that amount in ten months on lease, and since the machines remained on lease for years, the 914 was described by financial analysts as a "money pump." The growth of copying, fueled by the ease and desirability of copying onto ordinary paper, created a new market for the Xerox Corporation. The 914 Copier achieved the enviable status of being one of the most successful commercial products ever produced.

What Happened?

Throughout the 1960s and 1970s, the challenge for Xerox was to manage explosive growth. Sales grew from $40 million in 1960 by twenty-eight hundred employees to $1.7 billion in 1970 by sixty thousand employees. The firm dominated the market through the uniqueness of its products and the thicket of patents developed around the xerographic technology. Holders of Haloid stock became multimillionaires, and stories of instant wealth in the Rochester community remain part of the folklore of that area.

In 1970, IBM entered the market with a competitive plain-paper copier, and five years later, Kodak reentered with a viable copier that also provided an alternative to Xerox copiers and duplicators. The IBM device introduced several new features, such as automatic document feed, enlargement and reduction, automatic collation, and two-sided copying. The Kodak copier was the first to use a microcomputer to control the internal operations of the machine.

Although competition from two of America's premier corporations, IBM and Kodak, was enough to get the attention of Xerox senior management, another problem occurred in the late 1970s to shake management's confidence further. The Japanese began to export to the U.S. low-volume markets desktop copiers that were fast, produced excellent copy quality, and were priced $700 below comparable Xerox models. The result was that Xerox began to lose its share of the low-volume market to the Japanese and its share of the high-volume market to IBM and Kodak. The company was in trouble!

What Did Xerox Do?

Xerox senior management recognized in the late 1970s that it had to change the way the company was managed. Task forces were formed, recommendations were made, and some small changes were implemented. Employee involvement and quality circles were started in 1978 in the Webster, New York, manufacturing facility. In 1979, a new concept of benchmarking internal practices against external sources was launched. In 1980, a small effort in employee involvement teams was piloted with field technicians in the Chicago area.

Still, these activities were insufficient to counter the buffeting that Xerox was receiving in the marketplace. Market share continued to slide. Employees were concerned about direction and company leadership and asked with increasing urgency, "Who's driving this bus?"

In response to these problems, Xerox launched a "business effectiveness" strategy in which individuals were designated in each division and operating company to identify ways to increase the effectiveness and efficiency of their respective units. These dedicated managers were simply assigned this enormous task without the necessary authority or even the support of the heads of their respective organizations. To say that this effort was "unsuccessful" would be using the kindest word possible.

In 1982, a small group of Xerox managers was invited to Japan to attend a Fuji-Xerox (FX) Quality Circle Convention. The FX convention is held annually in Tokyo to recognize the accomplishments of FX quality circles and to demonstrate the concept and application of employee participation. The group of visiting Xerox managers took advantage of the trip to visit other Japanese firms employing quality circles and a new concept called total quality control (TQC). The impact of observing the TQC management process and its apparent success in solving many of the same issues facing Xerox in the United States was startling. After the Xerox managers returned from Japan, they asked for and received an opportunity to meet with David Kearns, then president of Xerox.

Kearns was intrigued by the team's report, since their discussion of TQC answered many of the questions he had formulated through numerous prior visits to FX. Kearns knew about the remarkable recovery of FX after the oil shock in Japan in 1973, but he did not have details regarding specific management techniques that had been used at FX. He now understood and asked a small group to investigate TQC for possible application within Xerox Corporation. A task force was formed, and it developed a strategy that later became known as *leadership through quality*.

Leadership through Quality

The task team spent nearly one year preparing its recommendations to Kearns. The team contacted a number of organizations and visited those that had significantly improved performance through application of the principles of TQC. Management processes were studied, training strategies discussed, and successes and failures analyzed. The team attended quality seminars and listened to each of the quality gurus.

From all of this, a recommendation was prepared and presented, first to Kearns and then to the corporate management committee, the top twenty-five managers within Xerox. The name first used to describe the effort was "commitment to excellence." However, Paul Alair said that what was needed was a description of the company's management style and an example of how Xerox managers were going to be required to lead. The name of the project became "leadership through quality."

In early 1983, David Kearns convened a senior management meeting to review the completed leadership through quality strategy that the group had seen earlier in draft form. The meeting debated the pros, cons, difficulties, and opportunities that the strategy represented for the corporation. Kearns led the discussion and framed the meeting around the thirty-four key decisions the executives had to make to finalize the strategy and make it theirs. The strategy was finalized and published for all managers in the "green book" (the color of the cover denoted successive versions of the strategy during its formulation).

Throughout this demanding time for Xerox, the words of David Kearns provided the guidance that helped to motivate employees to accept this enormous task:

> Xerox is clearly in a period of transition. We are no longer the company we once were, and we are not yet the company that we must be. If we are to successfully complete this transition and continue our record of success, every individual in the corporation will have to work toward our common goals.
>
> *—David Kearns, 1983*

The Xerox Leadership Through Quality strategy is built on three elements:

1 Quality principles
2 Management actions and behaviors
3 Quality tools

Quality Principles

- Quality is the basic business principle for Xerox to continue to be a leadership company.
- We will understand our customers' existing and latent requirements.
- We will provide all our external and internal customers with products and services that meet their requirements.
- Employee involvement, through participative problem solving, is essential to improve quality.
- Error-free work is the most cost-effective way to improve quality.

Management Actions and Behaviors

- We will assure strategic clarity and consistency.
- We will provide visible supportive management practices, commitment, and leadership.
- We will set quality objectives and measurement standards.
- We will establish and reinforce a management style of openness, trust, respect, patience, and discipline.
- We will establish an environment in which each person can be responsible for quality.

Quality Tools

- The Xerox quality policy
- Competitive benchmarking and goal setting
- Systemic defect and error-prevention processes
- Training for leadership through quality
- Communication and recognition programs that reinforce leadership through quality
- A measure for cost of quality (or its lack)

Following the development of quality principles, management actions, and tools, Xerox senior management defined the goals it would strive to achieve and the activities it would strive to implement in the next five years. A detailed list of activities and expected results was compiled for each time period. As Xerox progressed through its training and other implementation phases, plans and accomplishments were reviewed to determine progress and to ascertain where corrective action was needed. Revised plans and expectations were subsequently communicated.

Was It Successful?

Manufacturing at Xerox was completely reorganized. New managers were brought in from other parts of the company. Processes and practices were benchmarked against the best in the world. Training on problem solving and process improvement was provided to over a hundred thousand employees worldwide. Formal customer satisfaction measurement systems were introduced to gauge the effect of these actions in the marketplace. Suppliers were narrowed from four thousand to four hundred, and each attended leadership through quality training. Key suppliers are now involved in the early stages of product design; they understand the objectives and share a common language with Xerox employees. Inventories shrank.

New-product designs now contain the features, characteristics, and reliability that the market has always expected from the firm that developed the original device that created the market.

This huge task of reshaping Xerox to become more competitive was rewarded with "considerable success."[5] Production costs were cut in half, and product quality, as measured in defects per hundred machines, improved dramatically. The onslaught of Japanese copiers was blunted, and the ability of the Japanese firms to move into the high-volume duplicating market was delayed by Xerox's actions.

Total Quality Management

"Xerox boasts it is the only American company that has lost market share to Japanese competition and reversed the trend without government assistance."[6]

Notes

1. R. Williams and B. Bertsch, *Stages in the Management of Quality Improvement Programmes* (Rotterdam, Netherlands: Erasmus University Department of Business and Organization, 1989).

2. Ibid., 2–3.

3. Ibid., 3.

4. *914 Copier* is a registered trademark of the Xerox Corporation.

5. M. L. Detouzoz, R. K. Lester, and R. M. Solow, *Made in America* (Cambridge, Mass.: MIT Commission on Industrial Productivity, MIT Press, 1989), 275.

6. Ibid.

References

Aubrey, C. A. *Quality Management in Financial Services*. Wheaton, Ill.: Hitchcock, 1988.

Dumas, R. A. "Organizationwide Quality: How to Avoid Common Pitfalls." *Quality Progress* 22, no. 5 (1989): 41–44.

Stratton, B. "What Makes It Take? What Makes It Break?" *Quality Progress* 23, no. 4 (1990): 14–18.

Index